STATE AND RURAL SOCIETY IN BANGLADESH

**Scandinavian Institute of Asian Studies
Monograph Series**

South Asia

SCANDINAVIAN INSTITUTE OF ASIAN STUDIES

MONOGRAPH SERIES   NO. 49

State and Rural Society in Bangladesh

A study in relationship

Kirsten Westergaard

Curzon Press

Scandinavian Institute of Asian Studies
Kejsergade 2, DK-1155 Copenhagen K

First published 1985

Curzon Press Ltd : London and Malmö

ISBN 0 7007 0166 4
ISSN 0069 1712

The publication of this book is supported by a grant from the Danish Social
Science Research Council

British Library Cataloguing in Publication Data

Westergaard, Kirsten
   State and rural society in Bangladesh: a study
   in relationship.—(Scandinavian Institute of
   Asian Studies monograph series, ISSN 0069-1712;
   No. 49)
   1. Bangladesh—Politics and government
   I. Title   II. Series
   320.9549'2   JQ631
   ISBN 0-7007-0166-4

Printed and bound in Great Britain by
Biddles Ltd, Guildford and King's Lynn

CONTENTS

PREFACE

Much of the data for this study were gathered during repeated visits to Bangladesh (and the former East Pakistan) between 1970 and 1981.

The purpose of the first visits to the area in 1970 and 1971 was to conduct a study of the social consequences of the Comilla rural development model. Because of the war in 1971, this project was never completed.

The next longer visit to the area was in 1975. For two months I acted as a consultant to the Comilla Rural Academy in connection with an evaluation of the Integrated Rural Development Programme in Comilla District. Between November 1975 and June 1976 I stayed in a village in Sherpur thanba, Bogra District. During this period I gathered most of the information for the local level apsects of this study.

In January/February 1977 I revisited Bangladesh, partly as a consultant to a DANIDA (Danish International Development Agency) mission in conection with a development project in Noakhali district, and partly to study the local council elections in Sherpur thana. Two brief visits were made to Bangladesh in 1978 and 1979, the purpose of the latter being to collect data in connection with the national elections which took place in February 1979. The data on *gram sarkar* (village governments introduced in 1980) were gathered during a visit to Bangladesh in 1981.

The blk of this book was written in 1979 and submitted to the University of Copenhagen as a requirement for my Ph.D., which was awarded in 1980. Revisions and additions were made in the spring of 1982.

A major part of the study has been financed by Riksbanken (Stockholm) through the Mobilization Project of the Institute for Peace and Conflict Research, Gothenburg University. This project financed the field-study undertaken during 1975 – 6 as well as the short visit in the spring of 1979.

The publication of this book has been made possible through a grant from the Danish Social Science Research Council.

May 1982   Kirsten Westergaard

I

INTRODUCTION

The genesis of this study was the author's participation in a major research project, undertaken by the Department for Peace and Conflict Research, Gothenburg University, on the mobilization of peoples. The purpose of the mobilization project is to develop a conceptual and theoretical framework for mobilization research through theoretical as well as comparative empirical studies.[1]

The concept of mobilization, while often used in the social sciences, is seldom clearly defined and is, moreover, associated with different connotations.[2] From being a negative concept, it has gradually developed into a concept with positive connotations, and the use of the concept adopted in the present study follows closely Rudebeck's definition: '1. social mobilization: ever on-going process whereby people's awareness of the structural conditions and contradictions of society is influenced by these conditions and contradictions themselves. 2. political mobilization: process involving the political organization of the people'.[3]

Mobilization is thus primarily a process related to social change and social development with a focus on the interaction between state and society. The model adopted for analysing this interaction is the centre-periphery frame of reference, in the sense that this concept is used in theories on imperialism, viz. as a structural dependency relation. As will be discussed in the chapter on theoretical issues relating to the nature of the state (Chapter II), the interaction between state and society concerns the spread of central institutions (economic, political and cultural) to the periphery, and the reaction of the latter to this process. It is regarding the ensuing centre-periphery contradictions that mobilization theory provides tools for analysing under which conditions conflicts are resolved or, alternatively, under which conditions the periphery is mobilized to resist the dominance from the centre.

Originally this study was conceived within the mobilization/centre-periphery model outlined above. Thus, the object of the field-work, conducted in a local area of northern Bangladesh during 1975 – 6 (Chapter VII), was to study—in a historical perspective—not only the changes which occurred in the periphery as a result of the economic, political and cultural policies emanating from the centre, but also the resistance to these changes, i.e. to which extent the population had become mobilized against central domination.

During the course of the analysis of the field data, the focus of the theoretical framework was shifted. While the original design included an analysis of the rural social structure within the theoretical discourse concerning the mode of production, the final analysis came to focus on this problematic.

The concept of mode of production is an abstract concept which refers to an articulated combination of relations and forces of production.[4] Here the relations of production define the relationship between the producing class and the exploiting class, or the mode of appropriation of surplus labour, and the forces of production the way in which a raw material is transformed into a determinate product, i.e. the labour process. Thus, relations of production refer to relationships between men and fellow men in society, and forces of production to relationships between man and nature through labour.[5]

As treated in the theoretical discussion of the field-data (Chapter VIII), the analysis is based on the analytical framework advanced by Alavi,[6] according to whom the structural characteristics of the small peasant farming economy can only be defined with reference to its integration into capitalism. The object of the investigation is thus to analyse the nature of this integration. As argued below, my own as well as other researchers' field data show that despite the economic penetration, there is no clear trend towards capitalist relations of production in agriculture in Bangladesh.

The historical analyses which will be discussed in this study show that during colonial rule the peasant economy was very responsive to the pull of the world market, and that although this subsumption under capitalism depressed the rural sector, the social structure remained 'seemingly unchanged'. During colonial rule the role of the peasant sector was to supply an exportable agricultural surplus at low prices. As shown in this study, during the Pakistan period, the role of the East Bengal agricultural sector remained unchanged, as it provided the bulk of the export earnings used for the building up of a modern industrial sector, primarily in West Pakistan. It is further argued that since the independence of Bangladesh, there has been no significant change in the role allotted to the agricultural sector. Not only must it provide foreign exchange through the export of cash crops, but it must also provide cheap grain for domestic consumption in the urban areas. Thus, the government's emphasis on agricultural growth should be analysed, not only in economic terms, but also in political terms, the latter implying the imperative of keeping urban consumption prices low, in order to secure political stability.

In the local area studied, it was found that politics had not crystallized along class lines. Rather, vertical alignments and factional politics—as they are known from Indian village studies[7]—predominate. Thus, local politics becomes the arena of power struggle among the upper peasantry.

As Alavi has pointed out, 'The structure of power within the village community derives not only from the economic and political structure of the community itself, but also from relationships that are established through structures of power and economic structures that encapsulate the village community. On the other hand, the larger polity in turn rests on its base in the rural power structure'.[8] As mentioned above, it was found that the problematic concerned with the mode of production provided the best framework for analysing the rural society. This framework also concerns the nature of the encapsulation process. Here, however, the analysis moves from the abstract concept of the mode of production to the concrete social formation.[9] Thus, from the original focus on the centre-periphery contradiction inherent in the mobilization model, the analysis was broadened to include an analysis of the nature of the state.

As will be discussed in Chapter II, this problematic is analysed within the framework of class relations. In order to undertake such an analysis, theories regarding the specific nature of class relations in peripheral (or post-colonial) social formations are introduced and applied throughout the empirical analysis.

Because of their centrality at the political level in the Pakistan/Bangladesh case—as in many other countries of the Third world—issues such as national integration and subnationalism are incorporated in the analysis, not as alternative explanatory models but as further tools for analysing the class relations.

As originally applied in the mobilization model, the centre-periphery frame of reference is central to the present analysis between state and society. As pointed out above, such as in theories on imperialism, the way the concept is used in the present study implies a structural dependency relation. In fact, the concept is used at different levels of analysis. In the most basic sense, the theoretical discourse concerns the nature of class relationships in Third World countries which have been penetrated by capitalist expansion from the metropolitan centre(s). It is the ensuing dependency relation which underlies the concept of peripheral societies. Furthermore, the analysis follows the extension of the concept as used in other theoretical approaches discussed in Chapter II. Here the concept is used hierarchically in the sense that the capital centres of the peripheral states are treated as sub-centres, while the hinterland becomes structurally dependent on the national centres, which are in turn dependent on the nature of global integration.

The present study on the relationship between state and society, in the area which today comprises the state of Bangladesh, is analysed in a historical perspective with the focus on class relationships and their determination of the social formation. Because of historical circumstances the geographical demarcation of the social whole under analysis shifts over time. Thus, during the colonial period, East Bengal was part of British India, while during the Pakistan period the sub-centre was shifted to West Pakistan, and today the social formation comprises only the former East Bengal. As, however, class relationships in Bangladesh were shaped and determined by relationships in the wider arena, the analysis of the preceding state formations constitutes an integral part of the study. Thus, Chapters III and IV focus on the development of class relations within the theoretical framework outlined in Chapter II. Chapter V analyses the social formation in present-day Bangladesh. In these chapters the relationship between state and society is central to the analysis, but the focus is on the state level.

Chapters VI to IX treat the state-society relationship with focus on the local level. This part of the study is limited to the rural society and includes a description of Bangladesh society (Chapter VI), followed by a detailed analysis of a local area (Chapter VII), based on the author's field-work. This is followed by a theoretical discussion centred on the problematic of the mode of production (Chapter VIII), and Chapter IX discusses local level politics with the focus on its relation to the larger polity.

While the bulk of the study analyses the relationship between state and society from either of the two levels, the focus of the concluding Chapter X is on the relationship between the two levels. Here the interaction between local economic and political structures and the structures of power and economic structures of the social whole are analysed with a view to determining the character of the specific social formation.

II

THEORETICAL DISCUSSION OF THE NATURE OF THE STATE

In recent years much research attention has been given to the specificities of
social formations in the countries of the so-called Third World. Much of this
work, however, is of a theoretical nature, and few empirical analyses have
been undertaken.

The theoretical approaches adopted in much recent debate on the social formations of these countries have focused on their specificities either as post-
colonial states—emphasizing their previous status as colonies—or as
peripheral states—emphasizing their complementary and subsidiary attachment to world capitalism. This analysis of the state of Bangladesh draws
heavily on these theories.

While the study draws primarily upon the theories applying Marxist
analytical tools and focusing upon the mode(s) of production as determinant
for social formations, the use of Marxist concepts are treated with caution, as
they were developed particularly with a view to analysing the capitalist mode
of production. As Hindess and Hirst have pointed out, 'In *Capital* we are
given the elaborated concept of a particular variant form of the general structure of production, namely, the capitalist mode of production. For the concepts of the other modes of production, we are merely given a series of brief
and partial indications which are mostly in the form of illustrative com-
parisons, designed to highlight certain features of capitalism'.[1] It will be
argued below in the historical analysis that Pakistan—and later
Bangladesh—at the time of independence were not dominated by the capitalist
mode of production.

Besides their specificities as post-colonial or peripheral states, many countries in the Third World are also characterized by the fact that they are in the
process of national integration. The study therefore also draws from theories
within the discipline of political development relating to nationalism, national
integration and social mobilization.

In the post-colonial phase of many countries in the Third World it is the
rising middle class, or petty bourgeoisie, which assumes formal political
power. The specificities of such regimes will be discussed at the end of this
chapter.

A.   *Social formations in the Third World*

(1)   The theory on post-colonial states

The first theoretical approach to an analysis of social formations in the Third
world was Hamza Alavi's article 'The State in Post-colonial Societies:
Pakistan and Bangladesh'.[2]

The focus of Alavi's analysis is on the special role of the military-bureaucratic oligarchy which, in his opinion, is a common phenomenon in post-colonial societies. Central to his theory is the notion of an 'overdeveloped' superstructure or state apparatus in these societies. The genesis of this overdeveloped superstructure he ascribes to the colonial past, where the task of carrying out the bourgeois revolution was undertaken by the metropolitan centre in the process of imposition of colonial rule. In that process it was necessary for the colonial power to create a state apparatus which was sufficiently powerful to subordinate the native social classes. At the time of independence the post-colonial state 'inherits the overdeveloped state apparatus and its institutionalized practices through which the operations of the indigenous social classes are regulated and controlled'.[3]

Alavi points out that the role of the bureaucratic-military oligarchy in post-colonial societies is determined within the matrix of a class society. However, at the time of independence no single class had exclusive command over the state,[4] and thus 'the state in the post-colonial society is not the instrument of a single class. It is relatively autonomous and it mediates the competing interests of the three propertied classes—the metropolitan bourgeoisie, the indigenous bourgeoisie, and the landed classes—while at the same time acting on behalf of all of them in order to preserve the social order in which their interests are embedded, namely, the institution of private property and the capitalist mode as the dominant mode of production'.[5]

The politicians and political parties may challenge the relative autonomy and the mediatory role of the bureaucratic-military oligarchy, but, as Alavi points out, in post-colonial societies the relationship between the two is often complementary, and the political parties play the role of partners, 'a third component of the oligarchy'.[6] In his own analysis of Pakistan, Alavi argues that most of the political parties played such a complementary role. The exception was the political movements which drew their strength from people of underprivileged regions and demanded regional autonomy.[7]

In the post-colonial societies the relationship between 'feudal' landowning classes and the native bourgeoisie is different from that in the metropolitan countries at the time of the bourgeois revolution. Based on the argument that the bourgeois revolution in the colonies was already established by the metropolitan centre in the process of colonial rule, the 'native bourgeoisie is not confronted with the historical task . . . to subordinate feudal power for the purpose of establishing the nation-state'.[8] So, not only does the state mediate the interests of these classes, there is furthermore an accommodation between them, as the landowning classes complement 'the political purposes of the native bourgeoisie in the "democratic" running of the post-colonial state, because it plays a key role in establishing links between the state at the national level and the local level power structures in the rural areas which it dominates', and where it 'contains' potentially revolutionary forces and helps to maintain the 'political equilibrium' of the post-colonial system.[9]

Complementary to the relative autonomy of the military-bureaucratic state apparatus in the political sphere is, in Alavi's theory, the notion of 'a new and relatively autonomous *economic* role'. In the post-colonial societies the state 'directly appropriates a very large part of the economic surplus and deploys it in bureaucratically directed economic activity in the name of promoting economic development'.[10]

As will be shown below, the economic development policy of the Pakistan government was very much in the interest of all three propertied classes of West Pakistan, whereas the demand for regional autonomy by East Bengal was partly in response to the economic policy of the military-bureaucratic oligarchy centred in the West.

Subsequent to the publication of the article, Alavi's theory concerning the state in post-colonial societies has been the object of a considerable debate, especially in an African context. One participant in the debate has, with certain reservations, more or less taken over and further elaborated on Alavi's theoretical approach.

In analysing the Tanzanian experience Saul outlines three points which define the crucial significance of the state in post-colonial societies.[11] Two relate to the concepts advanced by Alavi, viz. the notion of the 'overdeveloped state', and that of a new and relatively autonomous economic role of the state apparatus. To these Saul adds a third feature, viz. the special ideological function of the state. In the post-colonial states this ideological function is of special significance, as the state's hegemonic position 'must be created within territorial boundaries which often appear as quite artificial entities'. The state thus comes to play an important role in creating territorial unity and legitimacy, and according to Saul, 'the post-colonial state's centrality to the process of creating these conditions (like its centrality in promoting economic development) further reinforces Alavi's point about the state's importance'.[12] The notion of the 'centrality of the state' in fact becomes crucial to his analysis of the post-colonial social formations, as this leads him to focus on 'the importance of those who staff the state apparatus'. As will be discussed below, Saul does question some of Alavi's propositions regarding the nature and extent of the autonomy of the state and those who staff it *vis-à-vis* the classes directly rooted in the production process.

However, most of the participants in the debate regarding the state in post-colonial societies have criticized the theoretical approach advanced by Alavi. One of these is Colin Leys who rejects the entire notion of the 'overdeveloped state'.[13] First of all, he questions the argument that the inherited military and administrative machinery was excessive for the task of domination in the situation which existed by the time formal independence was achieved. In fact he argues that it seems more plausible 'that the colonial state, after the initial resistance to conquest had been overcome, disposed of less military force than it would have required, if it had not been able to rely on reinforcements from the metropole or other parts of the colonial empire, whenever the need arose'. He further points out that on the Indian subcontinent and elsewhere 'the civil service and armed forces were expanded more rapidly than either national income or population in the years following 1947'.[14] Regarding the Tanzanian case, Leys finds the notion of the overdeveloped state even less plausible than on the Indian subcontinent, for here—as Saul himself has pointed out—there were no strong classes to defend their interests in the old social formations.

Having rejected the arguments for the existence of an overdeveloped state, Leys in turn rejects the notion of a specific 'centrality' of the state in post-colonial societies, a notion which he finds just another empty word.[15]

However, Leys' criticism goes much deeper than arguing against the existence of a specific overdeveloped or central state in the post-colonial societies. He in fact rejects the whole approach to an analysis of the state in those societies: 'But the important point is not so much that the idea of the "overdeveloped" state is empty; it is really that this whole way of approaching the question of the significance of any state, i.e. of starting out from its structure or scope, whether inherited from an earlier situation or not, is a mistake'.[16]

One problem inherent in the concept of the post-colonial state is that it focuses on the superstructure. As Alavi himself points out, his argument is 'premised on the historical specificity of the post-colonial societies, which arises from (1) structural changes brought about by the colonial experience and alignments of classes and superstructures of political and administrative institutions established in that context, and (2) radical realignments of class forces which have been brought about in the post-colonial situation'.[17] Taken alone, his paper thus does not sufficiently explain the inherent dynamic of the social formation. However, the focus on the superstructure does have some explanatory value. As will be shown in the historical analysis, at the time of independence from the British, the mere existence of a developed (if not overdeveloped) state apparatus in Pakistan with its institutionalized practices was of importance for the political development.

It should be pointed out that to criticize Alavi for focusing on the superstructure to a large extent misses the mark. In many other contexts he has written extensively on the mode(s) of production, especially as regards the Indian subcontinent.[18]

(2)   *The theory on peripheral states*

While the theories on the post-colonial aspects of the state focus on the superstructure, the theories on the peripheral aspects emphasize the economic structures. Ziemann and Lanzendörfer[19] have outlined some of the specificities of peripheral states. Their article is written as a critique of Saul's analysis of Tanzania, based on the concept of the post-colonial state, and they set themselves out to provide an alternative framework for explaining the increasing concentration of political power in the state apparatus.

Ziemann and Lanzendörfer point out that the peripheral societies are historically determined by their integration in an international economic system following European colonial expansion, and as a result of this integration, 'the elements of the pre-existing, or now historical peripheral social formation synthesize in the form with the exogenous conditions of development'.[20] Their line of argument thus parallels the theories advanced by Amin regarding accumulation on a world scale.[21] Following European capitalist expansion, the economic structures in the peripheries were disrupted, and in the process the 'self-contained development of the peripheral societies was transformed . . . into a complementary and subsidiary system attached to the metropolitan system'.[22] The analysis referred to in Chapter VIII of the development process in Bengal very well illustrates the complementary and subsidiary system emerging as a result of colonial rule.[23]

As a result of its complementary and subsidiary role within the world capitalist system, peripheral reproduction has three distinctive features, according to Ziemann and Lanzendörfer, viz. (a) structural distortion of economic development, (b) structural dependency of the peripheral economy, (c) the heterogeneity of the economic structure, in particular heterogeneous relations of production. The preservation of 'traditional modes of production are not shortcomings, signs of backwardness in the periphery . . ., they are necessary components of peripheral reproduction'.[24]

Regarding Alavi's suggestion of the post-colonial state's relative autonomous role in relation to the three propertied classes, Ziemann and Lanzendörfer point out that this is not a special feature of post-colonial societies but an 'integral part of the "classical" Marxist view of the (capitalist) state, namely its relative autonomy *vis-à-vis* fractions of capital'.[25] They further point out that 'only by examining the relationships of state and society can the *significance* and the relative autonomy of the state be perceived'.[26] And in their view 'the varying significance of the state in the society depends on how far the economy is self-regulating or is subject to state intervention. Only in this sense does the state in the peripheral social formations hold a more significant (or more "central") position than the state in the metropolis'.[27]

Referring to the three distinctive features of peripheral reproduction, Ziemann and Lanzendörfer maintain that the result is a fragmented, weak and unstable class-structure, and therefore the interests of the various classes and groupings are not accommodated within the social process but mediated by the state. As a consequence 'The state becomes the actual forum of class struggle and class relations. This is manifested in a process of increasing concentration of political power in the state apparatus'.[28]

This theory concerning the concentration of political power in the state apparatus is quite similar to Sonntag's theory of what he calls 'the state of underdeveloped capitalism', to which the authors also refer. Sonntag also emphasizes the economic dependence on the metropolis and the heterogeneity of the economic structures in the peripheral societies, and according to him the consequent weak economic structure has the result that 'the economic allots the essential role for a long time to the political'.[29]

By focusing their analysis on the economic structure of the peripheral states, Ziemann and Lanzendörfer in fact provide a better framework also for analysing the existence and necessity of military-bureaucratic-technocratic types of regimes in these societies.

As pointed out above it is the distorted, dependent and heterogeneous nature of the peripheral economic structures and the resultant weak class-structure which gives rise to the state's mediating role and, as argued in this case study on the Pakistan period, the concentration of political power in the state apparatus. They further argue that it is the various demands on the state stemming from the complex of social reproduction which 'assume concrete form in the relative autonomy of the state'.[30] This leads them to advance a proposition regarding specific aspects of statehood which exist simultaneously and are logically not separable. As this proposition seems very relevant for analysing the Bangladesh case, the specific aspects of statehood characteristic of peripheral societies will be briefly outlined below.

Due to the heterogeneity and dependent nature of the economic structure, the peripheral states are *weak*. This characteristic may be manifested, e.g. in political instability (see below), regional disintegration, restricted effectiveness of government resources.

The *political instability* of peripheral states is manifested through frequent changes in state forms, in the constitution, and in the interchangeability of political institutions. With particular interests being realized via the state, the growth of a state clientele and of corruption leads to its becoming the private preserve and instrument of ever-changing partial interests, and this political instability often takes the form of a permanent political crisis. When the interests of the weaker sections of society are impinged upon, acute political crises may arise. These may be covered up temporarily through political manipulation (populist or nationalist ideology) or limited reforms.

Most peripheral states enjoy only *limited legitimacy* which is manifested through authoritarian forms of government, employing *ad hoc* laws, ideological manipulation and crude force.

Finally, peripheral states are forced to be '*strong*'. This is manifested primarily in the 'development policies' through massive intervention in production and through its domination over the propertyless masses.

According to Ziemann and Lanzendörfer these four aspects of statehood comprise a unity. However, the result is a 'permanent economic crisis in the shape of an unbalanced economy, (and) a permanent political crisis in the shape of political imbalance'.[31] These imbalances in turn force the state to make constant intervention in the economic and political processes. The consequence is to aggravate the social contradictions and conflicts, which lead to further intervention. Thus, peripheral societies are also characterized by *permanent intervention*, and this 'can only be based on a paternalistic regime of military-bureaucratic-technocratic type'.[32] It is this relationship between state and society which, according to Ziemann and Lanzendörfer, explains the concentration of political power in the state apparatus.

Whereas Alavi maintains that the state acts on behalf of the propertied classes to preserve the social order in which their interests are embedded, namely, the institution of private property and the capitalist mode as the dominant mode of production, Ziemann and Lanzendörfer argue that 'the state is both "midwife" of the capitalist mode of production and also provides a "crutch" for the non-capitalist modes, and also both modern capitalist conditions as well as "social and political anachronisms" are produced and reproduced'.[33] As will be pointed out in the historical analysis, this latter argument provides a good analytical framework for explaining the Pakistan case during the period following independence.

Besides their different analytical approaches (i.e. focus on superstructure and economic structure, respectively), the theoretical approaches adopted by Alavi and Ziemann and Lanzendörfer are also different. While Alavi argues within a framework of what he calls 'classical' Marxist theory of the state, Ziemann and Lanzendörfer maintain that such a theory does not exist.[34] Here they follow Poulantzas' argument and, like the latter, they attempt to construct a theory. This relates to the points raised above regarding the use of Marxist concepts. However, while Alavi may differ from Ziemann and Lanzendörfer regarding the status of the Marxist theory of the bourgeois (capitalist) state, his work is as much as theirs an attempt to construct a theory regarding the specificities of social formations in the Third World. Besides, unlike e.g. Ziemann and Lanzendörfer, his theoretical works are always related to concrete historical situations.

B.   *The bureaucracy*

In the analysis of the state's political functions the relationship between those who staff the state apparatus and the dominant class or classes in a given social formation is central. As pointed out above, the focus of Alavi's analysis was on the special role of the military-bureaucratic oligarchy in post-colonial societies.

This part of the debate is quite confusing, as the bureaucracy (or oligarchy) is often referred to in nebulous terms, e.g. as a special social category or a special class. In the latter case it is not clear whether the members constitute a class by virtue of their class origin, or because they belong to the bureaucracy. Secondly, the distinction between the state apparatus and state power is not always clear.

On some of these aspects Poulantzas is quite clear. To him the bureaucracy constitutes not a class but a social category, defined as a social ensemble whose distinguishing feature is based on their specific and over-determining relation to structures other than economic ones (here the political).[35] Secondly, the bureaucracy 'always concerns the state apparatus and not state power. In particular, the bureaucracy, as a specific social category, depends on the concrete functioning of the state apparatus and not on its own state power'. And further, 'the functioning of the bureaucracy is specified by its particular relation to the state', for 'so-called "bureaucratic power" is in fact the mere exercise of the state's functions, since the state is not the foundation of political power but the *centre of political power* belonging to determinate classes',[36] to whose interests the state corresponds.

As Michaela von Freyhold has pointed out, a distinction should be made between the ruling class and the governing class.[37]

Poulantzas allows for the possibility that in the developing countries the state bourgeoisie 'may, through the state, establish a specific place for itself in the existing relations of production, or even in the not-yet-existing relations of production. But in that case, it does not constitute a class by virtue of being the bureaucracy, but by virtue of being an effective class'.[38] During the later analysis of Pakistan's economic and political development it will be shown that the state bourgeoisie did establish such a specific place for itself. At the time of independence, however, it was not the case.

In his discussion of the transition to the capitalist mode of production in Europe, Poulantzas has some remarks which are relevant for the Pakistan case: 'In this case, because of the dominant role developing upon the political instance, because of the particular instability of the state power and because of the unstable and precarious equilibrium of the classes in struggle, the state apparatus's class affiliation can play a determinant role to the advantage of the non-hegemonic[39] classes in charge: it is not that this affiliation in itself confers political power on them, *but it creates the conditions for their accession to this power*' (italics in the original). Of the German case he writes that 'the bourgeois class established its hegemony *by means of the state apparatus*, although the class affiliation of the latter was to the landed nobility.' He adds that it 'is possible for the bureaucracy concretely to function in these ways, in so far as their operations depend strictly on the relation between the social forces and the state's role during the transition period'.[40]

In Alavi's analysis it is not quite clear whether he considers the military-bureaucratic oligarchy as a category concerning the state apparatus (governing) or state power (ruling). Throughout most of his analysis he refers to the 'historically specific role of the military and the bureaucracy, who constitute the state apparatus in post-colonial societies'.[41] However, in his analysis of the relationship to political parties—which he considers as part of the state apparatus in a competitive and complementary role *vis-à-vis* the oligarchy—he writes that the 'bureaucratic-military oligarchy . . . often prefers to *rule* through politicians so long as the latter do not impinge upon its own relative autonomy and power'.[42]

Although Alavi never refers to the oligarchy as a special class, his analysis is somewhat vague on this point. When he writes that 'at the moment of independence . . . those at the top of the hierarchy of the bureaucratic-military apparatus of the state are able to maintain and even extend their dominant power in society',[43] he almost gives the oligarchy the status of class. A similar interpretation may be read from his discussion of the oligarchy's economic role both in the network of controls in which the vested interests of the bureaucracy are embedded, and in the direct appropriation and disposition of a substantial proportion of the economic surplus. 'These constitute independent material bases of the autonomy of the bureaucratic-military oligarchy'.[44]

However, in other sections of the analysis the oligarchy is not given the status of class with a dominant role.

Ziemann and Lanzendörfer reject the notion of the bureaucracy constituting a special class. However, they do refer to the state bureaucracy's special economic and political interests in maintaining their positions, or status. To a large extent their special interests complement the functional tasks of the bureaucracy. It is in their interest to maintain and extend their economic privileges and social position and power. At the economic level it is both their function and in their own interest to guarantee and promote the process of value creation in the economy, to provide a source of state finance. At the political level both aspects are realized through the stabilization of the ruling order in the society, which involves maintaining the loyalty of the powerful social classes.

However, the functional tasks of the state bureaucracy may conflict with their own interests, as they may become involved in battles over the distribution of the state income.

They further point out that the relative autonomy of the state does give those who staff the state apparatus a certain freedom of action. This may give cause to various political actions which may be explained by the origin, interests and ideological orientation of its members.

As mentioned above, in his analysis Saul takes over Alavi's concept of the 'overdeveloped' state. He, however, has some reservations regarding the applicability of some of the analysis, at least as regards East Africa. For the Indian subcontinent, Alavi wrote about the need to subordinate the native social classes, whereas Saul points out that the colonial state in East Africa became 'overdeveloped' as a need to subordinate pre-capitalist, generally non-feudal, social formations. Here there is neither a landed class nor a developed indigenous bourgeoisie. In the East African context he thus does not find the mediating role as a satisfactory explanation for the relative autonomy of those elements which cluster around the state. He rather finds an autonomy rooted in what he has called the centrality of the state.[45]

As mentioned, the debate on the state's political function and the role of the bureaucracy is very confusing, and the concepts are not well defined.

Regarding the status of the bureaucracy, Alavi's analysis leads him to a theoretical framework akin to the proposition advanced by Poulantzas concerning the possibility of the state bureaucracy establishing a place for itself in the relations of production, and thus constituting a class.

The question relating to the special interest of those who staff the state apparatus is dealt with in Alavi's analysis of their feudal background.

C. *External linkages*

Ziemann and Lanzendörfer base their analysis on the economic structures in the peripheral states where the world market context is the 'primary, and hence essential framework of reproduction to which the economic cycle within the national borders is subordinated'.[46] They point out that at the time of independence the economic structure remained unchanged, and it is in this context that they refer to the state as the 'midwife' of the capitalist mode of production.

As mentioned above, Alavi's argument is apposite in that he argues that the bourgeois revolution was established in the colonies during colonial rule. This in fact implies that he postulates the dominance of the capitalist mode of production in the social formation at the time of independence. As pointed out above, the former proposition provides a better framework for analysis, at least for the Pakistan case.

Despite their different analyses regarding the social formation, the two schools reach similar conclusions regarding the state's role *vis-à-vis* the metropolitan bourgeoisies. The state's mediating role *vis-à-vis* the three propertied classes, including the metropolitan bourgeoisies, as postulated by Alavi, is repeated by Ziemann and Lanzendörfer: 'Stemming from this special structure of peripheral society, alongside the mediating of political differences among the classes and fractions of classes at home (the state also acts) as intermediary in political differences between the synthesised national interests with the interests of the external bourgeoisie and their states'.[47]

A study on the relationship between multinational corporations and the state in Kenya further elaborates this argument. In his analysis of this relationship Steven Langdon writes that 'the state is also proving to be the instrument by which the African petty bourgeoisie is being meshed into the structure of MNC . . . The symbiosis emerging in Kenya integrates together the state foreign capital and elements of local African capital . . .'[48]

Corresponding to Ziemann's and Lanzendörfer's proposition regarding the periphery's complementary and subsidiary attachment to the metropolitan system, Alavi's analysis of the superstructure leads him to a similar conclusion: 'Neo-colonialism is probably the greatest beneficiary of the relative autonomy of the bureaucratic-military oligarchy. It is precisely such a relatively autonomous role that renders the government of the post-colonial society sufficiently open to admit the successful intrusion of neo-colonial interests in the formulation of public policy'.[49]

Although empirically these propositions may be proven valid, theoretically they do not advance the analysis very far. Here Alavi's analysis of the collaborative relationship of the native bourgeoisie towards imperialism seems more to the point; but in each concrete situation the structural necessity of such collaboration needs to be analysed in order to incorporate the external linkages as explanatory characteristics of peripheral societies.

It should be pointed out that Alavi repeatedly stresses the interest of both internal and external propertied classes in the maintenance of the social order based on the institution of private property and the capitalist mode as the dominant mode of production. As this interest is backed up by the states of the metropolitan countries, neo-imperialism becomes an important aspect of the analysis. As will be shown in Chapter IV, the relationship with the United States from the 1950s had an important impact on the political development of Pakistan.

D. *Theories relating to political development*

(1) National integration and social movements

In the above discussion on social formation in the Third World, attention was drawn to the concept of the 'centrality of the state' which, according to Saul, refers to the state's ideological function in creating territorial unity and legitimacy.

Unity and legitimacy to a large extent concern the question of nationality and the nation-state. In his *Nationalism and Social Communication*[50] Deutsch discusses the interplay of society (relating to labour process), community (collectivity of individuals sharing habits and channels of culture) and nationality. A large collectivity is referred to as a people, and 'in the age of nationalism, *nationality* is a people pressing to acquire a measure of effective control over the behaviour of its members'.[51]

Many states in the Third World are made up of different nationalities[52] and after the attainment of independence, the task of nation-building becomes a central political issue. In the theory of political development, nation-building includes the creation of a sense of territorial nationality, the establishing of a national central authority, the creation of value consensus, and the establishment of integrative institutions and behaviour.[53]

As many states are made up of diverse regional groups or nationalities which do not necessarily give their first loyalty to the nation-state, the very process of nation-building often leads to severe political conflicts. This has been witnessed in many of the newly-independent countries of Africa and Asia, where the national boundaries were drawn by the ex-colonial powers with little regard to the wishes of the people. As will be shown in the following chapter, at the political level, the central conflicts in Pakistan were over nation-building, and Pakistan is an extreme example of the 'failure of national integration'.[54]

As mentioned, the process of nation-building includes the creation of value consensus. This dimension is central in Wertheim's analysis of human emancipation.[55] He is concerned with value norms, and his central proposition is that in all societies there is more than one set of values. However, one is dominant and protected by those in power by means of social control. Besides, there are contrary sets of values which may function as a kind of counterpoint. A countervalue starts to threaten the established authority when it has grown into a more or less consistent set of countervalues, openly professed by a social category. In such a case, it should not be called a counterpoint any more, but a social protest movement.[56]

Regarding the situation in the Third World, Wertheim discusses, among other factors, the political situation. Here he has some valuable points regarding populism with its ideology of unity rather than class divisions. This will be discussed in Chapter IV and Chapter V in the analysis of the Bengali nationalist movement. His arguments regarding military dictatorships parallel those of Zieman and Lanzendörfer, as he points to their weakness and difficulty in transforming the economic system, as well as to their linkage to neo-colonialism. His prospect and argumentation for a general trend of political development where populist regimes are followed by military regimes fit the Bangladesh case very well, as will be argued in Chapter V.[57]

To a large extent nation-building relates to the relationship between a central government and regional groups or nationalities. Theoretically, this relationship can be analysed within the framework of the centre-periphery model.

In political science the centre-periphery concept is used in many contexts, and it is most often used to analyse the relationship between the Western capitalist centres and the Third World countries which have been penetrated by capitalist expansion. It is thus a key concept in many theories of imperialism which stress the structural dependency relationship.[58] It is this relationship which underlies the concept of peripheral societies which are structurally dependent on centre capitalism. However, recent theories on nation-building also make use of the centre and periphery concepts, for, as Kothari has pointed out, 'both the process of internal consolidation and external linkages can be explored with the help of these concepts'.[59]

With regard to external linkages, Kothari's operative model is one in which 'the centre (or super-centre) is located in the territory of a dominant political power, the sub-centre in the national capital, and . . . all the rest is reduced to a vast periphery'.[60] This model, in fact, is similar to Frank's model of the chain of interlinked metropolitan-satellite relationships and their position *vis-à-vis* the hinterland.[61] It is along the same lines that Ziemann and Lanzendörfer argue when they write about the periphery's integration in the world market as a 'ladder of domination between periphery and metropolis'.[62]

With respect to the national level Kothari points out that 'first there is the need for institutionalizing the state in terms of a national community—the establishment of a centre, its outward thrust of permeating the periphery, and its handling of the issue of legitimacy through the processes of democratic participation, political conflict, the intellectual dissent, and the response of the periphery to these processes by progressively mobilizing its own social structure and moving centreward through both struggle and coalition-making. The resulting structure of power and decision-making entails a whole line of political and cultural centres and subcentres built out of the erstwhile periphery—with a corresponding set of élites and counter-élites . . .'.[63]

It is the same use of the concepts which have been used in recent attempts at theorizing regarding the mobilization process. In an attempt to develop a conceptual and theoretical framework for the mobilization process Hettne and Friberg write, 'What mobilization seems to be about is precisely the way in which the periphery tries to reduce the control exercised by the center. Mobilization processes are basically expressions of CP-contradictions, of which class contradictions is a special case'.[64] Along with Jessop they define the centre as the 'structural aspect of power and comprises those organisations, groups and individuals . . . who exercise most 'power' in a given social system'.[65] The process of nation-building involves the penetration of central institutions downward from the centre to the periphery. The result of this penetration may be the assimilation and/or incorporation of the periphery in the central institutions. Alternatively, the penetration may generate a cleavage of conflict between the central national-building culture and the increasing resistance of the ethnically, linguistically or religiously distinct subject populations in the provinces and the peripheries. (The concept of cleavage patterns is based on Rokkan's analysis, and the cleavage between the centre and the periphery corresponds to one of the two cleavages he associates with the national revolution.[66]) It is in response to these cleavages that the local political élites mobilize the population politically, either *reactively*, i.e. in defence of rights believed to have been unjustly removed or denied, or *proactively*, i.e.

claiming new rights.[67] As will be shown in Chapter IV, in the course of the development of the relationship between the centre and the periphery the people of Bengal were mobilized both reactively and proactively.

(2) *Populism*

Both the theoretical discourse relating to the centre/periphery model as well as the analytical framework focusing on mobilization, concern the relationship between the state and the people. However, the concept of 'the people' is most often rather nebulous. In two essays on fascism and populism Laclau[68] has a thorough analysis of the relationship between class, 'the people', the power bloc (the state), and the role of ideology, relationships which are central to the approach adopted in the present analysis of the Bangladesh state which goes beyond a strict—or mechanic—class analysis, while at the same time reserving a central role for such an analysis.

Central to Laclau's analysis is his insistence that populism should be analysed in terms of ideology and not in terms of movement, in the sense that it is impossible to link 'the strictly populist element to the class nature of a determinate movement.'[69] According to Laclau the basic function of ideology is to interpellate—or constitute—individuals as subjects.[70] Thus ideology has an important function both in the maintenance of hegemony on the part of the power bloc as well as in movements challenging this hegemony. As far as the dominant class is concerned, ideology 'interpellates not only the members of that class but also members of the dominated classes . . . (and) it is hegemonic not so much to the extent that it is able to impose a uniform conception of the world on the rest of the society, but to the extent that it can articulate different visions of the world in such a way that their potential antagonism is neutralized'.[71] In other words, the dominant class uses ideology to obscure class differences. As will be pointed out below, a similar use is made of ideology in certain types of movements challenging the power bloc, i.e. in movements not based on specific structural class antagonisms.

In order to specify such movements, classes must be properly determined, and according to Laclau they are defined as 'the pose of antagonistic production relations'. In other words on the bases of economic relationships. From this he concludes that the class character of an ideology cannot be deducted from its content.

While classes are defined by Laclau at the economic level, they may exist at the ideological and political level in a process of articulation, i.e. 'ideological practices are determined not only by a view of the world consistent with the insertion of a given class in the process of production, but also by its relations with other classes and by the actual level of class struggle'.[72]

While the above assertions regarding the relationship between economic, political and ideological relationships are questionable—or rather unorthodox,[73] it does advance the understanding of certain class relationships in the process of political mobilization: 'If classes constitute themselves as such at the level of production relations, and if the articulating principle of a discourse is always a class principle, it follows that those sectors—such as the middle classes—which do not participate in the relations of production that are basic to a society, will lack an articulating principle of their own and the unification of their ideology will depend on other classes . . .[74]

It is from this principle of articulation that Laclau analyses specificities regarding populism. As was pointed out before, according to him it does not lie in the movement as such, nor in its characteristic ideological discourse, which always has a class belonging, but in the *specific non-class contradictions articulated into that discourse.*[75]

It was pointed out above that the basic function of ideology is to interpellate individuals as subjects, and in the populist ideological discourse individuals are interpellated with reference to 'the people', or other similar non-class references. In order to analyse this phenomenon Laclau makes a distinction between the dominant contradictions at the level of concrete social formations and at the level of mode of production. While the contradictions at the latter level constitute the domain of class struggle, the former concern 'people power bloc contradictions relating to political and ideological relations of domination, i.e. the domain of the popular-democratic struggle'. However, as the historical processes are determined in the last instance by the relations of production, i.e. by classes, and as the class struggle thus takes priority over popular-democratic struggles, it follows that the latter only exist articulated with class projects.[76] It is on the basis of this relationship that Laclau points out that 'it is possible to assert the class belonging of a movement or an ideology and, at the same time, to assert the non-class character of some of the interpellations which constitute it'.[77] As this assertion is crucial to the analysis of the relationship between class and political mobilization, it will be dealt with in more detail through the example provided by Laclau himself. He illustrates his argument through the example of a semi-colonial social formation, in which a dominant section of landowners exploits indigenous peasant communities. At the abstract level of mode of production landowners and peasants constitute the dominant contradiction. This antagonistic relationship may take on different forms in the political mobilization, i.e. either a direct confrontation between the two classes, or the mobilization of the dominated peasants by other classes challenging the domination of the landowning class. Such other classes may consist of a rising middle class or other classes not rooted in the relations of production basic to the society. In order to make their political opposition consistent and systematic, these other classes increasingly appeal to the symbols and values of peasant groups. But in the reformation of those symbols and values, the reference to the peasant social base is lost and is transformed into the ideological expression of the 'people'/power bloc confrontation. Thus, the symbols and values of peasant ideology are articulated into the ideological discourses of the most divergent classes.[78]

The above illustration shows how the basic contradiction between the two poles in the class struggle may be transformed into a people/power bloc confrontation, and the substitution of class for people is crucial in the ideological discourse. Thus, the presence of 'the people' in the ideological discourse constitutes one element of populism. However, this presence in itself does not make an ideology populist. Also the structural content and the concrete historical experience of the social formation is crucial, and according to Laclau 'populism starts at the point where popular-democratic elements are presented as an antagonistic option against the ideology of the dominant bloc',[79] (or more obscurely: populism consists in presentation of popular-democratic interpellations as a synthetic-antagonistic complex with respect of the dominant ideology').[80]

From this it follows that the 'emergence of populism is historically linked to a crisis of the dominant ideological discourse which is in turn part of a more general social crisis'.[81] While this last conclusion does not advance the theoretical understanding, the basic approach of the analysis—with the limitations pointed out above—does provide tools for analysing the crucial relationship between 'the people', classes and ideology beyond the level of mechanistic reductionism and structural determinism.[82]

(3) Petty bourgeois regimes in the Third World

In the example provided by Laclau he referred to the specificities of political mobilization undertaken by a rising middle class not rooted in the relations of production basic to the society. Based on similar lines of arguments Saul has analysed the specificities of political regimes controlled by the rising middle class, or petty bourgeoisie, in an African context where 'it is precisely this class which assumes formal political power in the post-colonial phase'.[83] As this is also true for newly-independent countries in other parts of the world, including Bangladesh, some of his insights will be outlined below and referred to in the empirical analysis.

Saul draws on other writers who have analysed the class-structure of newly-independent African regimes. The concept of the petty bourgeoisie in the African context has a broader meaning than in the classical European context. It not only has the usual meaning of small capitalists, but also includes rich farmers as well as salaried employers, including civil servants of the state. To Saul these groups belong to a single class, which is, however, fragmented and unformed.

Saul further takes over Murray's concept of a 'political class', referring to those who staff the state at the most overtly political level. In petty bourgeois regimes, 'the partial and "transitional" character of this political class expresses itself in its absence of a determinate class standpoint grounded upon its site in the process of production'.[84] And he argues that 'this class—this circle of political activists—is one which exemplifies particularly graphically the basic attributes of the African petty bourgeoisie identified above, its relatively undefined and unformed nature and its ambiguous over-lapping of the various fractions conceivable within such a class'.[85]

Once in control of the post-colonial state, the state itself becomes 'an important prize, well-situated to arbitrate for aspirant Africans the terms and methods of capital accumulation in the new economies, as well as the uses to which various surpluses and scarce resources are put'.[86] Furthermore, the intra-class competition for control of the state and for economic advantage activates the diversity of factions at the political level. As pointed out, these factions are not rooted in the production process itself, but are based on diverse grounds, be they ethnic, cultural or religious. The petty bourgeoisie may also be divided into ideological factions, but because of the class nature of the petty bourgeoisie, leftist ideology tends 'all too easily to collapse into a vague, even opportunistic, populism—one more ploy of building a broader popular constituency'.[87]

Saul's analysis of petty bourgeois governments in the post-colonial phase provides a useful framework for understanding the economic policies of these countries. Many of his arguments coincide with those used by Kalecki[88] and Raj[89] in their analyses of 'intermediate regimes', a concept which they use to refer to governments in which the lower middle class and the rich peasantry could be identified as performing the role of the ruling classes. Such governments are likely to emerge in 'underdeveloped countries' where the lower middle class is numerically dominant at the time of independence, where the state is extensively involved in economic activity, and where credits are available from abroad (in Kalecki's version, from socialist countries). In order to stay in power intermediate regimes will have to gain independence from foreign capital, carry out land reform, and assure continuous economic growth. An economic policy based on the promotion of economic development through the public sector would be advantageous to both the lower middle class and the rich peasants, for the following reasons: 'state capitalism concentrates investment on the expansion of the productive potential of the country. Thus there is no danger of forcing the small firms out of business, which is a characteristic feature of the early stage of industrialization under *laissez faire*. Next, the rapid development of state enterprises creates executive and technical openings for ambitious young men of the numerous ruling class. Finally, the land reform, which is not preceded by an agrarian revolution, is conducted in such a way that the middle class which directly exploits the poor peasants—i.e. the money lenders and merchants—maintains its position, while the rich peasantry achieves considerable gains in the process'.[90]

Synthesis

In his criticism of Laclau, Mouzelis points out that 'concepts such as political mobilization and integration can and should be taken into account in a Marxist theory of third-world populism'.[91] In fact, in analysing the short-comings of Laclau's approach, Mouzelis raises some valid points which are extremely important for the epistemological problem inherent in the approach adopted in this theoretical introduction. He cautions against dismissing altogether 'bourgeois' concepts from Marxist analyses. In this context he points out: 'One should in fact stay clear of two equally unacceptable extreme positions: first, an *ad hoc* eclecticism which brings together concepts derived from different paradigms *without any serious attempt at theoretical reworking and reconceptualization*; secondly, a paradigmatic purism or sectarianism which insists that one should never "contaminate" the Marxist discourse with so-called bourgeois concepts . . . I feel impelled, therefore, to draw a parallel between the fact that popular interpellations can be articulated into a variety of different ideological discourses, with radically different political consequences, and the fact that crucial concepts such as political mobilization and integration can be articulated into a variety of different theoretical discourses, with very different theoretical effects'.[92]

As is apparent from the preceding pages, the approach adopted here obviously stays quite clear of the second extreme position. Similarly, the approach aims at also avoiding the first extreme position. The theoretical discourse adopted relates to the problematic of class relations and the nature of the state. However, as a Bengali political scientist has pointed out regarding political practice, 'one of the major doctrinal lapses of Marxist international communism has been the non-recognition of the force of nationalism as a factor in the change of history . . . East Pakistan Communist revolutionaries, while thrashing out their tactical moves, failed at the beginning to take into consideration the force of East Pakistan nationalism . . .'[93] In order to avoid similar lapses at the analytical level, it is therefore necessary to supplement the class analysis with concepts relating to political phenomena which are of relevance for concrete social formations. It is in this sense that the various theories discussed in the preceding pages are not to be considered as alternative analytical tools. It is my contention that, taken alone, none of the theoretical discourses discussed above provide tools for an analysis of the relationship between state and society. Neither does the sum of these discourses provide an adequate analytical framework. Rather, the discourses are regarded as supplementary, in the sense that they are all articulated into the fundamental theoretical discourse of class relations and the nature of the state.

It is in this sense that Laclau's analysis of the role of ideology and the relationship between class, 'the people', and the state provides a framework for the articulation of the concepts discussed above. In Pakistan/Bangladesh, as in most newly independent countries, the role of ideology on the part of the power bloc is closely linked to the issue of national integration, cf. Saul's discussion of the centrality of the state. However, in the attempt to maintain hegemony the power bloc acts on behalf of its own class interests. As pointed out during the discussion of mobilization theory, the penetration from the centre may generate cleavages giving rise to antagonistic relationships which may lead to e.g. sub-national movements, as was the case in the Bengal nationalist movement. However, though the issue of nationalism (or sub-nationalism) or other counterpoint values are often central in political movements directed against the attempts at national integration on the part of the state, it is often found that the issue of class relations plays an important role. Thus the concepts of national integration and sub-nationalism become central to the analysis, but these are regarded as supplementary to the class analysis, into which discourse they are articulated.

As mentioned above, Laclau points out that populism is historically associated with a general social crisis, and he also refers to the fact that populism occurs more frequently in peripheral capitalist social formations.

But, as Mouzelis points out, Laclau's own analysis does not allow him to explain why this is so.[94] The theories discussed above regarding the specificities of these social formations (referred to as post-colonial or peripheral) provide an analytical framework for analysing not only the nature of the social crises—which may or may not give rise to the emergence of populism—but also their frequency. As pointed out by Ziemann and Lanzendörfer, the economic structure of these societies is characterized by heterogeneity and dependence, resulting in permanent economic and political crises. And Alavi has shown how the class alignments in post-colonial states differ from those in the metropolitan centre. Central to both Ziemann and Lanzendörfer and Alavi's theories is the complementary and subsidiary nature of these societies vis-à-vis the metropolitan system. Thus, the political crises are closely linked to the specific class relations of these countries which are determined by the nature of the integration of pre-existing modes of production into capitalism.[95] The analysis of this integration is central to the fundamental theoretical discourse adopted in this study.

The approach adopted for the present study has thus been to focus on the socio-economic structure of the social formations at the given moments in the historical existence of the Bangladesh people, and at the same time to highlight the importance of nation and nationality.

By focusing on the different dimensions of the social conflicts during the course of the political history of a specific people, it is thus possible to provide a more comprehensive framework for analysing the societies of the Third World than is possible by an analysis limited to class relationships.

The nature of the integration of pre-existing modes of production into capitalism is treated separately in the theoretical discussion of the mode of production in Bangladesh, which deals primarily with the local level of rural society. The theories discussed in the present chapter deal primarily with the state level, and these theories are applied throughout the empirical analysis in the following three chapters.

III

THE COLONIAL IMPACT

A. *Introduction*

In his illuminating essay 'Peasant Mobilization in Twentieth Century Bengal' Broomfield wrote: 'Economic depression, war, and famine did not produce revolution in Bengal'.[1] This statement refers to the situation just prior to the partition of British India into the two separate states of India and Pakistan in 1947, but it still holds today when the population of the area has lived through severe economic depressions, famine and yet another war.

In an attempt to understand why this is so, Broomfield provides several answers, one of which is that 'in Bengal, as elsewhere, peasants are often mobilized through institutions that serve to sustain, not threaten, the structures of power'.[2] But what are the structures of power, and what are the economic and political forces on which they are based? This will be object of analysis in this and the following two chapters.

In many respects Bangladesh is a unique object of study for the relationship between state and society as well as for a study of mobilization of people. As Rounaq Janan has pointed out, 'the birth of Bangladesh was in many ways a unique phenomenon, for Bangladesh was the first country to emerge out of a successful national liberation movement waged against "internal colonialism" in the new states'.[3]

In order to understand the structures of power emerging from this liberation movement it is, however, necessary to go back to an analysis of the roles played by the various classes in Bengal during the previous liberation, or independence movement, viz. the movement for an independent Pakistan. The role played by the various classes was rooted in the socio-economic structure resulting from two centuries of colonial rule.

B. *Development of social classes*

Under British rule the province of Bengal was included in the Permanent Settlement of 1793. This meant that most of the land was parcelled out in estates, and ownership rights were given primarily to a group of persons called *zamindars* who had during the Moghul empire acted as tax-collectors for the state. The tax-collection obligations continued under the British, and the amount paid from each estate was permanently fixed. Within the estates, taxes were collected from the actual cultivators, some of whom held various tenancy rights, and others were share-croppers. Zamindari rights could be bought and sold, or they could be leased to subsidiary landlords, a system which over time led to considerable subinfeudation. The entire land-tenure system in Bengal became legally very complicated but, as Broomfield has pointed out, these

23

legal categories can be misleading for the analysis of the social structure. What is really important is to look at the means by which power was acquired and held, and here the first requirement was secure control, direct or indirect, of good arable land. Cultivators with some surplus 'could rapidly combine all three roles of peasant, money-lender, and landlord, and sustain these roles indefinitely. Moreover, the level of the tenure that they purchased depended less on its rank order in the legal hierarchy, than upon the access which it gave to good land and control of people on the land'.[4] As will be outlined in a later chapter on the mode of production, the Rays have shown that within the village community the socio-economic relations had a self-perpetuating tendency, for the political and economic control of the dominant village groups was based on usury and crop sharing.[5]

Bengal was inhabited by both Hindus and Muslims, but the latter were initially held in suspicion by the British who regarded them as direct representatives of the previous rulers. It was primarily the Hindus who became employed by the East India Company, and as its agents 'this group gained a strong footing in the economic organization of Bengal through dealing in its merchandise and other products'.[6] Many of these used their surplus for investment in land, i.e. they bought up zamindari estates, many of which were put on auction, as the traditional zamindars were unable to meet their tax obligations. As most of the peasants in East Bengal were Muslims, the class difference coincided with the religious division in the form of Hindu landlords versus Muslim peasants.

It was primarily the Hindus who availed themselves of the educational facilities instituted by the British, and thus most of the Bengalis employed as government clerks in British mercantile firms were Hindus, and these made up the core of the middle class by the end of the nineteenth century.

However, around that time the demand for the agricultural products of Bengal rose, especially the demand for jute, the acreage of which almost quadrupled during the last quarter of the century.[7] This significantly improved the economic situation of those cultivators who were in control of land, viz. the peasant-money-lender-landlord category who made up the dominant village groups. In East Bengal the majority of these were Muslims who began to send their sons for higher education and invest in business in the rural towns. This process gave rise to the emergence of a Bengali-speaking Muslim middle class, especially in the post-1920 period. Until that time the politically vocal Muslim community had been limited to the upper classes, especially the landed aristocracy, which was primarily Urdu-speaking. This upper class had since 1863 been organized in the Muhammadan Literary Society where lectures were delivered in Urdu, Persian, Arabic or English. As has been pointed out, the use of these languages clearly shows that the Bengali masses were not connected with this organization, for these mostly spoke Bengali.[8]

Thus, during the last two decades prior to independence from the British the Muslim élite in Bengal was divided into three factions, representing different socio-economic strata and with different socio-geographical roots. As mentioned above, the traditional Muslim élite was made up primarily of the landed aristocracy (i.e. the remaining Muslim zamindars) which was non-Bengali in orientation. This Urdu-speaking élite had cultural affinities with the Muslims of northern India. At the time of independence the politically most influential person was Kwaja Nazimuddin whose family had settled in eastern Bengal as traders and later established themselves as zamindars. Although this family's political base was Dacca, their 'spiritual home' was among the Urdu-speaking Muslim élite outside Bengal. After returning from law studies in England in the 1920s, Nazimuddin's career was rapidly advanced by the British who at that time favoured the Muslims, and especially the loyal landed aristocracy. Besides, as one of his biographers points out, the British were especially favourably inclined towards Nazimuddin because of his link with the European trading community.[9]

Another Muslim élite of political importance was the Calcutta-based urban cosmopolitans. Like the landed aristocracy this élite was non-vernacular[10] and drew its strength from the modernized sections of the urban areas, especially intellectuals and students. The most influential person in Bengal politics from this élite at that time was Shaheed Suhrawardy, the son of a Calcutta advocate. Like Nazimuddin he became important in politics after his return from law studies in England in the early 1920s.

The third faction of the Muslim élite had its base in the rural areas of East Bengal. Unlike the other two factions, this élite was vernacular and was drawn from among the middle class emerging from the up-country towns in the 1920s. The champion of this class was the small-town lawyer and landlord Fazlul Huq, who played an important part in Bengal politics during the first 60 years of this century. For this faction the issues of community and class clearly overlapped, in the sense that the emancipation (mobilization) of the vernacular élite was rooted both in the cultural (national) process as well as in the political ascendance of this class.

By the 1920s and 1930s the various sections of the Muslim population of Bengal clearly had developed separate class interests as well as geographical affinities. At the same time the different Muslim social classes had common interests with the respective sections of the Hindu population. In fact there were indications that the various social classes were starting to organize across religious lines. In 1909 Hindu and Muslim zamindars formed the Imperial League against the rising popular movements,[11] and in some areas there was support for the Muslims among the lower-caste Hindus who felt oppressed by the upper castes of their religious community. Also the middle classes of the two religious communities had common interests both *vis-à-vis* the British and the aristocracy, as well as *vis-à-vis* the impoverished poor peasants.

C. *The Bengal involvement in the Pakistan Movement*

The rise of cultural and political consciousness among the Bengal Muslims was, however, very much connected with and influenced by the developments within the independence movement in the whole of British India. At the end of the nineteenth century the Congress was organized by well-educated Indians. This became the principal organization for the independence movement against the British. Although both Hindus and Muslims were members, the Hindu dominance became increasingly resented by the Muslims. In the early years of this century two developments contributed to the increased political consciousness among the Muslims. One was the British decision in 1905 to partition the province of Bengal. The upper-caste Hindus violently objected to this and launched a mass movement which in turn created reaction among sections of the Muslim élite. At the same time the British announced the plan to enlarge the Indian Legislative Councils, and the Muslims decided to use this opportunity to create a political organization in order to press their demands before the government. Leading Muslims among the landlords and trading communities in northern India approached the Bengal Muslims, and in 1906 the All-India Muslim League was formed in Dacca. Among the Bengalis it was especially the representatives of the Muslim landed aristocracy who joined the Muslim League and favoured partition of Bengal. Other sections among the Muslim élite were against partition, and several persons joined together and formed the Indian Mussalman Association which stressed the common interests of Hindus and Muslims.[12]

In 1911 the British yielded to the agitation against partition, and Bengal was reunited. During the war the Muslim League and the Congress reached an agreement in 1916, and until the middle thirties the two organizations worked together.

However, the provincial assembly election scheduled for 1937[13] again aroused the political consciousness of the Muslims, and after taking over the organization of the Muslim League in 1935, Jinnah ran the election campaign. At that time there was no Bengal branch of the Muslim League, but under the leadership of the Nawab of Dacca the landed aristocracy and upper middle-class Muslims had formed the Bengal United Muslim Party. When Jinnah visited Calcutta, this was converted into the Muslim League, and twelve members were nominated for the Muslim League Parliamentary Board from among the landed aristocracy, the urban Bengali élite as well as from the non-Bengali business community, and Suhrawardy became the secretary. The only important Muslim political leader who did not join was Fazlul Huq, who had become president of the *Krishak Praja Party* (peasants and tenants party).[14]

At the all-India level the 1937 elections was a great disappointment to the Muslim League which won only 109 out of 485 seats awarded to the Muslims.[15] However, in Bengal the Muslim League and the Krishak Praja Party together had a majority.[16] Fazlul Huq had fought the election primarily on the issue of peasants versus zamindars, and in his own constituency he won a great victory over Nazimuddin. Although his party only came in as the third largest, he was asked to form a government, and soon afterwards he joined the Muslim League and became the president of its Bengal branch with Suhrawardy as secretary.

During the Muslim League government in Bengal under Fazlul Huq several bills were passed to ameliorate the lot of the peasants, such as the Bengal Tenancy Act, the Bengal Money-Lenders Act, etc. Most of these reforms, however, benefited the upper peasants, for as Broomfield has pointed out, 'that the Huq government's achievement did not match its pre-election rhetoric will come as little surprise, particularly when we note that Huq—a lawyer and tenure-holder from East Bengal—and all his influential party colleagues, were from that class of small-town notables who had so much invested in the existing system. A strengthening of the position of the rural middle rung at the expense of the biggest men they would welcome, but fundamental change in the system they would not'.[17]

During the Fazlul Huq government reforms were also introduced with respect to education, and the Muslims were reserved 50 per cent of the seats in the provincial services. This 'created a new generation of middle-class people, a generation who by 1946 became the inner heart of the Pakistan movement.'[18]

As mentioned, at the all-India level the Muslim League had not done well during the 1937 elections, and a general session of the party was called in Lahore in 1940. It was during this session that Jinnah advanced the two-nation theory and the demand for a Muslim homeland. The session passed a resolution, later to be known as the Pakistan Resolution, demanding independent and sovereign states[19] in the Muslim majority areas of north-east and north-west India. From this period on, the Muslim League fought for independence from the British on the basis of the Pakistan Resolution.[20]

The Pakistan Resolution gave the Muslims of Bengal a sense of identity, and the middle and lower classes were mobilized for the cause of Pakistan under the leadership of the Muslim League. As has been pointed out, it was especially the moderately affluent farmers who were used as 'levers by which to move the rural masses. With a son in school or college, with more land than he can cultivate by family labour, and growing more crops than he needs for family consumption, [the affluent farmer] could be approached and mobilized, and could be trusted, particularly with a little bit of communal tensions, to mobilize the poorer peasants also for Allah and the Muslim League'.[21] The case-study from Bogra (Chapter IX) very much confirms this general trend. Here the ancestors of the richest family in the village as well as of other affluent peasant families had been very active in the movement for Pakistan.

The rising political consciousness among the Muslim masses just prior to independence led to increased religious agitation, which was in turn met by agitation on the part of Hindus; and during the 1940s communal riots were frequent in Bengal. Thus, as independence approached, the ethnic and cultural ties which bound the Bengali people together were completely overshadowed by the religious question. To this was added the economic competition among the two religious communities. Although the Muslims controlled the provincial assembly, it could not compete with the Hindus' entrenched positions both in the economy and within the bureaucracy. The Muslim League's appeal for a Muslim homeland gathered strength from various strata of the Muslim population: 'Muslim officers, who could not expect any promotion in India because of senior and more efficient Hindu officers, expected to get speedier promotions in Pakistan. The Muslim traders and industrialists, who could not hope to flourish competing with the more experienced and clever Hindu traders and industrialists in India backed the Pakistan movement for the same reasons'.[22] To the peasants it was primarily a struggle against the

Hindu zamindars. Towards the end Hindus and Muslims increasingly used their respective religion to safeguard their economic interests. 'It was really a class struggle which . . . was converted into communal rivalry'.[23]

When it was realized that the province of Bengal would be partitioned, a group of non-communal Hindu and Muslim leaders advocated the establishment of an independent and united Bengal. Among the Muslims, this movement was especially supported by the Calcutta-based urban cosmopolitans under the leadership of Suhrawardy. The Congress leadership was strongly against an independent Bengal, and the movement further strained the relationship between Suhrawardy and the central Muslim League leadership.

The rise of political consciousness among the Muslims of Bengal in the first half of this century had many facets. As mentioned, towards the end of British rule the religious question became the predominant issue; but throughout the period the religious issue in East Bengal was very much intertwined with the economic emancipation of the Muslim peasants. As pointed out above, however, the Muslim political élite represented different social classes; and as the development in Bengal was a part of the political development at the all-India level, the relationship between the various factions of the Bengal political leadership and the all-India Muslim League leadership had a decisive impact on the course of political events in Bengal.

In the Muslim League Council, landowners represented the largest single group;[24] and as also the Muslim trading communities played an important role in the central leadership, it was quite natural that the all-India Muslim League leadership favoured that section of the Bengali Muslims which represented similar class interests, viz. the landed aristocracy represented by Nazimuddin and the non-Bengali trading community centred in Calcutta. Although this faction of the Bengal Muslim League was never able to win in popular elections, it nevertheless occupied important political posts.

After adoption of the Pakistan Resolution the power of the central Working Committee of the Muslim League was increased by an amendment to the party constitution, which gave the Working Committee the power 'to control, direct and regulate all activities of the various provincial leagues'.[25] On several occasions the Working Committee interfered in Bengal politics. Thus, when Fazlul Huq and Jinnah disagreed in 1943 (when the former had joined the National Defence Council of the British), Nazimuddin was installed as prime minister in Bengal. He was ousted after the provincial election in 1946, when Suhrawardy became prime minister; but when Pakistan became independent in August 1947, the Muslim League made Nazimuddin the first chief minister of East Bengal (which was later named East Pakistan).

Synthesis

After two centuries of British rule, considerable social and economic changes had taken place in Bengal. With a few exceptions, such as the nawabs of Bogra and Dacca (Nazimuddin's family), most of the zamindar estates had come into the hands of the Hindus, who also constituted almost the entire middle class until the turn of the nineteenth century. With the improved economic situation for the dominant village groups from the beginning of the twentieth century, the sons of the Muslim upper peasantry began to join the middle class in the rural towns, and it was this group which was especially active, not only in Bengal Muslim politics but also in the Pakistan movement. Through their influence in the countryside they mobilized the peasants.

In the political mobilization of the Muslims, these were interpellated primarily as members of their religious community. Thus, at the ideological level, the religious issue predominated, and the Islamic conception of obedience to God and His Commandments had an important impact.[26] This subservience coupled with a fatalistic attitude among the impoverished peasants played into the hands of the Muslim League Leadership. As has been pointed out, such attitudes produce fertile grounds for political manipulation.[27] For the rising Muslim petty bourgeoisie, the independence movement was also part of an intra-class competition against their Hindu counterparts and, as pointed out by Saul,[28] such intra-class competition for control often gives rise to political factions not rooted in the production process itself, but based on ethnic, religious or other non-economic grounds.

However, although the emergent rural middle-class had become politically conscious during the movement for Pakistan, they accepted a political leadership which did not represent their class interest. Neither at the state level nor at the provincial level did this class get positions of power commensurate with their local political strength.

At the time of the establishment of the state of Pakistan the social formation was a complex one. This will be discussed in the following chapter, but before concluding the analysis of the emergence of Pakistan, it should be pointed out that the social formation at the all-Pakistan level at the time of independence was determined by the dominant mode of production in the western provinces. Here the dominant mode of production was the feudal one, which at the political level was reflected in the leadership of the Muslim League made up primarily of the landed aristocracy 'supported by their own tribes or tenants'.[29] Within the social formation of West Pakistan, the capitalist mode of production had not taken root at the time of independence.[30] Unlike the situation in India there was no industrialist class in the area which became Pakistan. Before partition the Muslims had been active in trade—representing merchant capital—and many of these migrated to Pakistan during the time of independence. Although they were influential in the Muslim League, they had no local power base.

In East Bengal the situation was quite different. Although legally the land was under the ownership of the zamindars, the social structure, which developed during colonial rule, was much more complicated than reflected by the legal categories regarding landownership. The peasants had become petty commodity producers and, as shown above, around the turn of the century, the economic situation of the well-to-do peasants improved. During the 1930s the political influence of this section of the peasantry increased at the provincial level. However, neither in East Bengal was the mode of production characterized by capitalist relationships. As will be shown in the chapter on the mode of production, the integration of the Bengal peasantry in the world market economy took place without any change in the mode of production. The economic control of the affluent peasants was based on usury and crop sharing. Thus, while the upper peasants sought to wrest economic and political control from the zamindars, it was not in their interest to bring about fundamental changes in the social structure.[31] In other words, the economic interests of the upper peasants were not based on a clear-cut contradiction to the existing mode of production.[32]

As mentioned in Chapter I, at the economic level, the concept of the mode of production refers to an articulated combination of relations and forces of production. Besides, the complex whole of a mode of production also comprises a political, as well as an ideological and theoretical level. Every mode of production has a dominant level or instance (determined in the last instance by the economic), and 'in the feudal mode of production, it is ideology in its religious form which plays the dominant role . . .'[33] This dominance has been shown in the above pages. The interrelationship between economic and religious issues was complex; the ideological dimension dominated, and the conflicting interests of the different social classes among the Bengali Muslims became submerged in the ideological drive for unity among the Muslims during the mobilization for Pakistan.

IV

THE PAKISTAN PERIOD

A.   The 'parliamentary' period

(1)   Economic base and social classes

As mentioned in the preceding chapters, the social formation in the whole of Pakistan was determined by the dominant mode of production in West Pakistan. Thus, in order to understand the political developments in East Pakistan (Bengal) it is necessary first to analyse the socio-political structure at the all-Pakistan state level and to devote attention to an anlysis of the social matrix in West Pakistan.

During the colonial period the economic role of the regions which came to constitute the Pakistan state in 1947 had been to supply raw materials to industries located elsewhere on the Indian subcontinent and in Britain. East Bengal supplied raw jute, and the regions in West Pakistan had supplied cotton.[1] Most of the population lived in the countryside which was dominated by feudal relations of production. This economic relationship entails a vertical alignment of economic dependence, where the structural conditions at the village level are such that political alignments are dominated by the economic and political power of the big feudal landlords. This local power is reinforced by the links of the feudal landlords with the bureaucracy and the dominant political parties.[2] As mentioned in Chapter III, the largest group in the Muslim League was that of the landowners, who emerged as the most powerful class politically at the time of independence.

Although the landlords constituted the most powerful class, they were not well organized politically. During the struggle for independence, the Muslim League had performed the role of a nationalist movement under the personal leadership of Jinnah, who became Pakistan's first governor-general. After independence it did not transform itself into a genuine political party,[3] and when Jinnah died in 1948 there was no well-organized party machinery, and many of the leading members of the party were feudal landlords who 'were involved in feuds with each other dating back several decades . . . (and) to them politics with its competition for jobs and patronage became another outlet for pursuing their old feuds'.[4]

In pre-partitioned India the emergent industrial class was made up of Hindus and other non-Muslims. However, in certain parts of India, especially Gujarat and Bombay, Muslim communities (such as the Menons, the Bohras, and the Khojas) had been active in trade. At the time of partition these migrated to Pakistan, but because of their small size, narrow community base and lack of roots in Pakistan, they were unable to assert themselves as a political force.[5] These trading communities were reluctant to undertake risks

31

with their capital on their own,[6] but depended on government patronage in the form of licences; and thus during the course of Pakistan's industrialization they were in a client relationship to the bureaucracy.[7]

At the time of independence the situation was chaotic in Pakistan, not least because of the immigration of close to eight million Muslim refugees (about 10 per cent of the entire population) from areas—especially in the Punjab—which came under India. Although the army itself also suffered from dislocations because of reorganization, it was able to establish a situation of internal security and thus came out as the custodian of the nation's integrity, a role it was to repeat several times during the course of Pakistan's history.[8]

From a constitutional point of view the office of the governor-general was invested with immense powers. It was he who picked the cabinet ministers and distributed portfolios among the ministers, and he could establish control over the entire mechanism of government.[9] Because of the inexperience of the Muslim League ministers, Jinnah as governor-general, and Liaquat Ali Khan, Pakistan's first prime minister, relied heavily on the civil servants who had the administrative experience necessary for the proper functioning of government. Especially in the provinces the governors were in a powerful position (in the early period three out of four provincial governors were British), and like the former Viceroys under British rule, Jinnah 'received fortnightly letters from his governors which gave him a detailed account of everything ranging from intrigues in the provincial cabinets to details of refugee rehabilitation or the food problem'.[10] Thus, the supremacy of the bureaucracy at the expense of the politicians was established from the very beginning, and, as has been pointed out, Pakistan adopted the British viceregal system in India, under which the bureaucrats had exercised their power most of the time without any interference from politicians.[11] It should be pointed out that the members of the Constituent Assembly had been elected in 1946, before the establishment of Pakistan. They had been elected indirectly by the members of the provincial assemblies, and many lacked grass-root support.

Jinnah and Liaquat Ali Khan relied on the civil servants not only as bureaucrats, but also they gave some of them important posts in the government. Thus, the office of finance minister was given to a former officer in the Indian Civil Service, Ghulam Mohammed, who later became governor-general in 1951. The very dynamic and politically conservative bureaucrat Chaudhri Muhammad Ali was given the post of secretary-general to the government with powers to co-ordinate all activities of the government. In 1951, after the death of Liaquat Ali Khan, he became minister of finance, and in 1955 prime minister.

The relationship between the landed aristocracy, the executive arm of the government and the civil and military bureaucracy was a complex one. As has been shown above, at the national level the dominance of the landlords as politicans was overshadowed by bureaucratic rule, but because of their control of the rural areas the landlords played a key role in establishing links between the state at the national level and the local level power structure.[12] Moreover, their link to the executive branch was very direct, as the top oligarchy of the army and the civil service came from the same social background as the landlords. They had gone to the same schools and belonged to the same social clubs.[13]

Alavi has maintained that at the time of independence the post-colonial states inherit an overdeveloped state apparatus. As was pointed out in Chapter II, several writers have criticized the notion of 'overdevelopment', and given the nature of the administrative tasks at the time of independence, including the refugee problem, the notion does not appear very appropriate. However, one can agree with Alavi that Pakistan (and India) inherited a powerful and organized bureaucracy; and even a strong critic of the Pakistan regime, like Sayeed, grants that 'there is no doubt that it was the inspiring leadership of Jinnah and the dedicated efforts of the civil servants which enabled Pakistan to succeed in this struggle for survival. It was felt that Pakistan could not overcome these difficulties by relying on the ability and skill of politicians'.[14] In the power vacuum created by the departure of the British, the bureaucracy—trained and equipped to administer a modern state—became an effective political force in its own right.[15] Furthermore, at the national level, 'because of the virtual absence of capitalists, feudal landlords, bureaucracy, and the military in East Pakistan, the West Pakistani power structure became the national power structure as well, ruling the eastern part with the collaboration of the dying Muslim aristocracy'.[16]

Alavi has also maintained that in the post-colonial states the interests of the feudal landowning class and the native bourgeoisie are complementary and competing, and that both are interested to preserve the social order in which their interests are embedded, namely the institution of private property and the capitalist mode as the dominant mode of production.

It is true that, during colonial rule, the legal framework necessary for capitalist development was established, but certainly feudal power—based on the feudal mode of production—was not subordinated, and it is not directly obvious that the interest of the feudal lords is embedded in a social order based on capitalism as the dominant mode of production. It only becomes obvious to the extent that such a social order is better equipped to contain and repress potentially revolutionary forces.

Thus, while the propertied classes were interested—politically—in a social order based on private property and the capitalist mode as the dominant mode of production, at the time of independence this mode of production, as shown above, was not dominant. As in some European countries during the transition to the capitalist mode of production, state power—as pointed out by Poulantzas—was unstable, and the bureaucracy was able to play a determinant role. And it became the role of the state to act as 'midwife' of the capitalist mode of production, to use Ziemann and Lanzendörfer's expression.

In order to pave the way for the capitalist mode of production, economic development thus became a key factor in Pakistan's politics. At the same time, economic development was one strategy to further national integration. Another was the attempt to create integrative institutions, including a constitutional framework.

(2) Nation-building

As mentioned in Chapter III, Pakistan was established as a nation on the basis of the demand for a homeland for the Muslims in north-western and north-eastern India. As such the nation was established according to the wishes of the people, and Islam did provide a value consensus. However, apart from the religious consensus, there was very little which kept the country together.

Pakistan has often been described as a monstrosity, especially because of the separation of its two wings by 1,000 miles of Indian territory. While the population of the eastern wing had a national identity based on Bengali culture and language, this was not the case of the sub-nationalities in the western wing which consisted of Punjabis, Pushtus, Sindis, and Baluchis with separate cultures and with their own languages. At the time of independence, the eastern wing of the country constituted one province, and the western wing three. Besides, certain tribal areas as well as Baluchistan and the town of Karachi were under the direct jurisdiction of the central government.

From the very beginning there were great political controversies in Pakistan about how to establish integrative institutions and create a national identity, i.e. how to solve the problem of nation-building among the diverse regional groups. The problem was compounded by the fact that within the various regions, class differences also reflected different attitudes regarding the nature of integration. It was shown above that during the independence movement, the landed aristocracy in Bengal was more willing to co-operate with the central Muslim League than were the other factions of the Bengal political élite, and similar differences existed in the western provinces.

Many of the problems regarding nation-building or national integration in Pakistan were reflected in the disagreements regarding the country's constitution. Although there was agreement that the country should have a federal type of government,[17] the central issue was the degree of autonomy to be given to the provinces. On this question the people were divided into two groups, the centralists who wanted a highly centralized government, and the autonomists who wanted wide autonomy for the provinces. Geographically, Sind, the Northwest Frontier and Bengal wanted autonomy, whereas the Punjabis (who constituted two thirds of the population in the western wing) wanted a strong central government. This geographical division to a large extent coincided with occupational divisions. The Punjabis dominated the civil service and to a large degree also the army. Both these groups were in the favour of a strong central government. The same applies to the trading communities which were located primarily in Karachi. During the course of the constitutional controversies there developed an axis between Bengal, Sind and the Northwest Frontier because of their common resentment against Punjabi domination.[18]

Another issue which became very controversial in the course of the constitutional debates was the language issue. As mentioned above, the various nationalities constituting the population of the western wing spoke different languages, and in the eastern wing the language was Bengali. Besides, Urdu was spoken by a section of the middle class. It had been the *lingua franca* among the upper-class Muslims in undivided India, and was the first language of the trading communities, and it was also spoken by the immigrants, the army personnel and, to a lesser extent, by the civil bureaucrats. In an attempt to integrate the population, the government decided to make Urdu the one and only state language in Pakistan. Although the language was not spoken by the great majority in the western wing, it was especially in East Bengal that the language issue became a central issue in the relation between the province and the central government. The Bengalis made up 56 per cent of the population of all Pakistan, and they claimed that Bengali should also be given the status of a state language in the constitution.

As will be shown in the section below, it was the government's very attempts at nation-building which, instead of creating a sense of territorial nationality, increased the sense of regionalism in Pakistan. The government sought to create integrative institutions in all spheres, but the response to this economic, political and cultural penetration was regional political mobilization for the demand for autonomy.

(3) Bengali counterpoint values

As pointed out in the preceding chapter, at the political level the emergent Muslim middle class of Bengal did not get positions of power commensurate with their local political strength. The Muslim League dominated the Constituent Assembly which had been indirectly elected in 1946. During Jinnah's lifetime, the party was centrally controlled by him, and as shown above, he relied more on the bureaucracy than on the elected ministers, both at the national and at the provincial levels. After his death, the party was left without a strong organization, and its leaders 'were not courageous enough to take a stand against the bureaucracy or the government of the day',[19] and with the frequent changes of government, the power of the bureaucracy increased. At the provincial level in Bengal, Nazimuddin, the representative of the landed aristocracy, was installed as chief minister, and neither Suhrawardy nor Fazlul Huq held any political office.

The urban middle-class Bengali Muslims had opted for Pakistan, partly because they resented Hindu domination in industry and in the civil service. However, with the departure of the Hindus, the key positions in the East Bengal administration were given to either Punjabi or Urdu-speaking Muslim civil servants who had migrated from India. This political and bureaucratic dominance from the centre was resented by the Bengalis, and six months after independence a Bengali member declared in the Constituent Assembly of Pakistan, that 'a feeling is growing among the Eastern Pakistanis that Eastern Pakistan is being neglected and treated merely as a colony of Western Pakistan'.[20] Several writers have commented on the 'colonial' policy of West Pakistan vis-à-vis Bengal. Thus Feroz Ahmed writes that 'the colonization of East Bengal was inherent in the power vacuum created by partition . . .'[21]

The first political manifestation of the Bengali's resentment against the centre's dominance at the political level and in the bureaucracy was over the language issue. In March 1948 a Committee of Action was formed to press the demand that Bengali should be accepted as one of the state languages in

Pakistan. The demand was followed by demonstrations, first by students in Dacca, but later it spread to the provinces. It was the first step in the mobilization of the people of Bengal against the central government. It was led by the newly-formed East Pakistan Students' League, and its leaders were to become influential in the Bengal nationalist movement in the 1960s.[22] The movement gathered momentum a few weeks later, when during a visit to Dacca Jinnah declared that Urdu must be the only state language.

The second political manifestation against the centre was in response to the first Draft of the Basic Principles Committee appointed by the Constituent Assembly to draw up a constitution for Pakistan. The draft which was published in February 1950 was strongly resented in East Bengal on the ground that it did not provide the province with an overall majority in the federal legislature on the basis of population and might even give it a minority in a joint session of the two houses. (The draft provided for a bi-cameral system consisting of a House of Units representing the legislatures of the units, and a House of the People elected by the people.[23]) The response was the convening of a Grand National Convention in Dacca which drew up an alternative constitution based on a republican form of government with two autonomous regional governments for the eastern and western units and one central parliament on the basis of population with powers to deal with foreign affairs, currency and defence only.[24] This Bengali proposal for maximum autonomy 'remained the sheet-anchor of all the popular movements for the first two decades after independence'.[25]

Meanwhile, the political élite in Bengal had become increasingly dissatisfied with the Muslim League, and in June 1949 they formed an opposition party, the Awami (people's) League. The initiator and first president of the party was Maulana Bhashani, a peasant leader who had been active in the independence movement in Assam. The leadership also included members of the Krishak Praja party. The vernacular élite was thus very influential in the party, and one of the joint secretaries was Sheikh Mujibur Rahman (who later became Bangladesh's first president). He belonged to the rural middle class, and had studied in Calcutta. Soon after the formation of the party, Suhrawardy took over the leadership, and many of his supporters, representing also the urban-based non-vernacular élite, became the hard core of the Awami League. The party thus became the platform of both sections of the middle class.

Although the Awami League had been formed, the political initiative remained with the students, especially concerning the language issue. In 1951 Nazimuddin had become prime minister of Pakistan, and during a visit to Dacca in 1952 he repeated Jinnah's claim that Urdu alone should be the state language of Pakistan.[26] Although the politicians were included in a Committee of Action formed to protest against this repeated declaration, they hesitated to join a general strike launched by the students on 21 February 1952. The demonstrations were met by police firing, and several persons were killed. Since then, 21 February has been observed in East Bengal as *Shaheed* (Martyrs') Day, and its symbolic importance in creating counterpoint values was considerable in that it reminded the population that 'it was the central government dominated by West Pakistanis which tried to impose the Urdu language on East Pakistan and in resisting this policy successfully East Pakistanis had to face death'.[27]

Within a few years of the formation of Pakistan it was thus clear that the population of Bengal resented the political and cultural domination from the centre. The political élite and especially the students had demonstrated against the policy of the central government. However, it was not until 1954 that the relationship between the province and the central government was put to a real test. This test was the first popular election to the provincial assembly which took place in March 1954. Already the previous year a United Front was formed against the Muslim League by the Awami League Party and the Krishak Praja Party which had been reivived by Fazlul Huq under the name of Krishak Sramik (peasants and workers) Party. Although by that time Suhrawardy had become more interested in central politics, he nevertheless took on the chairmanship of the steering committee of the Front. The United Front fought the election on a 21-point programme which included complete autonomy for East Bengal and the acceptance of Bengali as a state language.[28]

The result of the provincial election was the utter defeat of the Muslim League which got only 9 out of 309 seats, the remainder going to the United Front. It was thus clear that the population of East Bengal had been mobilized against the centre, and that the Bengali nationalist movement had grown into a social protest movement.[29] A United Front government with Fazlul Huq as the chief minister was formed, but it was only allowed to remain in office for a few months, and in May governor's rule was imposed in the province.[30]

At that time the political situation in the West and at the Centre had deteriorated. In 1953 there had been religious agitation among various Muslim sects, and Martial Law had been declared in the city of Lahore. In 1952 the Basic Principles Committee presented a second draft constitution also recommending a bi-cameral system and based on parity between East and West Pakistan. This draft was especially resented by the Punjabi members of the Constituent Assembly who feared that parity might lead to Bengali dominance.[31] By that time Ghulam Mohammed had become governor-general of Pakistan, and in 1954 he strongly supported a Punjabi proposal for integrating all the provinces of the western wing into one single province. According to the One Unit Documents, West Pakistan, in its confrontation with East Bengal, should speak as one entity.[32] The one-unit scheme was thus an attempt to sever the Bengal, Sind, North-West province axis. It was resented by the smaller provinces in the West, where ministries opposing the scheme were dismissed by the governor-general.[33]

At the national level it led to a power struggle between the Constituent Assembly and the governor-general who finally dismissed the Constituent Assembly in October 1954.[34] This created a constitutional crisis,[35] but finally a new Constituent Assembly was set up in May 1955, constituted by members indirectly elected from the provincial assemblies. Its major purpose—like the previous one—was to draft a constitution for Pakistan. The constitution which was finally adopted by February 1956 was based on compromises, and the framers were guided by an 'interplay of personal, group and provincial ambitions'.[36] Even before the constitution was framed, various deals had been made between the groups. In return for joining, Fazlul Huq and the new prime minister, Chaudhri Muhammad Ali, agreed to lift governor's rule in Bengal, and a new Krishak Sramik government was formed. Suhrawardy had become Law Minister in the central cabinet, and Major-General Izkandar Mirza became governor-general.[37]

Before the Constitution was passed, the Constituent Assembly passed a bill for the unification of the Western provinces, henceforth called West Pakistan. At the same time East Bengal was renamed East Pakistan. This bill was resented by the small provinces in the west as well as by the political élite in Bengal, with the exception of Suhrawardy who supported it strongly.[38]

As pointed out, the constitution of 1956 was based on compromises, including the acceptance of Bengali as one of two state languages (Urdu being the other). Unlike the previous drafts, it was based on only one chamber, called the National Assembly, to be elected on a basis of parity between East and West. However, it provided for a strong central government, and this was widely resented, especially in East Pakistan where the faction of the Awami League which was under the leadership of Bhashani declared that East Pakistan might have to think in terms of secession.[39]

The lack of cultural consensus and nationalist commitment among the various peoples in Pakistan was so great that it took its leaders nine years to frame a constitution which should be the institutional framework for nation-building. In the political struggle among the centralists and the autonomists, the centralists prevailed, but they were not able to govern the country on the basis of the constitution. In other words, the dominant classes of West Pakistan were only hegemonic to the extent that they could *impose* their uniform conception of the world on the rest of society, but not in a real sense, as it was unable to articulate different visions of the world in such a way that their potential antagonism was neutralized. Because of this inability, antagonistic interpellations against the ideology of the dominant bloc increased.[40] Before the army finally imposed martial law and took over power in October 1958, there had been as many as four different prime ministers in the intervening two and a half years.

The parliamentary system failed to solve the basic relationship between the centre and the periphery in creating integrative institutions. It has been maintained that after the imposition of Martial Law the country 'began to be governed by an authoritarian system'.[41] However, it seems closer to actual facts to argue that Pakistan had had an authoritarian system governed by civil servants from the beginning, and later by civil servants and the army. It was pointed out above that already in the first cabinet a leading civil servant, Ghulam Mohammed, was made minister of finance. He later became governor-general. Another high-ranking civil bureaucrat, Chaudhri Muhammad Ali started out with a politically influential position as secretary-general under Jinnah, and ended up as prime minister in 1955. In that year the office of governor-general went from a civil bureaucrat to Major-General Izkandar Mirza. Also in 1955 Ayub Khan, who had become commander-in-chief of the army in 1951, was made minister of defence. Thus Alavi's analysis seems more to the point when he argues that the bureaucratic military oligarchy had been in effective control of state power from the inception of the state. During the 'period of "parliamentary government", the true role of the bureaucratic military oligarchy was obscured by the political fiction under which it operated. After 1958, its dominant and decisive role became manifest'.[42]

(4) Political realignments in Bengal

Before the attempts of nation-building through the parliamentarian process was stopped by the army, political realignments took place in East Pakistan. It was mentioned above the Bhashani had threatened secession in 1956. The final split up of the Awami League came in 1957, when Suhrawardy was prime minister at the national level. He supported the 1956 constitution on the grounds that it had guaranteed ninety-eight per cent provincial autonomy. Besides, as mentioned, he supported the one-unit scheme for West Pakistan. Both these policies, as well as his foreign policy, were opposed by the Bhashani faction, and in 1957, along with some leftist groups, they formed the National Awami Party which was based on socialism and internationalism.[43]

Thus, during the first decade of Pakistan the various sections of the Bengali Muslim élite had crystallized more sharply. The upper class, the landed aristocracy, had completely lost its political influence as a result of the 1954 provincial election. The two sections of the middle class competed for control during the period. The urban-based (previously Calcutta-based) section supporting Suhrawardy became less involved in regional politics, whereas it was primarily the vernacular élite which pressed the demand for regional autonomy. As pointed out, it was especially the students who provided the leadership in the language movement which was 'crucial to the development of the vernacular élite'.[44] A survey[45] undertaken in the early sixties showed that about three-quarters of the students came from villages or small towns and about half of them from peasant families. This rural background of the students explains the support from the peasants, as witnessed especially during the 1954 provincial election.

It has been pointed out that during the late 1950s there were signs in East Pakistan that the Krashak Sramik Party, the Awami League, and the religious Nizam-i-Islam Party would join together in one moderate/conservative party opposed by the more radical National Awami Party with its base among peasants and industrial workers.[46] However, by the time of imposition of martial law the class alliances within the different parties were not very clear-cut, and when party politics was resumed in the mid-60s, the nationalist issue dominated Bengal politics, to a large extent cutting across class lines.

(5) *Economic policy and development of new social classes*

a. *Industrialization policy*

It was pointed out in the introduction to this chapter that before independence the areas which came to constitute Pakistan had primarily been exporters of agricultural commodities, and there was hardly any industry, its contribution to national income being less than one per cent.[47] Partition interrupted transportation, communication and trade, and there were no links between the two wings.

Like all the newly-independent nations, Pakistan wanted to become a modern industrialized state.[48] Besides, it was believed that economic development would further the nation-building process, as it would bring greater interdependence.[49] Both politicans and civil bureaucrats were in favour of an economic development strategy based on private ownership of the means of production,[50] i.e. the capitalist path. However, government control over actual investment has been considerable. About 40 per cent of gross monetary investment has been public, and these investments have gone to industrial undertakings where no private interest existed, and to infrastructure required by industry.[51] The establishment of private enterprises was often given an initial push through semi-autonomous bodies, e.g. through the Pakistan Industrial Development Corporation which was set up in 1950. This corporation was financed and controlled by the state which would initiate and establish enterprises and then turn them over to private ownership, once they were in progress.[52]

The absence of industrialization meant that there was no native bourgeoisie in Pakistan at the time of partition. Thus, in order to industrialize the country on the basis of free enterprise, the government had to rely on the immigrant trading communities as agents of its industrialization programme.[53] As pointed out above, these were reluctant to take long-term risks with their capital. In order to induce them to take such risks the government introduced various measures which would provide incentives for private investment, primarily in import-substitution industries.

The most important measure adopted to ensure industrialization was to rely on export earnings from cash crops, especially raw jute from Bengal. This strategy was implemented by complementary measures, the use of differential exchange rates and control of imports. Through this system the price of exports was kept low, and the exporters furthermore had to surrender their exchange earnings to the government. Through an import licensing system the government then allocated the foreign exchange to the importation of capital goods. This made it possible to sell domestic manufactures at high prices, thus providing incentives for investment. The net result of these measures was to turn the terms of trade against agriculture by transferring real income from the agricultural sector to the import and import-substituting sector. The measures also affected the price of agricultural products in the home market, and throughout the period up to 1958, the terms of trade facing agriculture was less than one half of what it would have been, had agricultural products been traded in world markets.

These measures thus provided the incentives necessary to risk capital investment, for 'the deterioration of agriculture's terms of trade increased industrial profitability because (i) the price of wage goods was kept down, thus keeping pressure off money wages, and (ii) the industrial sector had access to the foreign exchange earned by the agricultural sector at less than the opportunity cost to the economy. This access to foreign exchange was for imports of both capital goods and raw materials. In effect, the agricultural sector was selling its output to the manufacturing sector in exchange for manufactured goods at a set of prices that were very disadvantageous to agriculture, and the manufacturing sector was receiving a substantial windfall on each transaction'.[54]

As East Bengal contributed between one half and almost three quarters of the foreign exchange earnings during the first decade (50 per cent 1950 – 55 and 61 per cent during 1956 – 60),[55] it was especially the eastern wing which bore the cost of the exchange policy and the squeezing of the peasants.[56]

It was, however, not only the adverse terms of trade against agriculture which resulted in a disproportionate share of the industrialization policy being borne by the Bengalis. Another factor which resulted in the economic exploitation of the eastern wing was that most investments took place in West Pakistan, as East Pakistan received less than one-third of the total domestic investment, and less than one-third of commodity imports.[57] As interwing trade increased and manufactures were exported from the western to the eastern wing at inflated prices (due to tariff barriers resulting in domestic prices exceeding world market prices by 150 per cent at an average),[58] a further outflow of resources from east to west took place.

There were several reasons why industrial investment took place primarily in the West. For one thing most of the immigrant traders-turned-industrialists had settled in the West, especially in Karachi. Secondly, the central government was located in Karachi, and with resources and licences being controlled by the government, easy access and personal contacts to government were of great importance.[59] Finally, as the civil service dominated the government, and West Pakistanis dominated the civil service, these had a bias towards public investment in the West, especially as regards urban power and transport development.[60]

By traditional indices the government's industrial policy was a success; between 1949 and 1964 the output of the modern manufacturing sector increased at an average rate of 15 per cent per year.[61] The various measures adopted had provided sufficient incentives for private investment—incentives which provided profit rates of up to 100 per cent of invested capital in a single year.[62] That it was especially the traditional trading communities which took advantage of these opportunities is seen from Table 4.1.

As seen from the table, these traditional trading communities controlled about half of all industrial assets. The table further shows that although a little less than one-third of the investment took place in the eastern wing, only 11 per cent of the industrial assets were controlled by Bengalis, and of these less than one-third by the Muslims. This meant that much of the wealth created in

Table 4.1. Approximate percentage of industrial assets by 'community' 1959

Community	Private Muslim firms only	All firms	Share of population
%	%	%	%
Muslim trading communities	74.5	50.5	0.5
Bengali Muslim	3.5	2.5	43.0
Other Muslim	22.0	14.0	
Bengali Hindu		8.5	10.0
Other private non-Muslim		5.5	2.5
British		7.5	
Other foreign		1.0	
Public enterprises		12.0	

Source: adapted from Papanek, table II, p. 42.

Bengali industries was taken out of the province in forms of interest and profits, etc.

Not only was a substantial share of industrial assets controlled by the small trading communities. Data also show that by 1959 seven individuals, families, or foreign corporations controlled one-quarter of all private industrial assets. In addition, about 15 units owned about three-quarters of all the shares in banks and insurance companies.[63]

As Papanek—who was influential in formulating Pakistan's economic policy—has pointed out, 'concentration gave to a small group tremendous economic power, translatable into political influence'.[64]

The most powerful political influence was exerted through the Federation of Chambers of Commerce and Industries which represented West Pakistani business interests and controlled 96 per cent of Muslim-owned private industries, and 'its managing committee became the most powerful pressure group in the capital'.[65] Their main pressure was to secure foreign exchange and licences, and on several occasions they were responsible for the fall of cabinets. Thus, it was partly due to their pressure that Suhrawardy had to resign, as he had introduced parity between east and west in the allocation of foreign exchange and gave preference to import licences to under-represented areas, including East Pakistan.[66]

b. *Agricultural policy*

It was shown above that the government's economic policy was focused on industrial development, and that the strategy included squeezing the agricultural sector. This would lead one to expect a contradiction between the emergent capitalist interests and those of the feudal landlords. However, an analysis of the government's policy shows that it was not directed against the feudal landlords. For one thing, the government did not press for land reforms. Secondly, agricultural income remained exempt from income tax.

Furthermore, the big landlords received most of the government's subsidies in agriculture, and it was thus possible to increase the 'agricultural surplus required to sustain industrialization and urbanization as well as of expanding the domestic market for manufactured goods. Pressures for radical action [had] diminished, while those for mutual accommodation [had] increased'.[67]

As both the army and the civil service recruited their senior officers from the big landlords in the West, these maintained a built-in position in the bureaucracy. At the same time the bureaucracy had a class interest in the privileges of the landlords.

The absence of a serious contradiction between the emergent capitalist interests and the feudal landlords and the tendency towards mutual economic and political accommodation, however, only applied to the relationship between those two classes in West Pakistan. As pointed out in Chapter III, to the peasants of Bengal the movement for national liberation from the British was primarily a struggle against the Hindu zamindars. This contradiction to a large extent was resolved by the East Bengal State Acquisition and Tenancy Act passed by the East Bengal Legislative Assembly in early 1950. The major features of the act were to eliminate rent-receiving interests and to redistribute land. While it did abolish the zamindari system, its redistributive impact was 'quite negligible. There was a redistribution, but it was not from rich land-owners to poor raiyats (cultivators). The main effect of the Act was a redistribution of income from a class of rural intermediaries to the (urban middle-class based) provincial government'.[68]

In analysing the mode of production in Bengal resulting from the British intervention, in the economy, Alamgir has referred to it as semi-feudal,[69] the major characteristics of which are (1) sharecropping, (2) multiplex social roles of dominant groups, (3) perpetual indebtedness of small tenants, and (4) distress sale of assets and produce by small tenants.[70] While under feudalism the principal contradiction is between feudal lords and the peasantry, under semi-feudalism, it is between rich peasants, merchants, traders and middlemen and usurers (money-lenders) on the one hand, and poor peasants and agricultural labourers on the other.[71]

With the abolition of the zamindari system in 1950 the legal superstructure of feudalism was removed, while the semi-feudal relations of production (which had in fact co-existed with feudal relations throughout the British period)[72] became dominant. This further enhanced the position of the peasant-money-lender landlord category in the rural areas.

Because of the economic exploitation, resulting from the economic policy of Pakistan outlined above, East Pakistan was turned into a society which Alamgir has described as semi-colonial and semi-feudal. The semi-colonial aspect meant that surplus was extracted from the peasantry in East Pakistan and transferred to West Pakistan, and at the same time 'the West Pakistani bourgeoisie intervened in a manner such that it preserved perpetuated semi-feudal exploitation in the countryside'.[73]

This process resulted in a number of contradictions, among others (1) the contradiction between poor peasants and landless labourers on the one hand, and semi-feudal interests on the other, and (2) the contradiction between West

Pakistan and East Bengal. As will be shown at the end of this chapter, it also resulted in the ideological discourse of Bengali nationalism which came to predominate.

B. Military rule

(1) Consolidation of power

Alavi has pointed out that the bureaucratic military oligarchy does not necessarily prefer to rule directly; rather, 'it often prefers to rule through politicians, as long as the latter do not impinge upon its own relative autonomy and power'.[74]

Through this strategy of indirect rule the military had been in effective control of state power during the first decade of Pakistan. The politicians supporting the regime in 1958 were, however, unlikely to win the general elections scheduled for the spring of 1959, and the military *coup d'état* in October 1958 was primarily aimed at forestalling these elections, which were feared to give the majority to regional politicians, not only from East Pakistan, but also from the various regions in the western wing.[75] Thus, in order to maintain their power unchallenged, the military had to rule directly.

In order to evaluate the policies pursued by the military under the leadership of Ayub Khan, it may be useful to look into his political philosophy. Ayub Khan had nothing but contempt for politicians, who—according to him— 'used provincial feelings, sectarian, religious, and racial differences to set a Pakistani against a Pakistani'.[76] Besides, he had no faith in the western political system, which he found unsuited for Pakistan. As early as 1954—after becoming defence minister—he wrote a memorandum regarding his views of the 'Present and Future Problems of Pakistan'.[77] According to Ayub Khan, Pakistan needed a constitution suiting the genius of the people. The two central points in the constitution envisaged by him was first and foremost the concentration of power in the office of the president: 'The president should be made the final custodian of power on the country's behalf, and should be able to put things right in both the provinces and the Centre—should they go wrong. Laws should be operative only if certified by the president, except in cases where they are passed by three-fourths majority. No change in the constitution should be made, unless agreed to by the president'.[78] Secondly, he envisaged a system of indirect election. As will be shown below, the 1962 constitution to a large extent adopted the original 1954 outline.

However, before a new constitution could be adopted, he followed the immediate aim outlined in the 1954 memorandum, viz. to take certain preliminary steps that 'will provide for the setting for the unhindered evolution of such a constitution. The taking of such preliminary steps therefore becomes the *immediate* aim of Pakistan'.[79]

Several of the first steps taken by the military regime were directed against the politicians. The most important step was the Elective Bodies (Disqualification) Ordinance which disqualified approximately seven thousand people from political life.[80]

(2) Mobilization of political support

In order to justify the military take-over by unconstitutional means, the regime had to legitimize itself, and for this it needed a support base apart from the military. After having repressed the vocal opposition by disqualifying the political leaders, the regime took steps to generate a new group of leaders who—it was hoped—would mobilize mass support for the government.[81] The steps adopted very closely followed the guidelines Ayub had provided in his 1954 memorandum. In order to bypass the politicians he had suggested that 'it would be advisable to enable people to elect a college of people in each sub-unit who in turn elect members for the Provincial and Central legislatures. Such an electoral system would be more easily manageable, and would make for a good deal of responsibility'.[82] It was such a manageable system which was introduced by the Basic Democracy's Order, which was promulgated in October 1959, one year after the military coup. The Basic Democracies system served a dual purpose in that it provided for local self-government, and at the same time it acted as an electoral college for presidential and assembly elections.

Soon after the Order was promulgated, the elections of Basic Democrats took place during December 1959 and January 1960. Despite the considerable publicity given to the election, including Ayub's extensive tour of both wings, the voter turn-out was low in East Pakistan and in the major cities,[83] and as many as 25 per cent of the seats were uncontested. Because of the Disqualification Order, it was not surprising that only seven per cent of those elected in East Pakistan had previous party affiliation.

The above argument, that one of the primary purposes of the Basic Democracies system was to legitimize the regime, is confirmed by the fact that one month after their election the Basic Democrats, as an electoral college, were called upon to vote whether or not they had confidence in President Ayub Khan. The president's manageable body voted overwhelmingly in favour, 96 per cent of those voting confirming their confidence in the president, who then declared himself the first elected president of Pakistan.[84]

Having taken the preliminary steps, the President then appointed a Constitution Commission, and, as he was not satisfied with their views, two additional advisory committees were later appointed. However, in the final analysis, and despite the recommendations of the various bodies, the final constitution as promulgated in March 1962 closely followed Ayub's 1954 recommendation of a presidential system with political power concentrated in the office of the president, and indirect elections through an electoral college for the office of the president, as well as for the national and provincial assemblies.[85] As was observed by an East Pakistani politician, it was 'a government of the President, by the President, and for the President'.[86]

Von Vorys aptly characterized Ayub Khan's system as a guided democracy, the main feature of which was a guided process where each step was accompanied by control mechanisms. He has described the process as follows: 'Every new step was introduced with special reference to the past and to the future, and all the media of communication were concentrated on disseminating this impression. The Revolution was caused by the disintegration of the political structure, and brought about a military interregnum. The system of Basic Democracies was caused by the consolidation. The Constitution was caused by the successful operation of the Basic Democracies and would bring about the lifting of martial law'.[87]

Having introduced the Basic Democracies system, which was largely controlled by the bureaucracy as far as local self-government was concerned, and by the indirect election procedure through the electoral college, and having prepared the 1962 constitution with the power concentrated in the presidency, he then embarked on the next step, viz. the holding of elections to the national and provincial assemblies.

The polling by the electoral college for the members of the National Assembly took place at the end of April, and for the members of the provincial assemblies in early May 1962. These elections took place at a time when political parties were not allowed, when several national political leaders were in jail, and others disqualified; and the elections did not arouse a lot of interest. That the electoral system turned out to be manageable is evidenced by the fact that, of the 76 members elected to the National Assembly from East Pakistan, 43 had been actively associated with the Muslim League in the past.[88-9]

The newly-elected National Assembly met on 7 June. On the same day the new constitution came into effect, and martial law was lifted.

As mentioned, under the new constitution political power was concentrated in the office of the president, who had the backing of the army and the bureaucracy. The control of the latter was by no means diminished; a number of parliamentary secretaries were appointed—drawn from the membership of the National Assembly—to maintain liaison between the Assembly, the cabinet ministers and the administrative secretaries. In effect, 'like the Basic Democracies which were linked to and dominated by the bureaucracy, the legislatures were brought under administrative influence'.[90]

At the provincial level the control of the president was assured through the governor who was appointed by the president.[91]

The rationale behind the guided democracy introduced by Ayub Khan was that it would work and be controlled without a political party. However, although the electoral system assured that manageable members became elected, it could not control the mounting opposition to the construction. The absence of a government political party deprived the government of an organizational framework for mass mobilization on behalf of the government.

Thus, in July, a bill permitting political parties was passed, but the Disqualification Order from 1959 remained in force. A few months later the government took over the old Muslim League Party at a Convention. This party was later called Convention Muslim League. In March 1963 Ayub Khan himself was elected president of the Convention Muslim League.

Although the introduction of a government-controlled political party headed by the president increased Ayub Khan's power of control, and facilitated mass mobilization in support of the government, the change was in fact a great concession on his part. For one thing, the party was introduced from the top, and thus did not work from below gradually going to the top, as he had announced when he introduced the Basic Democracies Order. Secondly, he was forced to rely on the political party system which he had 'castigated . . . as a bane of the past'.[92]

Ayub Khan's efforts to change the political system to suit the genius of the people thus had limited success. The constitutional provisions did provide the president with vast power, and the electoral system, along with the Disqualifications Order, did disenfranchise the leading opposition politicians. As far as East Pakistan was concerned, this meant that the vernacular élite, which had dominated Bengal politics during the fifties, was barred from voicing its opposition in the elected assemblies. However, outside these bodies, they continued their opposition to the government, and in the autumn of 1962 Suhrawardy formed the National Democratic Front, which included leading opposition politicians from both West and East Pakistan. Especially in East Pakistan, the meetings of the Front drew large crowds, and the appeal of the opposition can be measured from the acceleration of coercive measures in both West and East Pakistan.[93]

The regime's response to the political opposition was twofold. As pointed out above, the president was not able to manage the political system without resort to military and legal repression. At the same time, the president continued the efforts to build up a new group of leaders through the Basic Democracies system. The success of these efforts is witnessed by the result of the 1965 presidential elections.

The central issue in this election was the political system. For Ayub Khan the presidential election was primarily a means to demonstrate his legitimacy by public endorsement, which would also symbolize popular ratification of the constitution. The opposition parties joined together in a front of Combined Opposition Parties (COP), who nominated Miss Fatima Jinnah, the sister of Muhammad Ali Jinnah, as their candidate. She contested the election on the COP nine-point programme, calling for the restoration of democracy, including a parliamentary system.

The presidential election was preceded by an election of Basic Democrats who were to elect the president. Whereas there had been little public interest in the 1959 Basic Democracies election, the 1964 election was accompanied by a lot of political campaigning, both on the part of the president and of the COP. One reason was the forthcoming presidential election, and another was the fact that the channelling of development funds—especially under the works programme—through the Union Councils gave the Basic Democrats considerable economic and political power, and the seats were keenly contested.[94]

Despite the heavy involvement of both major presidential candidates in the Basic Democracies election, local issues remained important in the election, and empirical studies show that personal abilities rather than party affiliation were important in the elections.[95] So, when the Basic Democracies election was finished in November 1964, the party loyalty of those elected was unknown, and consequently the result of the presidential election scheduled for January 1965 was by no means a foregone conclusion, as indicated by the fact that both parties claimed the election to be a victory for their respective candidates. As has been pointed out, it is probable that, 'at this time, a substantial number, if not most, of successful candidates simply did not have party commitment. They were open to persuasion'.[96] Between the completion of the Basic Democracies election in November and the presidential election in January 1965, both candidates toured the country. The COP politicians were quite optimistic because of the much larger crowds attending Miss Jinnah's meetings. However, while Miss Jinnah concentrated on public rallies, Ayub Khan had more meetings with specialized groups, including the Basic Democrats, i.e. the members of the electorial college. The final result was a significant victory for the president, who got 63 per cent of the votes. The victory was highest in West Pakistan, where he received 73 per cent of the votes, but even in East Pakistan he pulled over half, viz. 53 per cent of the votes.[97]

As pointed out above, the election of Basic Democrats was heavily contested, not least because of the considerable economic and political power accruing to the members of the Union Boards through the development programmes. Thus, it is not surprising that the majority of the councillors were committed to the regime, and voted for Ayub Khan.

Thus, although Ayub Khan had to resort to the despised political party system to mobilize support for his regime, the results of the 1965 presidential election show that he did succeed in building up a power base outside the military. In order to evaluate the—short-term—success, it is necessary to analyse his economic policy as well as the inner dynamics of the Basic Democracies system.

(3) Economic policy

The economic policy of the Ayub Khan regime had three political purposes. One was a legitimating one, i.e. if he could demonstrate the regime's ability to secure economic development, the seizure of power would be justified. Closely related to this purpose was the integrative function, where economic development was considered an important instrument in securing national integration. Both these purposes were in fact a continuation of the policy of the previous regimes. Thirdly, he also used his economic development policy to secure a political support base outside the military.

The economic development policy of the Ayub Khan regime differed in two respects from the policy of the previous regime. Firstly, according to the government's own claim, there was a shift in favour of private enterprise. This claim was substantiated by the increase in commercial credit, transfer of industries operated by the Pakistan Industrial Development Corporation, tax holidays, and better arrangements for private entrepreneurs and importers.[98] Secondly, the government recognized the necessity of removing the disparities between the provinces, a policy which became incorporated in the 1962 Constitution.[99]

In order to improve the economic situation in East Pakistan various measures were adopted. In 1962 the Pakistan Industrial Development Corporation was bifurcated, and the East Pakistan Industrial Development

Corporation established. Secondly, there was an increase in the allocation of resources allocated to East Pakistan. Thus, public sector allocations to East Pakistan increased from 35 per cent during 1955 – 60 to 45 per cent during 1960 – 5, and after 1965 it was above fifty per cent of total public sector expenditure. Also, the share of development loans allocated to East Pakistan increased during the sixties, and the province received about two-thirds of such loans by the middle of the decade. The same holds true for foreign project assistance, which increased from about one-third during the 1950s to an average of 44 per cent during 1960 – 6.[100]

The decade of Ayub Khan's rule has been termed the development decade.[101] From the point of view of economic growth, this characterization is quite appropriate. The annual rate of growth of g.n.p. increased from 2.4 per cent during 1955 – 60 to 5.3 per cent during 1960 – 5.[102] As far as the Eastern wing was concerned, the economic performance showed a significant improvement over the previous decade. The annual rate of growth of gross domestic product in East Pakistan increased from 1.7 per cent during 1955 – 60 to 5.2 per cent during 1960 – 5, and the per capita annual growth rate went from 0.6 per cent to 2.6 per cent during the respective periods.[103] Besides, there are some indices that the exploitation of East Pakistan by West Pakistan was less pronounced during the 1960s than during the preceding period: East Pakistan's share of total export earnings declined from 70 per cent during 1960 – 1 to 55 per cent during 1965 – 6, due primarily to a greater increase in West Pakistan's export earnings.[104] Thus, the contribution of East Pakistan to the industrialization of the West decreased. Secondly, while the terms of trade against agriculture remained considerable, especially against East Pakistan, the squeeze was ameliorated, during the early 1960s. While during 1955—8 East Pakistan agriculture received only 45 per cent of what it would have received on the world market, the proportion was increased to 59 per cent during 1961 – 4.[105]

However, despite the improved economic situation, inequalities were growing, not only between various sections of the population, but also between the two wings. On a national basis, civil servants, businessmen and some big peasants improved their economic situation, while the 'losers included the bulk of the population—families dependent on agriculture, and particularly, landless workers'.[106] (It should be pointed out that this general trend does not apply internally in East Pakistan. While the bulk of the population were losers on a national scale, the data reveal some reduction in inequality as far as income distribution is concerned during the mid-sixties, both in the rural and the urban areas.[107])

Comparing the two wings of the country, the data show that in terms of meeting the aim of decreasing disparity between the two wings, the result was not a success. Although the growth in gross domestic product in East Pakistan was significant in the early 60s, the rate was even higher in the western wing, with a yearly per capita growth rate of 4.4 per cent (compared to 2.6 per cent for East Pakistan). The disparity index rose throughout the 1960s.[108]

In terms of fulfilling the political purpose, the economic policy thus had some degree of success, at least in the short run. The economic performance, in terms of economic growth, did provide the regime with legitimacy. As far as national integration is concerned, the results were less clear-cut. While the economy of East Pakistan improved considerably over the previous decade, disparity continued to increase, a development which became of major political importance in the latter half of the 1960s.

In terms of securing political support outside the military and bureaucracy, the regime's economic policy had some success, not least in West Pakistan, where the new entrepreneurial class was strongly behind the Ayub government. As mentioned, the military government had strongly promoted private enterprise by granting tax holidays and other concessions, and the growth rate was especially high for the industrial sector (about 13 per cent annually for large-scale manufacture during the period 1960 – 5).[109] The industrialists clearly benefited from the government's policy, and they supported a strong and stable government. Most of Ayub's supporters in the big industrial cities in West Pakistan were business magnates.[110]

In West Pakistan the President was also supported by the landlords. Although the regime's land reform measures were more effective than those undertaken by the previous governments, only 5 per cent of the land owned by the biggest landowners possessing above 500 acres were distributed. Secondly, the land ceilings were kept high, primarily not to alienate the middle-sized landlords, from which class most of the army officers were recruited.[111]

The government was also able to exercise control over the landlords, not least through the immense power of the governor. At the same time the landlords depended on the bureaucracy, 'without whose good-will and support it would be difficult . . . to carry on their activities and control their tenants'.[112]

As regards East Pakistan, the government had purposely encouraged the growth of a Bengali industrialist and business class. These received substantial support from the government in form of loans from the Industrial Development Board and the East Pakistan Development Corporation. In terms of the proportion of total investment going to East Pakistan, there was no change between the two periods: the percentage of fixed investment in East Pakistan actually declined from 34 per cent in 1959 – 60 to 31 per cent in 1965 – 6,[113] and private investment in East Pakistan never rose above 24 per cent of total private investment during the 1960s.[114] However, in terms of actual investments in East Pakistan, the amounts doubled between 1960 and 1965.[115] Thus, the rising Bengali industrialists owed their newly-acquired wealth to the Ayub regime. At the same time they faced severe competition from the West Pakistani industrialists.[116] The support of this class to the Ayub regime was ambivalent. As will be shown below, the representation of the class, both in the National Assembly and in the local councils under the Basic Democracies system, increased during the 1960s, and it is to be assumed that those seeking election by and large supported the system.

Thus, while the economic policy of the regime did not reduce disparities between the two wings, it did create a small group of entrepreneurs with sufficient influence in the electorial bodies to secure the victory of Ayub Khan during the 1965 presidential election.

In addition—as will be shown below—the government's policy regarding the rural economy also brought to power a group of farmers owing their economic prosperity to the regime.

(4) Basic democracies system

As the Basic Democracies system had an important impact on both economic and political development in East Pakistan, it will be dealt with in detail.

In East Pakistan local self-government was not new. Some kind of local councils existed in the pre-British period, when the village panchayats (councils) were responsible for the management of rural administration. During the colonial period the British took several steps to train the people in local self-government through the enactment of various laws, the latest being the Village Self-Government Act of 1919, which replaced an earlier three-tier system with a two-tier system consisting of Union Boards and District Boards in the rural areas. The Union Boards had various functions, the maintenance of a rural police being the most important one. Besides, most of them undertook works for public health, waterworks, water supply, etc. The Union Boards had self-taxation powers to finance their duties, and they were entrusted with some judicial functions. During the early Pakistan period the local bodies did not perform very well, primarily due to lack of resources, and lack of co-ordination with national planning. So, as far as local self-government was concerned, the introduction of Basic Democracies was in fact a revitalization of the pre-existing local bodies.

The new system consisted of a four-tier structure, the lowest and most important tier being the Union Council, covering an area of eight to twelve square miles, and with a population of 8,000 to 12,000. Election to this body was on the basis of universal adult franchise with one councillor or Basic Democrat representing 800 to 1,500 persons. A total of 40,000 Basic Democrats were to be elected from East Pakistan, and a similar number from the western wing. Above the Union Council was the thana Council (covering 8 – 15 unions), which consisted of the chairman of the Union Councils, and an equal number of nominated government officials. Further up the hierarchy was the District Council, where half the members were nominated, and half indirectely elected by the chairman of the Union Councils. The top tier was the Divisional Council, also with half of its members nominated, and the other half indirectly elected by the elected members of the District Council.[117]

In the towns and the cities, the lowest tier was called town (or union) committee. As most of the population in East Pakistan lived (and lives) in the rural areas, the vast majority of the Basic Democrats were elected in rural areas. Thus, the system was manageable to the extent that it bypassed the vocal opposition, which was especially strong in the cities. That this was a clear aim of the government is indicated by Ayub's statement to the effect that '. . . the council which will be formed will be free from the curse of party intrigues, political pressures and tub-thumping politicians that characterized the Assemblies in our country in the past'.[118]

As mentioned above, the political purpose of the Basic Democracies system was to legitimize the regime by building up a rural support base. The system was also used as a vehicle for bringing the government close to the people. Here the purpose was twofold: one was to involve the population in decisions on local issues, and the other to control these decisions. The latter purpose was achieved through the bureaucracy. As has been pointed out, 'the most important feature of the four-tier system of Basic Democracies is the presence of officials at all the three levels, except the Union Councils'.[119] As the chairman of every council, except the Union Council, was an official (i.e. a bureaucrat), and as the lower bodies were required to perform their functions under the close supevision and control of officials and the respective higher councils and committees,[120] the influence and control of the bureaucrats was considerable. As will be shown below, through their actual involvement in the political process, their influence was further enhanced.

Both the local political power of the councillors, as well as the control of the bureaucracy, was enhanced through the government's local rural development programmes, which were administered through the councillors and the local level officials. The most important of these programmes was the Rural Works Programme, which was introduced all over East Pakistan during 1962–3.[121-2]

The control over development funds put the Basic Democrats in a position to dispense of financial patronage by virtue of their power to select those employed at the programme. This strengthened their economic power, and thus, further increased their political power. Moreover, the control over development funds also opened up avenues for personal enrichment. As has been pointed out, 'This combination of enhanced economic, and hence political power, along with the scope for direct financial enrichment, made the government in general, and the Works Programme in particular, irresistible to the Basic Democrats'.[123] This also made the position of the Basic Democrats very attractive, and after the introduction of the Works Programme, competition for seats in the local bodies became much more pronounced. Whereas 25 per cent of the seats were uncontested in 1959, fewer than 6 per cent were uncontested during the 1964 Basic Democracies election.[124]

In order to understand the full impact of the Basic Democracies system at the local level in East Pakistan, it is necessary to analyse it within the framework of the socio-economic structure. Data on income and land ownership (which are highly correlated) show that it is the upper peasantry which dominated the local councils. During the early 1960s about 3 per cent of the landowners in East Pakistan owned above 12.5 acres of land, while 42 per cent of the Basic Democrats owned above this acreage.[125] As far as income is concerned, about 15 per cent of the income earners had incomes above Rs. 3,000 against 46 per cent of the Basic Democrats elected in 1964. And for the chairman of the union councils, 59 per cent had annual incomes above Rs. 5,000.

As regards occupational background, there seems to have been a change. Given the dominance of agriculture in rural East Pakistan, it is not surprising to find that the majority of the members of the local bodies were farmers (the average being around 80 per cent for both the previous union boards and the union councils of 1959 and 1964). However, while lawyers and other professionals constituted about 10 per cent of the councillors in the pre-1959 union boards, their representation declined to about 2.8 per cent in 1964. At the same time, the representation of the businessmen or contractors increased from 11 per cent during the 1950s to 16 per cent in 1959 and 17 per cent in 1964. Among the chairmen elected in 1964, as much as 24 per cent were businessmen or contractors, and at the district level this group constituted as much as 42 per cent.[126]

Whereas all analyses of the Basic Democrats confirm the above conclusion that the local bodies (and hence the electoral college) were dominated by the upper peasantry, there seems to be some uncertainty regarding the family background of this class in the sixties. One analysis concludes that it was no longer possible to have local bodies dominated by traditional families, such as zamindars and taluqdars. In fact, the author found that 86 per cent of the union council members came from families other than the traditional ones.[127] If one restricts the definition of traditional families exclusively to zamindars and taluqdars, there seems little reason to question the above findings. However, as pointed out in Chapter III, during the first half of this century the upper peasantry had been mobilized through Fazlul Huq's Krishak Praja Party, and it was this group which wielded power in the countryside.[128] Thus, the change in rural leadership seems to predate the Ayub Khan period by at least four decades. The power of this class was entrenched during the Muslim League government of Bengal in the late 1930s, and in the absence of contradictory evidence, it seems reasonable to argue that it was from among this socio-economic group that the Basic Democrats were recruited. This argument is substantiated by the case history of local-level politics from the area studied during 1975 – 6.[129] It is also confirmed by a study on the local people's opinion regarding the causes of success and failure of the Basic Democrats. As many as 88 per cent of those interviewed listed hereditary influence as the cause for success of sitting Basic Democrats. The author concludes that 'It reaffirms the notion of a sort of rural élite who over the years have had an option on village politics. This class being more often than not the well-off or 'surplus' farmers whose influence is synonymous with wealth above the average'.[130]

The same study shows that, while 77 per cent of the sitting members contested the 1964 Basic Democracies election, only 48 per cent of the sitting members were returned, and less than half (44 per cent) received more than 50 per cent of the votes in their constituency. The author interprets the data as a negative vote against the system, where the small farmers and landless voiced their frustration against the immediate representatives, viz. the sitting Basic Democrats. And he concludes, 'for all practical purposes the election was more in the nature of a palace revolution. The class composition of the elected members remained unchanged, only the faces changed. The new incumbents cashed in on the resentment against the old members and the general sense of frustration, and rode to victory on the wings of social unrest. As far as the poor villagers were concerned, they had achieved a temporary catharsis, but in the long run they remained under the heels of their traditional oppressors'.

As far as the relationship between the various socio-economic groups in the rural areas is concerned, one cannot but agree with the conclusion drawn from the above study: 'It now appears that the economic domination of this same class of high income "surplus" farmers has been reinforced by their political domination of the rural areas'. Especially the control over the landless or land-poor labourers was increased, for it 'was this class of villager who was most dependent on the "surplus" farmer for a bit of land to farm, or for implements, or for casual jobs during harvest. Now this landlord and creditor also became the arbiter of whether he would work and hence eat in the winter months. Thus, the stranglehold was complete, and the labourer became the virtual serf of the "surplus" farmer.'[131] Thus, semi-feudal exploitation was perpetuated and strengthened.

It was pointed out above that the bureaucracy was represented at all levels of the Basic Democracies system except the union councils, where, however, their influence increased with the planning and implementation of development programmes. The development programmes entrenched the position of bureaucrats in the rural area, and at the same time the government could make use of this group at times of election. Interview data show that in some areas a large majority of the voters were approached by government officials, and asked to vote for a specific candidate.[132] Also, during the presidential and assembly elections, the bureaucracy put pressure on the Basic Democrats to vote for the government party. Like the Basic Democrats themselves, the bureaucracy's power of persuasion and pressure was considerable by virtue of their power to dispense favours and patronage.[133]

It thus seems safe to conclude that the introduction of the Basic Democracies at the local political level, along with the development programmes at the economic level, significantly increased the government's control. This control was exercised partly through specific socio-economic groups. In the rural areas it was the 'surplus' farmers, and in the urban areas, to a large extent, the businessmen and contractors. Since both groups had a vested interest in the economic policy of the Ayub regime, and thus, in the continuation of the system, the strategy of building up a loyal support base in East Pakistan was successful in the short run.

C. *The bureaucracy and the army*

Gunnar Myrdal has pointed out that 'Because of its decision to relinquish its political hold in the area, Britain was able to preserve all its financial, industrial and commercial positions in India and Pakistan practically intact. It also maintained much of its political and cultural influence in these two countries'.[134]

The British were able to maintain this influence by aligning themselves with and transferring power to the newly-emerging élite classes of professionals, landowners, and industrialists who had 'come in touch with western ideas of nationalism, parliamentary democracy, and industrial development'.[135]

From the turn of the century the British had recruited the army personnel from the landed aristocracy with the object to 'attach the higher ranks of

Indian society, and more especially the old aristocratic families to the British government by closer and more cordial ties'.[136] Furthermore, in order to ensure the political reliability of the army, the recruitment policy emphasized political conservatism. Thus, most officers were recruited from politically backward regions, and a myth was propagated of the so-called martial races of India, who were supposed to have unique fighting qualities. Thus, a large number of Pathans, Baluchis and Punjabi Muslims were recruited, whereas the Bengalis were deliberately excluded. During the Indianization of the army, top officers were sent for training at the Royal Military College at Sandhurst. One of these was Ayub Khan who, as mentioned above, became president after the army had taken over complete control of the country in 1958.

Also, the top civil servants were trained by the British. The Civil Service of Pakistan inherited the élitist tradition of the Indian Civil Service, and after independence it remained a tightly-knit and cohesive cadre. It was almost self-perpetuating, as most of the recruits were the sons of government servants.[137]

As was shown above, the economic power of the civil servants was considerable. Not only were they directors of government enterprises, but through their control of import and export they decided where to locate industries and to whom licences would be given.

This economic power of the civil servants was important not only in terms of their role as bureaucrats, but also in terms of class formation, i.e. their place in the social formation. As has been pointed out by several analysts, civil servants 'have made full use of their talents and the connections they have built up during their careers and thus have become leading industrialists',[138] 'accumulating profits directly and joining the ranks of the bourgeoisie'.[139-40]

The same alliance has taken place between private industry and the army bureaucracy, as 'big businessmen in Pakistan have adopted the practice of awarding profitable directorships to retiring generals'.[141]

Thus, while the business community does not exert political power through any specific party representing their interest, their political influence is through 'direct contact with and influence on the bureaucracy itself'.[142]

Through its direct involvement in the production process the state bourgeoisie (civil and military) established a place for itself in the emergent relations of production and came to constitute an effective class, to use Poulantzas's analytical framework. Its interests were identical with those of the rising industrial class, and to the extent that the civil-military oligarchy controlled state power—as argued above—it would be in their interest to exercise this power to the mutual interest of both sections of the bourgeoisie (the state and the industrial bourgeoisie).

As argued above, the bureaucratic-military oligarchy had been in effective control of state power since the inception of the state of Pakistan. After the military take-over in 1958, not only was the position of the military itself strengthened, but also the position of the bureaucracy was further entrenched, not least through the control of the local bodies set up as part of the Basic Democracies system. The increased emphasis on rural development and the involvement of the local bodies during the Ayub Khan regime in fact meant that the bureaucratic control was expanded vertically.

However, during the 1960s there was a significant change in the composition of the bureaucracy. In order to placate the political discontent in East Pakistan, the government increased the number of East Pakistanis in the Civil Service of Pakistan, and especially in the provincial secretariat, where, by 1964, 15 of 19 secretaries were East Pakistanis. At the time of Partition there were only a couple of East Pakistanis in the Civil Service of Pakistan, but by 1965 their proportion of the entire service had increased to 35 per cent. Given the immense decision-making powers of the civil servants under bureaucratic-military rule, this increase was important; but as the West Pakistani civil servants still held the key positions, the improvement fell short of placating the grievance of the East Pakistani political élite.[143]

Also, with the increase of East Pakistani bureaucrats in the provincial service, the homogeneity of the bureaucracy was broken. While the majority of the West Pakistani civil servants came from upper-class conservative backgrounds, their East Pakistani counterparts were predominantly from lower middle-class families, many of whom had kinship ties with the non-vernacular élite.[144] With the radicalization of the Bengal nationalist movement, the position of this group became ambiguous.

As far as army recruitment was concerned, the representation of East Pakistanis was not significantly increased during the Ayub Khan regime, especially as regards top-ranking officers. By the mid-sixties East Pakistanis constituted only 5 per cent of the officers of the Pakistani army, and only one had the rank of major general (of which there were 14 in all, and above these two lieutenant-generals and one general). The East Pakistanis complained that the government continued the British policy of recruiting primarily the so-called martial races.[145] However, as will be shown below, many of the officers and enlisted men from East Bengal came to play an important role during the war for national liberation.

D. *External linkages*

As pointed out above, during colonial rule the regions which came to constitute the Pakistan state had become integrated into the world capitalist system as suppliers of raw materials.

With the granting of independence to the colonies the colonial powers made sure that this integration was not severed, but was allowed to continue and to be strengthened.

The British handed over power to the ruling classes who, like themselves, were eager to 'prevent a popular socialist movement from materializing after the end of colonial rule'.[146]

The British influence in the army continued after independence through the British-trained top army officers. Besides, the first two commanders-in-chief of the Pakistan army were British, and as late as 1951 there were 200 British officers in the army.[147] As mentioned, British civil servants also stayed on after independence, including the important posts as provincial governors.

During the first decade, foreign investment in industry remained almost exclusively in British hands.

After World War II the power and influence of Britain was on the decline, and the United States was emerging as the leading western power, economically as well as politically. Internationally the United States soon became preoccupied with the containment of communism, especially after the communist take-over in China in 1949 and the Korean war; and one of the major global strategies of the United States was to seek Cold War Allies, not least in Asia.

Ever since Partition, relations between India and Pakistan were hostile. In the Cold War, India took a definite neutral position (Nehru was one of the leaders of the non-aligned nations). Pakistan was eager to secure allies against India, and thus needed little persuasion to become an ally of the United States, especially because of the obvious benefits in the form of military assistance.

After the 1952 election in the United States when John Foster Dulles became Secretary of State, close ties developed between the United States and Pakistan, especially the army, through Ayub Khan who had become commander-in-chief in 1951. In 1953 an Army Planning Board was set up to reorganize the army, and in 1954 a U.S. Military Assistance Advisory Group was established in Pakistan. In the same year Pakistan joined the South East Asia Treaty Organization (SEATO), and the U.S. Department of Defense could declare 'From a political viewpoint, U.S. military aid has strengthened Pakistan's armed services, the greatest stablizing force in the country, and has encouraged Pakistan to participate in collective defense agreements'.[148]

The relationship between the U.S. and the Pakistan army was so close that Ayub Khan consulted Washington before declaring Martial Law in 1958.[149]

Thus the external linkages were very influential in securing the ascendancy of the army in the political affairs of Pakistan, and during the 1960s the government's military expenditure increased significantly.[150]

Pakistan's external linkages, and the economic and political development described above, very well fit the pattern of other countries in the Third World during the neo-colonial phase, where 'national independence and the formation of the national state led to the creation of social strata between imperial capitalism and the labour force . . . rooted in the state bureaucracy it has access to powers of the state, including revenues and expenditures'.[151] As argued above, the army and the bureaucracy had an interest in preserving the social order based on private property and the *development* of the capitalist mode as the dominant mode of production. (The word *development* is emphasized, as it was argued above that the capitalist mode was not the dominant mode at the time of independence.) Petras has outlined three strategies available to the national regime in order to secure capital accumulation, viz. (1) 'dependent neo-colonialism' involving close collaboration with imperial firms, (2) 'national developmental' which limits imperial involvement and concentrates the surplus in the hand of state and/or private national entrepreneurs, and (3) 'national popular' involving nationalization and income distribution.[152]

The second strategy is also referred to as national developmentalism without redistribution and is characterized by concentration of income at the top of the national class hierarchy, and it very well fits the Pakistan model, although it also made use of elements of the first strategy, especially after the mid-1960s.

Some writers have maintained that the rising industrialists 'sought collaboration with foreign capital in order to increase their fortunes, and were willing to offer benefits to the imperialist powers at the expense of the people of Pakistan'.[153] However, a close look at investment patterns reveals that it was not primarily through foreign investment that foreign interests made their influence felt. By the mid-sixties foreign investment was less than 10 per cent of the fixed investment in manufacturing enterprises.[154]

The economic influence was exerted more through development and military assistance, especially from the United States which started giving aid to Pakistan in 1951. Between 1950 and 1959 the total foreign exchange payments made by the government of Pakistan exceeded the payments made abroad for imports on private account, and 54 per cent of these government foreign exchange payments went to the United States.[155] The inflow of foreign resources increased during the 1960s, and by the middle sixties financed 40 per cent of gross investment, compared to 30 per cent in the late fifties.[156]

In terms of the class interests of the power bloc, the close alliance of Pakistan with the United States thus was beneficial, as it secured an increased inflow of economic assistance. Furthermore it secured military assistance, particulary through the SEATO membership. However, as regards foreign policy, the priorities of the countries were not similar. While the United States had supplied arms to their SEATO allies in order to counter communist aggression, Pakistan regarded India as its main enemy, and had joined the treaty to secury allies in case of Indian aggression.[157]

The Indo-Chinese border dispute had repercussions on Pakistan's relations with the United States, primarily because of the latter's shift in policy towards India, who then became a recipient of United Stated foreign aid. The situation was aggravated, when the United States took a neutral stand in the war between India and Pakistan over Kashmir in 1965. Not only did the United States declare that the war was outside SEATO jurisdiction, but it also suspended its military assistance to Pakistan as well as to India.

The outcome of the war with India had several repercussions. Internationally, the relationship to the United States deteriorated temporarily, while the relationship with China improved. Already in 1963 Pakistan had signed a border agreement with China, and in 1965 Ayub had visited China, which supplied arms to Pakistan during the war with India. The pro-China policy was advocated by Bhutto, who had been a member of the Ayub cabinets from 1958, and Foreign Minister in 1963.

By the time of the civil war in Pakistan and the war with India in 1971 international alignments had shifted. The first approaches had taken place between China and the United States (Kissinger made his first trip to China through Pakistan); and India and the Soviet Union had become close allies. Neither the expansion of the Soviet sphere of influence nor the disintegration of Pakistan

were in the interests of China and the United States which therefore both
supported Pakistan in 1971.

E. *National Disintegration*

Also, internally the war with India had several repercussions. While Ayub
Khan was supported by the various powerful interest groups and factions
within these, these groups and factions did not support each other. As was the
case during the previous regime, especially among the feudal landlords there
were internal factions. In fact the unity of the regime was held together by the
leadership of the president only.[158] The outcome of the war broke this
superficial unity. When Ayub signed the Tashkent Agreement in January 1966
calling for the withdrawal of both Indian and Pakistani troups, this decision
was severely criticized, especially in West Pakistan, where there were riots in
the major cities, and there was pressure from opposition leaders for the
resignation of Ayub Khan. Bhutto had been against the Tashkent Agreement,
and in the summer of 1966 he resigned from the government. In 1967 he
formed an opposition party, the People's Party, which was to become the
largest party in West Pakistan. Although the core of the party consisted of
feudal lords from Sind (Bhutto's province) and the rising middle class in the
Punjab, the socialist manifesto of the party programme attracted the left and
the students.

The support given to the People's Party was also indirectly related to the
war, as the cost of the war, coupled with decreased U.S. aid, forced the
government to cut down developmental expenditures. This accentuated the
social costs of the government's economic development policy, as the
substantial growth had not benefited the lower-middle class and the
peasants,[159] and the demonstrations against the regime increased during the
latter half of the 1960s. In November of 1967 there was an attempt to
assassinate Ayub Khan at a mass rally in West Pakistan. The incident was
followed by the arrest of leaders of the People's Party, including Bhutto, and
the National Awami Party, but the demonstrations continued.

When Ayub Khan resigned in March 1969, Pakistan (West as well as East)
was on the verge of a civil war.

After about two decades of independence it was clear that the policies of the
different regimes in Pakistan had failed. Its attempts at national integration
were unsuccessful, and in the end it turned out that the nation could not even
be held together through force. Its economic policy had shown good results in
terms of economic growth, but only a few had benefited, and disparities had
grown not only between social classes in West Pakistan but also between the
two wings of the country. Although a national bourgeoisie had developed
during the period of study, it is not clear-cut whether the capitalist mode had
become the dominant mode of production. It seems more appropriate to
describe it as the colonial mode, in the sense used by Alavi. Some of the
characteristics of this mode of production are the lack of conflict between

feudal and capitalist interests and a class alliance between foreign imperialist bourgeoisie, indigenous bourgeoisie and landlords.[160-1]

In East Pakistan the repercussions of the Indo-Pakistan war were very different. The East Pakistani politicians did not attach a great importance to the Kashmir issue, but the war highlighted the vulnerability of the eastern province. Without their own defence the province was unable to resist foreign aggression, and the need for a regional defence force—originally proposed in 1954—seemed more crucial than ever.

While in West Pakistan the political movements in the latter half of the 1960s were directed against Ayub Khan, in East Pakistan the revitalized and radicalized nationalist movement was aimed at a fundamental change in the political system, and the relationship between the centre and the province.

F.   Bengal Nationalist Movement

(1)   From reactive to proactive mobilization

The defeat of the opposition in the 1965 presidential election marked a turning point in the Bengal nationalist movement. Until that time, the Bengal political élite had put forward their demands within the constitutional framework, or tried to influence the constitutional framework, the aim being to change the national system. As Jahan has pointed out, 'during the Ayub decade political movements in East Pakistan changed from movements for competitive participation in the national system to radical autonomy movements'.[162]

In terms of mobilization theory, the development within the Bengal political movement confirms the hypotheses advanced by Hettne and Friberg regarding reactive and proactive mobilization. As pointed out in Chapter II, a mobilization is termed reactive when it is undertaken in defence of rights believed to have been unjustly removed or denied. This was clearly the situation during the fifties, where the defence of cultural rights, symbolized in the language movement, was in focus. Similarly during the early Ayub Khan period, mobilization was in defence of constitutional rights and participation in the political system. As Hettne and Friberg point out, penetration initially leads to reactive mobilization, which may result in assimilation and incorporation, i.e. national integration. If assimilation does not take place, the outcome is either repression or proactive mobilization, meaning the demands of new rights which the groups were not previously entitled to. In such situations proactive mobilization will take on a revolutionary character leading either to separatism or revolution.[163]

During the mobilization for Pakistan in the first half of the century, the mobilization was of a proactive type, and as will be shown below, their failure to become incorporated in the national system of Pakistan led the Bengal political élite to mobilize the population more and more proactively. However, even during the final period, sections of the political élite vacillated between strategies aiming at incorporation (reactive mobilization), and more radical strategies leading to separatism (proactive mobilization). As the central government followed a strategy of increasing repression, and because of the internal dynamics of the mobilization movement, there was, in the end, no option for the political élite but to follow a strategy of proactive mobilization.

The final blow to the opposition took place during the election to the national and provincial assemblies which were conducted soon after the presidential elections in 1965. After some hesitation the COP decided to participate, but the campaign was at a low gear. The election results all but eliminated the opposition in the national assembly, where the Convention Muslim League obtained 120 out of the 150 seats. The opposition got 15 seats from East Pakistan, and one from West Pakistan, the remainder being independents.[164]

As in the National Assemblies elected in 1947 and 1955, the majority of the members from West Pakistan were landlords, and from East Pakistan the vernacular professionals dominated. However, from both parts of the country there was an increase in the numbers of businessmen and industrialists, their numbers from East Pakistan growing from 3 in 1955 to 9 in 1962 and 20 in the Assembly elected in 1965.[165]

Just before the army took over direct control of Pakistan, the Awami League had been split with the departure of the left-wing faction headed by Bhashani, who formed the National Awami Party. As mentioned above, the split was caused by Suhrawardy's pro-western foreign policy as well as his moderate stand on the autonomy issue.

However, the split was more fundamental. As Alavi has pointed out, there were two traditions in the Bengali nationalist movement, viz. a petty bourgeois élitist tradition comprised of persons aspiring for senior posts in the bureaucracy, or to become rich businessmen, and a rural populist tradition articulating the frustrations of the poor peasantry.[166] With the departure of the Bhashani wing of the Awami League, the party came under the dominance of the élitist tradition.

When the ban on political parties was lifted in Pakistan in 1964, Suhrawardy had died, and the general secretary of the party, Sheikh Mujibur Rahman, revitalized the party. Although he was firmly committed to the élitist tradition, he managed to retain the mass populist base, thus bridging the gap between the two traditions.

With the failure of the Combined Opposition Parties to change the political system through the electoral system, the Awami League adopted a more radical strategy, and prepared for a proactive mobilization of the masses in support of full automony. Soon after the war, Sheikh Mujib had declared that 'The question of autonomy appears to be more important after the war. Time has come for making East Pakistan self-sufficient in all respects',[167] and in March 1966 the Awami League put forward its Six-Point Programme for regional autonomy which included the following demands:

1. The constitution should provide for a Federation of Pakistan in its true sense on the basis of the Labore Resolution and the parliamentary form of government with supremacy of a Legislature directly elected on the basis of universal adult franchise.

2. The federal government should deal with only two subjects: Defence and Foreign Affairs, and all other residuary subjects shall be vested in the federating states.

3. Two separate, but freely convertible currencies for two wings should be introduced; or if this is not feasible, there should be one currency for the whole country, but effective constitutional provisions should be introduced to stop the flight of capital from East to West Pakistan. Furthermore, a separate Banking Reserve should be established and separate fiscal and monetary policy be adopted for East Pakistan.

4. The power of taxation and revenue collection shall be vested in the federating units and the federal centre will have no such power. The federation will be entitled to a share in the state taxes to meet its expenditures.

5. There should be two separate accounts for the foreign exchange earnings of the two wings; the foreign exchange requirements of the federal government should be met by the two wings equally or in a ratio to be fixed; indigenous products should move free of duty between the two wings and the constitution should empower the units to establish trade links with foreign countries.

6. East Pakistan should have a separate militia or paramilitary force.[168]

In many respects the Six-Point Programme was more radical than the autonomy demands advanced during the 1950s, especially as regards economic issues, as the two wings of the country were, in fact, treated as two separate economies.[169]

Although the language question was not included in the demands,[170] linguistic nationalism and the stress on Bengali culture became a prominent part of the revitalized nationalist movement, especially among the students who had been active on the cultural front also during the martial law from 1958 – 62.[171]

The Six-Point Programme was met with enthusiasm by most sections in Bengal. Mujib was elected president of the party, and the student organization of the Awami League launched a mass campaign throughout Bengal. Especially the urban centres were 'in the grip of mass resolution',[172] and workers increasingly joined the demonstrations. The participation of the workers in turn radicalized the movement, not only in terms of strategy (from demonstrations to looting and confrontation with the police), but also in terms of political demands.

However, not all sections of the Bengal political élite were in favour of the resurgence of the Awami League and the demand for complete autonomy. The leftists under the leadership of Bhashani's National Awami Party (NAP),[173] argued that the programme did not reflect the aspiration of the poor. To the NAP leaders the autonomy issue could not be separated from the overall fight against imperialism, and they therefore rejected the programme. Secondly, Bhashani had disassociated himself from the struggle against Ayub, as he favoured the recent pro-Chinese policy adopted by the government.

Also, the moderate opposition politicians outside the Awami League were against the autonomy demand, which many feared would break up Pakistan.[174] Opposition leaders from both East and West Pakistan formed the Pakistan Democratic Movement, which adopted a compromise formula that would give equal participation to the two provinces at the Centre.

The government's response was increased repression and the threat of civil war, and in May, Mujib and several other Awami League leaders were arrested. Later, in December, the regime brought a case of conspiracy against leading Awami League politicians as well as members of the East Pakistan civil service and army officers.[175]

Meanwhile, the political situation had deteriorated in West Pakistan. After the assassination attempt on Ayub Khan in November 1968, the western wing was on the verge of civil war. In December the revolt against the regime spread to East Pakistan, where Bhashani took the initiative to call for a general strike, which was followed by mass uprisings throughout the province. In the rural areas the attacks were aimed at the Basic Democrats and government officials.

In February 1969, Ayub Khan announced that he was not going to seek re-election after the expiration of his term as president in 1970, and the following day Sheikh Mujib and other political prisoners were released. Ayub met with leaders of some of the opposition parties, including the Awami League. Bhutto and Bhashani had refused to join in the round-table conference, and after the talks the Awami League dissociated itself, as the autonomy issue was not resolved.

Meanwhile, both West Pakistan and East Pakistan were in chaos, and the protest movements took on increasingly radical demands. In East Pakistan factory workers had forced leading industrialists to increase wages.[176] In this situation Ayub Khan resigned in March 1969, and handed over control to the army; and again martial law was imposed.

To Ayub, the programme of the opposition parties would mean the liquidation of Pakistan. As has been pointed out, 'to say that Ayub failed, and was now about to leave a political vacuum, heightens the emphasis given to viceregal politics in Pakistan. It also explains why the military-bureaucratic nexus succeeded in perpetuating itself. And why this arrangement usually proves acceptable to the Pakistani people'.[177] In Ayub's own words: '. . . except for the Armed Forces, there is no constitutional and effective way to meet the situation'.[178]

(2) Radicalization of the movement

With the arrest of the Awami League leaders in the summer of 1966, the leadership of the nationalist movement was again taken over by the students. As mentioned above, the participation of the workers in the riots in 1966 had radicalized the movement, and when the various student organizations joined together in the Bengal Students Action Committee in 1968, their programme went beyond the demands advanced by Mujib in 1966. The 11-point pro-gramme put forward by the students included not only the 6-point demand for autonomy, but it also contained a socialist platform, including the nationalization of banks, insurance companies, and big industrial units (point 5). Besides, they claimed reduction of taxes upon agriculturalists (point 6), payment of proper wages to labourers (point 7), and the formulation of an independent foreign policy, including withdrawal from the CENTO and SEATO pacts (point 10).[179]

When Mujib was released from prison in February 1969, the movement had gone beyond his original claim, but, in order to remain in control of the movement, he declared that his party would work for the realization of both the 6-point and the 11-point programmes.[180] It was on the basis of these two programmes that Mujib in March 1969 presented a draft constitutional amendment to Ayub, a few days before martial law, was again imposed.

When the military took over direct rule in March 1969, Yahya Khan in his first address to the nation promised the restoration of parliamentary rule, and the holding of national elections on the basis of direct elections. In November elections were announced on the basis of population (i.e. the majority of the seats were given to East Pakistan). The elections were scheduled for October 1970, later postponed to December 1970, because of a severe cyclone in East Pakistan. In March 1970 a Legal Framework Order was proclaimed, according to which elections were to be held under Martial Law Order. The order outlined the role of the future National Assembly in framing a new Constitution where '. . . the Federal government shall also have adequate powers to discharge its responsibilities in relation to external and internal affairs, and to preserve the independence and territorial integrity of the country'.[181]

The Legal Framework Order was clearly addressed against the demands of the Awami League.

The Awami League, however, went ahead preparing for the coming elections which they declared to be a referendum on the party's programme for autonomy.[182] In their election campaign the nationalist issues were stressed, and the party nominees included leaders of all dominant interest groups. It was a national coalition party appealing to nationalist sentiments in non-class ideological terms, and combining the two traditions of the nationalist movement.

The majority of the Awami League nominees were lawyers (47 per cent), but more interesting is the fact that as much as 19 per cent of the nominees were businessmen.[183] Besides, the leader of the largest labour organization in East Pakistan was also appointed. This has lead one analyst to conclude that 'the Awami League had large-scale support from both business and labour'. The same author points out that 'like the national bourgeoisie in most former colonial countries, the majority of the Bengali businessmen and industrialists backed the liberation movement launched by the Awami League, and ultimately financed its election campaign'.[184]

Most analysts point out that the original 6-point programme was, in fact, a platform of the petty bourgeoisie and the emerging Bengali industrialists and businessmen, both of whom found their road to advancement blocked by their West Pakistani counterparts.[185] The autonomy demand was supported by the business community because of the competition from West Pakistani industrialists, and by the bureaucrats because of the fiscal control from the centre. However, not all agree that these same groups backed the liberation movement in its later phases. It has been maintained that the shift from a 6-point demand for autonomy to the 11-point demand for socialism was a threat to the bourgeoisie.[186] In fact, many members of the bourgeoisie collaborated with the Ayub Khan regime, which they regarded 'as a bulwark for the defence and protection of their own class interest'; and after the uprising in 1968–9, many of them transferred their assets to West Pakistan and abroad.[187]

As regards the support in the rural areas, the leadership of the nationalist movement was drawn from the same socio-economic groups as the Basic Democrats. Like their peers, the Basic Democrats, the rural cadres of the Awami League were drawn from the upper peasantry, but from the opposition factions in the local areas.[188] The rich peasant base of the Awami League leadership is seen from the data on the socio-economic background of the members elected to the Assembly in 1970. While 75 per cent of the farmers owned less than 3 acres of land, 71 per cent of the MPs elected in 1970 owned above 6.5 acres.[189] (As will be shown in the section on the social formation in Bangladesh, the Awami League's reliance on the affluent farmers for support in the rural areas had implications for the economic strategy of the new government.)

Writing in retrospect, an insider and a leading Bengali economist has summed up the situation as follows: 'In business, the big money was made by beneficiaries of Ayub's patronage . . . If there were political divisions cutting across class lines, they were between unsuccessful Awami League businessmen who remained in the ranks of the petty bourgeoisie through their lack of success, and supporters of the Ayub government who, by virtue of their patronage, graduated to the ranks of upper bourgeoisie. As the Awami League bandwagon started to roll in 1969 many big businessmen who had risen up the ladder under the benediction of the Ayub regime felt the need to restore their political cover, and sought to buy their way into the party . . . there is no doubt that at lower levels many ex-Basic Democrats and middle-level businessmen directly infiltrated the party in 1969, and many big businessmen, whilst not claiming party membership, contributed generously to the party coffers'.[190]

The result of the national elections was a complete victory to the Awami League, which won 160 of the 162 seats allotted to East Pakistan, and thus it got an absolute majority in the National Assembly with 300 seats.

There were several factors contributing to the success of the Awami League. By adopting the 11-point radical programme, the party to a great extent undercut the appeal from the left. And as has been pointed out, 'one of the major doctrinal lapses of Marxist international communism has been the non-recognition of the force of nationalism as a factor in the change of history . . . East Pakistan communist revolutionaries, while thrashing out their tactical moves, failed at the beginning to take into consideration the force of East Pakistan nationalism, . . . by siding with the Ayub Khan government on the ground of Ayub's pro-Chinese stand in foreign policy [they] even found it necessary to oppose the six-point autonomy movement, which ultimately gave the leadership of East Pakistan's liberation struggle to the Awami League.[191] Thus, when the NAP joined the anti-Ayub struggle in 1968, it was too late to recapture the leadership of the movement. By 1969 most leftist leaders refused to participate in the elections, and after the cyclone in East Pakistan in November 1970, Bhashani, in fact, unilaterally declared East Pakistan an independent country. The Awami League used the neglect of the central government during the cyclone as a further argument for autonomy.

The major political rivals of the Awami League were the National Awami Party and its splinter groups, whose leaders, including Bhashani, had initiated the ideological revolution that established secularism and socialism as dominant themes of the Bangladesh liberation movement.[192] By refusing to participate in the election, the strength of their support was not put to a test. However, it may be of relevance to note that the election turnout was not immense; only 58 per cent of registered voters in East Pakistan voted in the December 1970 National Assembly election.[193]

(3) Polarization between East and West Pakistan

While the Awami League won almost all seats in East Pakistan, it did not win a single seat in West Pakistan, where the majority (81 out of 140 seats) went to Bhutto's Pakistan People's Party, which had majority support in Sind and Punjab, but did not win any seats in East Pakistan or Baluchistan.[194]

The election results thus reflected the complete polarization between East and West Pakistan. Furthermore, with the majority of the seats in the National Assembly, the Awami League was in a position to dictate the new constitution, which it insisted should be on the basis of the autonomy programme. This was clearly not acceptable, neither to Bhutto, who had campaigned for a strong central government, a powerful army, and 'a thousand-year war with India', nor to the army itself.[195] Bhutto refused to attend the opening session of the National Assembly, and on 1 March 1971, Yahya Khan announced the postponement of the session.

Although the Awami League's 6-point and 11-point demands were considerably more radical than the demands put forward by the Bengalis during the 1950s, and were coupled with a proactive mobilization of the population for more rights to the Bengalis, at no time before the army crackdown did the Awami League leadership go beyond the demand for complete autonomy. However, the regime's refusal to accept the election result by postponing the opening of the National Assembly put the Awami League leadership in a very difficult position. As mentioned, in order to put weight behind their demands, the Awami League had mobilized the masses whose political consciousness and expectations had in turn been raised. Already in October 1970 Bhashani had declared East Pakistan an independent country, and after the postponement of the National Assembly, other leftist groups had followed suit, and Mujib was under tremendous pressure, especially from the student wing of the Awami League, to do the same.

However, Mujib decided for a compromise, and he called for a 'non-violent non-cooperation movement against the central government'. The support to this movement in Bengal was so strong that the Awami League leaders found themselves the *de facto* rulers of the province. All the government officials stayed away from work, including judges of the High Court and other senior officials.[196] However, despite the unity displayed during the non-cooperation period, the movement itself was not without its contradictions. With the students and workers taking the lead, and, in fact, acting as custodians for the new order, the situation of the middle-class supporters of the autonomy demand became more and more ambiguous: 'This new phase where the machinery of government and production were now subject to the authority of a "rebel" government was unique and unnerving to those who had for generations accepted the authority of the government of the day. Senior administrators felt that their whole career was at stake if they accepted Mujib's authority in the event of a restoration of authority by the central government . . . the Bengali owners were themselves shaken, and mostly unreliable in any confrontation. For them to see their own workers take up this positive and militant role in demanding independence and participating directly in non-cooperation made them more conscious of the fact that in an independent Bangladesh the workers were going to emerge as a powerful factor'.[197]

During the period between 1 and 25 March, three developments emerged simultaneously. One was the non-cooperation movement, where the pressure on Sheikh Mujib to declare Bangladesh independent was mounting every day; and it had become politically impossible for him to agree to a compromise with the central government, if he wanted to remain leader of the Bengal nationalist movement. During the same period there were negotiations in Dacca between the military represented by Yahya Khan, the Awami League leadership, and representatives from the political parties in West Pakistan, including Bhutto. Especially Bhutto could not accept the autonomy demand.[198]

While Yahya Khan was engaged in negotiations with the Awami League leadership, the army at the same time built up its strength in Bengal, sending reinforcements by air and sea from West Pakistan. It has been maintained from several quarters that Yahya Khan had very early decided to use the strategy advanced by Ayub Khan in 1966, viz. to use 'the language of weapons' against the Bengalis.[199]

The military crackdown took place in the evening of 25 March, and at the same time Sheikh Mujib was taken prisoner. The following day Bangladesh was declared independent in the name of Sheikh Mujib and the Awami League. This was the beginning of a civil war, the final outcome of which was the break-up of Pakistan.

Most of the leadership of the Awami League fled to India, where on 17 April they elected a government-in-exile. Meanwhile, a guerilla war was being fought inside the country. During the course of the civil war, or the liberation struggle, the contradictions within the nationalist movement were accentuated, both because of internal differences, and because of the internal dynamics of the fight itself.

(4)   Analysis of the nationalist movement

On the basis of the broad mass appeal of the Awami League, and of the personal style of Sheikh Mujib, several analysts have referred to the movement as a typical populist movement, and to Mujib as a populist leader.[200] While the above account has provided some analysis of the class belonging of the Bengal nationalist movement, the theoretical framework adopted by Laclau makes it possible to clarify further the relationship between class and people, as well as to analyse this relationship in terms of national integration—or disintegration—and political mobilization, both on the part of the power bloc, and on the part of the rising Bengal middle class.

Within the theoretical discourse used by Laclau, the dominant classes interpellated the members of the dominated classes in order to maintain their hegemony. This interpellation is exactly what national integration was all about, viz. the consistent appeal to Islam (on the basis of which the various classes were interpellated or mobilized in the first place), the appeal to a national identity through a common language (Urdu), and the use of economic integration as a vehicle for incorporation. The crisis in the dominant ideological discourse was a reflection of the utter failure of these interpellations, as the potential antagonisms were not neutralized. This failure was in turn part of a more general social crisis, the dominant feature of which was the failure of the economic policy *vis-à-vis* East Pakistan.

As Alamgir has pointed out, the semi-feudal/semi-colonial social formation of Pakistan gave rise to a number of contradictions in Bengal society, including (1) the contradiction between Bengali national bourgeoisie and the West Pakistani bourgeoisie, (2) the contradiction between the semi-proletariat (poor peasants and agricultural labourers) and the proletariat on the one hand and the semi-feudal interests and the bourgeoisie on the other, and (3) the contradiction between West Pakistan semi-colonialism and the Bengali nation.[201] It was the poor peasants and agricultural labourers who participated in the relations of production basic to the society. However, it was the middle class which challenged West Pakistani domination, and in the process of political mobilization this class was forced to appeal to the symbols and values of peasant groups (including building on the populist tradition articulating the frustrations of the poor peasantry) and to develop counterpoint values which would serve as antagonistic options against the ideology of the dominant bloc. Thus, while the basic contradiction was one of peasant exploitation, ideologically, it was transformed and articulated into the ideological discourse of divergent classes, including particularly the Bengali middle class. It is in this sense that the original 6-point programme of the Awami League could be interpreted, both as a radical political programme, and as the political platform of the middle class. The populist ideology was expressed as a counterpoint value in the substitution of Islam and Pakistani nationalism for secularism and Bengali sub-nationalism. This transformation was, in fact, a transformation at the ideological level to a 'people'/power bloc contradiction, expressed in terms of Bengali secular nationalism versus Muslim Pakistan.

However, the crucial contribution provided by Laclau is that only by analysing the basic contradictions at the level of the mode of production, is it possible to explain the class nature of the ideological struggle, in this case the peasant origin of the struggle. The same tools of analyses explain why the support of the urban middle class to the 11-point demand was ambiguous. In the course of the proactive mobilization the movement had, in fact, changed character, and the contradictions in the ideological discourse were no longer of a non-class nature. Through the demands for nationalization of industries and higher wages, individuals were interpellated, not only as national (Bengali) subjects, but also as political (class) subjects. In fact, some of the difficulties of the Awami League during the later phases of the nationalist movement—and even more so during their term of power in independent Bangladesh—were similar to the contradictions inherent in populism of the dominant classes. As Laclau points out, such experiences are dangerous, because the leaders try to develop the revolutionary potential of the people, and at the same time to keep it within certain limits.[202]

While the contradictions within the nationalist movement were, by and large, overshadowed by the consensus on nationalism during the period of opposition, they became manifested in the politics of the new state of Bangladesh. This will be dealt with in the following chapter.

V

THE BANGLADESH STATE

A. The liberation struggle

As mentioned in the previous chapter after the military crackdown on 25 March 1971 and the arrest of Sheikh Mujib in the evening of the same day, the majority of the Awami League leadership managed to escape to Calcutta. On 17 April they formed the Constituent Assembly of Bangladesh in exile, and with the assistance of the Indian government, this exile government began to prepare for the armed liberation of Bangladesh, under the command of Colonel Usmani, a former officer of the Pakistan army.

The first armed resistance came from Bengali members of the East Pakistan Rifles and the East Bengal Regiment, who had managed to escape.[1] Dacca town was in the complete control of the Pakistan army within a few days, but in other towns armed resistance lasted longer, including the city of Chittagong from where Major General Zia Rahman[2] declared on 28 March over the radio, Bangladesh to be an independent nation. Within a week all major towns had come under Pakistan control, and after the reinforcement of troops from Pakistan in April, the ill-equipped resistance groups gave up the defence of the countryside and fled to India, where they were placed in charge of the regular units of the *Mukti Bahini* (Liberation Army) under Colonel Usmani's control.

The nucleus from the East Pakistan Rifles and the East Bengal regiment was augmented by volunteers who joined the liberation war as Freedom Fighters. Labourers, small businessmen, and cultivators joined the Mukti Bahini, but the majority were students, many of whom had played an active political role in the preceding years. All new recruits were screened by the Awami League before they were sent to training camps in India. However, despite the political control, the experiences of the guerillas 'led them to a political orientation that was left of the regular Awami League. Indeed, the guerilla commandos and their rank-and-file were frequently critical of the more moderate A.L. leadership throughout 1971'.[3]

Also within the military command of the Mukti Bahini there were disagreements as to the direction of the liberation struggle. The 'official' line as advocated by Colonel Usmani adopted a conventional war strategy involving confronting Pakistani forces in cross-border raids from bases within India. Because of the numerical strength of the well-equipped Pakistani army, this strategy involved the ultimate reliance on an allied army. Politically this group regarded a rapid resolution of the war and the early installation of the Awami League government in Bangladesh as essential. This priority coincided with the interest of the Indian government which was interested not only in dividing Pakistan but also in a future Awami League government in Bangladesh.[4]

The role of the Indian government during the Liberation period has been the object of much debate. It seems beyond dispute that the civil war in Pakistan offered a unique possibility for weakening Pakistan through the establishment of a friendly Bangladesh at its eastern border. Because of international opinion it was, however, not possible to back the liberation openly from the outset. Instead they trained the Mukti Bahini and simultaneously used diplomatic channels to generate understanding for the refugee burden (about 10 million refugees—primarily Hindus—had come to India). When Pakistan declared war on India at the end of November, Indian troops had already been sent on raids across the border.

Two section commanders, Taher and Ziauddin, advocated an alternative strategy which would be based on a people's army dispersed within Bangladesh and with no foreign bases. This would involve a protracted war, the outcome of which would be the defeat of the Pakistani army by Bangladeshis, and not Indians. This group was very much opposed to an Indian military intervention, and had no great love for the Awami League leadership.

Besides the regular units of the Mukti Bahini and the—primarily Awami League—volunteers trained in India, there were numerous political groups operating inside Bangladesh. Many of these belonged to the various leftist parties, each with their own localized strength. Some of these groups co-operated with the Mukti Bahini, while others put more emphasis on the social revolutionary aspect of the struggle. As pointed out in the previous chapter, the pro-Peking left was split in many factions, and when China decided to support Pakistan against the Bengali liberation movement, these factions were at first completely paralyzed.

The pro-Moscow faction of the National Awami Party fully co-operated with the Mukti Bahini and supported the Awami League exile government. In September a Consultative Committee was formed by members of the Awami League, the pro-Moscow NAP and the pro-Moscow Bangladesh Communist Party as well as Maulana Bhashani (pro-Peking NAP).[5]

The atrocities committed by the Pakistani army in Bangladesh contributed greatly to the popular support to the liberation movement. However, sections of the upper-middle class vacillated, and many from the right-wing political parties joined the Pakistan-sponsored Peace Committees which served as intelligence networks for the army. In the rural areas, the Peace Committee members were by and large formed by the Basic Democrats. (It is difficult to judge the extent of active collaboration. There is no doubt that many collaborated voluntarily and believed in Pakistan, either for religious reasons or out of fear of a socialist Bangladesh. However, as has been pointed out with regard to the Bengali mill-owners who kept their factories in production: 'they probably had no choice since as long as they were in Bangladesh they were vulnerable to threats from the Pak army to keep their factories open'.[6] As regards the Basic Democrats, these were forced by the Pakistanis to form Peace Committees. As pointed out above, they owed their economic and political power to the Pakistani regime, and most likely they needed little persuasion. However, if they refused, they were killed, and if they collaborated they risked being killed by the guerilla forces.)[7]

As pointed out above, the Basic Democrats were primarily drawn from the upper peasantry, and as these became the primary targets—apart from the

Pakistani army—of the freedom fighters, the liberation movement could well have developed into a social revolutionary movement. It was exactly such a possibility that the 'official' line of the Mukti Bahini army command as well as the exile government wanted to avoid—thus their stress on a rapid resolution to the war.

However, with the radicalization of the rank-and-file within the Mukti Bahini, and with the existence of the many political resistance groups, it became increasingly difficult for the exile government to remain in control of the situation. In order to remedy the situation, some of Sheikh Mujib's closest student supporters formed the Mujib Bahini to preserve the interest of Sheikh Mujib and his closest supporters. Members of the Awami League student league were secretly recruited and given special training by the Indian army. Besides they were given political training in 'Mujibism', the four pillars of nationalism, secularism, socialism and democracy, which were to become the basis of the political ideology of independent Bangladesh under the Awami League.

Although the alternative strategy advocated by dissidents within the Mukti Bahini army command was not adopted as official military strategy, the inner dynamics of the resistance movement had its own momentum, and by September/October 1971 it was starting to develop into a people's liberation war. However, this development was interrupted by the active intervention of the Indian army on 3 December in support of the Mukti Bahini. The actual war between India and Pakistan lasted less than two weeks, and on 16 December the Pakistan army surrendered to a joint command of Indian and Bangladeshi forces, and Bangladesh had become an independent nation.

With the release of Sheikh Mujib from a Pakistani jail and his return to Bangladesh early in January 1972, the immediate struggle for power among the various army and civilian groups as well as among the Awami League exile government and the younger political cadres of the party was avoided. In the initial euphoria the contradictions which were apparent within the nationalist movement during the last years before independence, and which were accentuated during the liberation war, did not come to the surface. And—as will be shown below—the political strategy adopted by Mujib as leader of the new nation was to a large extent aimed at balancing between the conflicting interests.

B.   The Awami League government

(1)   Attempts at conflict resolution

a.   Political issues

As pointed out in the previous chapter, the Awami League emerged in the late sixties as the spearhead of the nationalist movement. While the original 6-point programme of the party was radical within the context of Pakistan policy, it was primarily the political platform of the Bengali middle class.

During the political mobilization of the Bengali population the movement was radicalized, as witnessed, e.g. by the 11-point programme of the students which included a socialist platform. In order to remain in control of the movement, the Awami League had to incorporate these demands in its platform.

As an opposition party the Awami League mobilized the masses primarily on the basis of Bengali nationalism. The other appeals used during the popular mobilization also concerned counterpoint values against the ideology of the West Pakistan dominated power bloc. It is in this context that the ideology of Mujibism, viz. the four pillars of nationalism, secularism, socialism and democracy should be viewed. As Jahan has noted with regard to democracy, the nationalist élite became committed to the model of parliamentary democracy because the promise of increased participation was a powerful slogan to mobilize mass support behind the nationalist movement. But, this commitment was eroded, as 'increased participation not only resulted in greater demands on the system, it also meant that the nationalist élite could be replaced by alternative leadership. Power, which was a means to an end with the nationalist élite before the independence, became an end in itself after independence'.[8] In other words, after independence, Bangladesh nationalism had turned into populism of the dominant classes, and the leadership was faced with the task of keeping the revolutionary potential of the people within certain—narrow—limits.[9]

However, given the long period of political mobilization of the people, followed by the increased political awareness as a consequence of the liberation struggle, the leadership was also forced to meet the expectations which had been generated, and to honour the pledges made to the people during the election in 1970.

At the same time the government was faced with tremendous problems in the aftermath of the liberation struggle, the most urgent of which was economic recovery. Besides, there was the resettlement of refugees and the issue of collaborators.

In addition to the many economic and political pressures on the regime, the Awami League was also faced with the problem of establishing its legitimacy as the ruling party. On his return to Bangladesh Sheikh Mujib was greeted as Bangabandhu, 'Father of the Nation', and his charismatic appeal was a great asset to the Awami League. However, the party leadership was accused by members of the Mukti Bahini of being a do-nothing-group which had lived in luxury in Calcutta.[10] Furthermore, its mandate from the people as the ruling party of independent Bangladesh was not clear. Although the Awami League had swept the polls in the election in 1970, its victory was based on the issue of autonomy and not on the basic principles of the new state.

As one of the first steps to establish its legitimacy, the government started to prepare a constitution for Bangladesh, which was drafted in less than six months. The Awami League was eager to pass a constitution as soon as possible, as it wanted it to reflect its own basic political framework according to its own preferences 'before serious controversies could arise'.[11]

The basic ideological principles of the constitution which came into effect on 16 December 1972—on the first anniversary of the liberation—were the four pillars of Mujibism which were declared in the preamble. As mentioned above, these principles reflected counterpoint values against the ideology of the previous Pakistan regime. At the same time they came to serve as the political platform of the Awami League party.

Regarding the principles of nationalism and secularism, there was little controversy in 1972. With respect to democracy the Constitution provided for a parliamentary form of government based on the Indian model, incorporating a number of provisions with an eye to ensure the stability of the system.[12] These provisions were criticized by the opposition which also objected to the extensive emergency powers permitted by the Constitution.[13]

b. Economic issues

Given the petty bourgeois nature of the Awami League leadership, the incorporation of socialism as one of the guiding principles in the Constitution is of special interest, not least because it reflects the basic contradictions within the party and the nationalism movement. As mentioned earlier, the Awami League had felt pressed to adopt socialism in its political platform in the late sixties in order to remain in control of the movement. After independence, this was one of the pledges which had to be honoured and, as has been pointed out, Sheikh Mujib was willing to yield to radical influences, 'as long as these did not prove inimical to his party interests'.[14]

Within the Awami League leadership there were conflicting views regarding the kind of socialism to be introduced in Bangladesh. One faction within the leadership, headed by the Finance Minister, Tajuddin Ahmed, was in favour of a socialist economy. This group was pro-Indian and pro-Soviet and against accepting aid from 'imperialist nations', especially the United States. Another major faction was led by Khondokar Mustaq Ahmad (Minister of Foreign Trade and Commerce) who was pro-American and in favour of a mixed economy as well as foreign aid.[15] This ambiguity among the party leadership was reflected in the constitution, as socialism was introduced as a general principle only, without any clear guidelines as to how to implement it or to the ultimate role of the public sector.[16]

The socialist measures and economic policy in general adopted by the Awami League government very well reflected the pattern of 'intermediate regimes', as this concept has been used by Kalecki and Raj to refer to government in which the lower-middle class and the rich peasantry could be identified as performing the role of the ruling classes.[17] In such regimes state capitalism plays an important role, and, as has been pointed out by Saul in an African context, the post-colonial state becomes an important prize for the petty bourgeoisie, among other things because of the absence of alternative sources of high income and status outside the government.[18] As will be shown below, these observations are equally relevant for the Bangladesh case in the post-colonial phase.

The government's economic policy thus reflected the petty bourgeois nature of the ruling party. However, as mentioned above, in order to remain in power, the government had also to meet the expectations raised during the course of political mobilization. In order to analyse the political and economic policies adopted by the Awami League government during the early years of independence, it is thus necessary also to evaluate the strength of the pressure from the various social groups as well as their relationship to the ruling party.

As pointed out in the previous chapter, the Awami League drew its support in the rural areas from among the surplus farmers, who constituted an important interest group. Also the trading and marketing intermediaries (mercantile class), small-scale entrepreneurs, as well as the industrial trade unions were economically and politically important. Besides, the various student groups put pressure on the new government. However, due to the economic policy of the Pakistan regime, there were few Bengali big industrialists, as most of big industry in the former East Pakistan had been in the hands of Pakistanis.[19]

In its populist discourse the radicalized Bengali nationalist movement had also become a movement against vested interests. In this context it is relevant to compare its 1970 election pledges to nationalize banking, insurance and major industries, and to implement land reform and land distribution, with its post-independence economic policy. In March 1972 the government took over public ownership of all industrial units abandoned by the Pakistanis with assets above Tk. 1.5 million. In addition it nationalized all units—including those owned by Bengalis—in large-scale cotton textile, jute and sugar manufacturing. As a result, 86 per cent of total industrial assets came under public ownership—as compared to 35 per cent before independence.[20] Furthermore, in July a ceiling of Tk. 2.5 million was imposed on private investment. With regard to private foreign investments, these were allowed only in participation with public enterprises.

The industrial policy was the major measure towards building up a socialist state undertaken by the government. This measure did alienate the Bengali industrialists, but as pointed out, these were few in number, and besides they were keeping a low profile at the time, 'uncertain whether they would be branded collaborators or taken to task and humiliated by their workers and subordinates for their lukewarm support of the war'.[21]

However, in no way did the regime in the early years introduce measures which seriously affected those groups on which the government depended for support. The mercantile interests were not touched, as trade remained within the private sector. More importantly, the pre-independence pledges regarding land reform and land distribution were not honoured. A ceiling of 100 bighas (33 acres) was imposed, and land revenue on small holdings (below 8 acres) was abolished. But there was no land reform, and the Planning Commission's suggestion that the ceiling on landownership should be reduced to 8 acres was rejected.[22] Furthermore, despite the high profits of the surplus farmers, proposals for taxation of this sector of the rural population were similarly rejected, as was the suggestion for the elimination of agricultural subsidies, which benefited primarily this group of farmers.[23]

Thus, as with its industrial policy, the agricultural policy of the Awami League government very much reflected the pattern of intermediate regimes with its neglect of an agrarian revolution and heavy reliance on agricultural subsidies.[24] In analysing the policies of the Awami League, one is reminded of Broomfield's comments regarding Fazlul Huq's policies during the 1930s. Broomfield was not surprised that the government's achievements at the time did not match its pre-election rhetoric. Then, as in the early seventies, the party leadership was middle class, who had much vested in the existing system. As he pointed out, a strengthening of the position of the middle-rung at the expense of the biggest men (here big, foreign business) they would welcome, but fundamental change in the system they would not.[25]

The economic policy outlined above thus reflected the government's dependence on the various pressure groups and was in fact based on tactical considerations in order to stay in power. The government had to balance between meeting the expectations raised during the liberation struggle and not to alienate important interest groups.

(2) Consolidation of power

a. The Awami League's relationship to the bureaucracy and the army

Besides the interest groups discussed above, the Awami League also had to establish its relationship to the traditional powerful interest groups, viz. the bureaucracy and the army.

As pointed out in Chapter IV, during the Pakistan period the bureaucracy, and especially the élite Civil Service of Pakistan, had significant influence on the decision-making process, in particular as regards economic policy. At the time of independence, however, the bureaucracy was rather weak, as it was divided in factions, among those who had fled to Calcutta (the 'patriots') and those who had stayed behind, whom the former branded as 'collaborators'. This rivalry was further accentuated later, when in 1973 many senior civil servants were repatriated from Pakistan. In this situation it was relatively easy for the Awami League leadership to curb the traditional power of the bureaucracy and to delegate to it a secondary role in the decision-making process. However, with the political control of the bureaucracy, this became caught in the factional conflicts within the Awami League.[26] The overall result was that the bureaucracy became less efficient in carrying out its functions, and although its decision-making power was curtailed, it could still block implementation of government policy, and it remained far from neutral—ideologically and politically.[27]

Whereas the bureaucracy was weak at the time of independence, the army, or rather the Mukti Bahini, was strong, and it was in fact a serious threat to the Awami League's claim to legitimacy. As pointed out above, the Mukti Bahini accused the Awami League leadership of being a do-nothing-group, while it had done the actual fighting and secured the independence of Bangladesh. However, also the Mukti Bahini was divided in various factions.

As pointed out above, during the liberation struggle there had been disagreements within the Mukti Bahini army command regarding the war strategy and the direction of the movement. These differences took on a new form in the post-independence period, when the government took steps to build up a conventional army, based on the colonial pattern. Taher and Ziauddin, who had been opposed to a conventional war strategy during the war, opposed the building up of such a traditional army. Instead they argued for the establishment of a 'productive army', where the soldiers should take active part in production. During the early months of 1972 they in fact established such productive army units in the Dacca and Comilla brigades, of which they were in command. However, when Ziauddin criticized the government, he was dismissed in the summer of 1972, and a few months later Taher was also dismissed from the army.

As mentioned earlier, both Ziauddin and Taher had been opposed to Indian intervention in the war, and their anti-Indian position was shared by other members of the Mukti Bahini, especially in the aftermath of the war, when equipment captured from the Pakistan army was taken to India. One major, Jalil, who publicly objected to the movement of captured weapons was arrested under pressure from India.[28] [Major Jalil later became president of a new opposition party, the JSD (National Socialist Party), while Ziauddin and Taher joined underground leftist parties.]

Although the most vocal critics within the army were removed, many army officers and soldiers remained strongly anti-Indian, and the Awami League government was never sure of the army's support. In order to remedy this situation, the government immediately after liberation set up a National Security Force, the Rakkhi Bahini, the members of which were recruited from the Mujib Bahini and other organizations loyal to the Awami League.

b. Party-building and elections

As pointed out above, among the many pressures on the Awami League in the post-independence period was the need for the party to establish its legitimacy as the ruling party. One step towards this aim was the passing of the constitution in December 1972, based on the party's ideology of Mujibism. The next step was the renewal of its mandate from the people through popular elections, which were announced immediately after the constitution came into effect, and the date was set for 7 March 1973.

One problem in this connection was the internal weakness of the Awami League party. As mentioned above, there were factions within the party leadership regarding the socialist platform and the country's relations to foreign countries, especially India, the Soviet Union and the United States. Besides, there were schisms between the old leadership, who were in the cabinet, and the younger party cadres, many of whom had taken active part in the liberation struggle. Like their senior colleagues, the latter were also split ideologically. In fact the party was held together by the person of Mujib who, initially, was able to maintain a balance between the various groups. On his return to Bangladesh, Mujib became Prime Minister,[29] and at the same time he took over the post of president of the party. In the latter capacity he immediately set out to revitalize and reorganize the Awami League with the help of former student leaders. One of the measures used in the party-building process was the strengthening of its various front organizations, especially the labour and youth fronts. The latter included not only the traditional Student League, but also a new Jubo League, headed by Mujib's nephew, Sheikh Moni, who had formulated the ideology of Mujibism during the liberation struggle. Besides, the use of patronage was wide-spread. Having captured the 'prize' of the post-colonial state, the Awami League as the ruling party was in a good position to dispense patronage through appointment of party members in the nationalized industries. In addition, it could distribute permits and licences.[30]

In the rural areas the Basic Democrats—many of whom had collaborated with the Pakistan regime—were dismissed and local loyal Awami Leaguers were installed as Relief chairmen to carry out the functions of the previous union council chairmen.

In March 1973 the elections took place as scheduled. The Awami League had been strengthened, and 'because of Mujib's appeal, his vigorous campaigning in all the towns and cities of Bangladesh, and the Awami League's association with the nationalist movement, the party's victory was really a foregone conclusion'.[31] In a House of three hundred, the Awami League won 291 seats, the pro-Moscow NAP 1, and the newly-formed JSD 1, while the rest went to independent candidates. The voting participation was 56 per cent, and the Awami League got 73 per cent of the votes cast.[32]

However, although the election victory for the Awami League was a foregone conclusion, nobody had expected it to be sweeping. This was due to the party's all-out effort to win all the seats, an effort which was undertaken with various strong-arm methods, such as false ballots, kidnapping of opposition candidates, etc. Thus, although the Awami League managed to establish its legitimacy as the ruling party through the elections, this legitimacy was considerably compromised by the tactics used.[33]

As two-thirds of the members elected to the new Parliament had been members of the Constituent Assembly (i.e. elected in 1970), there were no significant changes in their socio-economic background. Whereas 71 per cent of the MPs elected in 1970 owned above 6.5 acres (compared to 75 per cent below 3 acres for Bangladesh as a whole), 75 per cent of those elected in 1973 owned above this acreage, and also the percentage of bigger landowners was slightly higher in 1973 (51 per cent owning above 15 acres, compared to 42 per cent in 1970). As in the previous Parliament, lawyers and businessmen were the most important occupational groups (26 per cent and 24 per cent respectively, compared to 29 per cent and 27 per cent in 1970). The majority of the MPs were in middle-class occupations, and many members combined two or three occupations: law, business and farming.[34]

Unlike the Pakistan period where the civil bureaucracy played an important role in the local areas, it was the Awami League MPs who acted as brokers between the government and the people, not least in the distribution of relief materials, the granting of licences and permits, and the distribution of fertilizers and other inputs. This further strengthened the political support of the party in the rural areas, and given the dominance of the surplus farmers among the MPs, it is not surprising that they acted on behalf of this group and opposed land reforms.[35]

(3) Early opposition

As Kalecki and Raj have pointed out, in order for intermediate regimes to remain politically viable, one precondition is their ability to generate the economic surplus necessary for sustained economic growth. This the Awami League government was not able to do. In fact, long before the government had had a chance to revitalize the economy and put its economic policies to a test, popular discontent was increasing because of a rapid rise in the price index as well as the non-availability of basic consumer goods. Coupled with the conspicuous consumption of the *nouveaux riches* Awami League permit holders and other beneficiaries of the patronage scheme, the initial euphoria soon faded. As early as September 1972, the first demonstration against the government took place, in the form of a hunger-march organized by Bhashani (who had initially supported the Awami League government).[36]

The initial opposition to the Awami League, however, came from within its own ranks, namely from the most radical faction within the Student League. It was the group of student leaders who had radicalized the nationalist movement through the 11-point programme and who had—unsuccessfully—pressed Mujib to declare Bangladesh independent in March 1971, who early became disenchanted with the government's lack of commitment to socialism. In July 1971 the Student League split in a radical faction proclaiming a classless society and commitment to armed struggle to change the status quo, and a moderate faction committed to the transition to socialism through parliamentary means under Mujibism. As the party leadership was committed to parliamentary democracy and Mujibism, the radical faction withdrew its support from the party and set up a new party, the National Socialist Party (JSD), under the joint leadership of one of the student leaders and Major Jalil.[37-8] The JSD soon emerged as the major challenge to the government but, as mentioned above, the general election in 1973 returned only a handful of non-Awami League candidates, due to the strong-arm tactics used by the government, as well as to the charismatic appeal of Sheikh Mujib.

By the time of the election to the local councils in December 1973, the support for the Awami League had been considerably eroded. The Union Council candidates did not openly contest on a party ticket, but the political affiliation of most were known to the local people, and the Awami League campaigned for members loyal to the party. Although no systematic study has been made of the local elections in 1973, available information seems to indicate that most of the Relief Chairmen installed by the Awami League were voted out of office.[39]

Thus, the overwhelming victory which the Awami League received at the polls in March 1973 did by no means reflect support of the regime. After the election the intra-party conflicts became more pronounced, and the cabinet had to be enlarged to accommodate the various factions. But the threat from the opposition was more serious. Not only did the JSD attract many supporters, but also other leftist parties—although split among themselves—gained support in many local areas. By the autumn of 1973 the law and order situation in the countryside was serious, with numerous armed attacks on thana headquarters and police stations.

The government's response was increased repression, especially through the Rakkhi Bahini, the budget for which was doubled from 1972 – 3 to 1973 – 4.[40] Besides, various emergency provisions were adopted, starting with an amendment to the constitution in September 1973 empowering the president to declare a state of emergency.[41] This was followed in January 1974 by an act empowering the officers of the Rakkhi Bahini to arrest or search without warrant, and a Special Powers Act in February providing for preventive detention and the banning of political parties.[42]

Whilst most of the repressive measures were directed against the radical left, the government reacted differently towards the right. In order to widen its support base, the government decided to co-opt the Islamic nationalists, and in November 1973 a general amnesty was granted to collaborators, except those who were charged with murder, rape or arson. In an attempt to split the opposition the government formed a People's Unity Front with the two pro-Moscow parties, the Bangladesh Communist Party and the pro-Moscow NAP, the main aim of which was to fight the radical left.[43]

Thus, although initially Mujib managed to balance the various forces within Bangladesh society, the basic contradictions within the nationalist movement could not be resolved, once the Awami League came into power, due to the party's lack of commitment to radical changes. As a dominant class, the petty bourgeois leadership of the Awami League became pre-occupied with keeping the revolutionary potential of the people within narrow limits in order to remain in power. Although its ideological rhetoric remained leftist, its policies turned increasingly towards the right.

(4) Mounting economic crisis

In the Introduction to the First Five-Year Plan which was published in November 1973, one of the basic objectives listed was 'to reduce dependence on foreign aid over time through mobilization of domestic resources and the promotion of self-reliance'.[44] As pointed out, the transition to socialism was incorporated as one of the basic principles in the constitution, but as argued above, the government's commitment to socialism was ambiguous at best, and no measures were taken against the vested interests in agriculture. On the question of the agricultural sector, the following observation was made in the Plan: 'In an economy where more than 80 per cent of the activity is dependent on agriculture, it is inconceivable to bring in socialism without the socialization of agriculture'.[45]

While the socialization of agriculture was not even attempted, the objective of reducing dependence on foreign aid was not pursued very rigorously. When the first member of the Planning Commission resigned in late 1972, he severely attacked the government's lack of commitment to socialism and a self-reliant economy: 'On the morrow of the liberation, the Government of the People's Republic of Bangladesh had announced its intention not to accept aid from any country which had been hostile to its liberation struggle, no matter what this policy would cost the nation . . . This would have meant no US aid for Bangladesh, and thus the biggest single supply source of foreign aid would have been cut off . . . the nation would have been forced to adopt a more austere reconstruction and development policy than it has followed . . . But all this is fantasy. The radicals in the government did attempt a policy coup. The radical aid policy was followed by a ceiling on salaries . . . But the right-wing regrouped fast, and the "counter-revolution" was swift and decisive. Powerful right-wing pressure soon changed the aid policy and the door was thrown open to any donor who would now pose as a friend . . . By now, the country has firmly entered into a course of heavy indebtedness, particularly to the very country which had wanted the destruction of Bangladesh as a nation . . .'[46]

The points quoted above concerning foreign aid were substantiated by the figures released later by the government. Within the first two years of its existence (i.e. by 31 December 1973) Bangladesh had received food assistance worth 173 million dollars, multilateral aid worth 350 dollars, and bilateral aid worth 850 million dollars (with the US topping the list with 132 million dollars). As one observer has pointed out, this financial assistance 'was possibly the highest ever received by any underdeveloped country during such a short period in recent times'.[47] Much of the initial aid was given as relief operations following the war but, as will be shown below, due to the perpetual economic crisis during the Awami League regime, the country's reliance on foreign assistance did not diminish. Rather, as the economic situation continued to deteriorate, the need for foreign aid became desperate, and this need in turn further eroded the government's commitment to socialism.

As pointed out above, as early as the autumn of 1972 the first demonstration against the government took place due to the rising prices. These continued to soar, and by the end of 1973 the prices of essential consumer goods rose by 300 – 400 per cent over the 1969 – 70 level. By the middle of 1974 they had risen by 700 – 800 per cent.[48]

There were several reasons for the deteriorating economic situation. While some of these were rooted in the government's lack of commitment to self-reliance and austere reconstruction, others were in a more fundamental way beyond the control of the government. In the latter category is first and foremost the oil crisis which hit the world in those years, causing inflation in the Bangladesh economy as well as a scarcity of inputs, not least fertilizers for the agricultural sector. Another reason was the smuggling of goods, particularly rice and jute to India (encouraged by the unequal real value of the currency of the two countries, and by different pricing policies).

The government's economic policy aggravated the crisis. As pointed out above, most of the administrators in the nationalized industries were political appointees of the Awami League who had no knowledge of either a socialist or a capitalist system, and most were more interested in fast personal enrichment than in the performance of the industries.

The result was that the industrial sector stagnated, or even deteriorated. A few industries did well, but as especially the two major industries, jute and cotton textiles, lagged behind, 'the overall performance of the nationalised sector (was) far from satisfactory',[49] and the index for industrial production never reached the pre-independence level during the first half of the 1970s.[50] Moreover, three of the biggest nationalized industries, including jute, made consistent losses.[51]

Moreover, the government's decision to keep trade in the private sector also had an inflationary effect. Although the prices of manufactures were fixed by the government (most were essential consumer goods), it had no control over distribution, with the result 'that actual prices paid by the final users or consumers reflected their scarcity and were above the controlled prices', and these scarcity premiums were earned by the trading intermediaries.[52]

By June 1974 the situation had deteriorated so badly, that the Finance Minister had to announce publicly that the economy of the country had almost broken down.[53] On top of it all, Bangladesh was hit by serious floods during July and August, causing damage to more than 1 million tons of food grains and to about 15 million dollars worth of jute exports. A 'near famine condition' was prevailing, and deaths due to starvation were reported from many parts of the country. The country's food shortage was almost doubled, and thus the need for increased foreign assistance.[54]

Although flooding was severe in many parts of the country, investigations have shown that at least in some areas the shortage of food grains was caused by leakage through smuggling and hoarding. This caused some observations that the famine was to a large degree man-made.[55] In fact, at the time it was alleged in various quarters that the government played up the damage caused by floods in order to secure increased foreign assistance to save the government.[56]

Thus, by the middle of 1974 the economy of the country had nearly collapsed, and the government was under pressure from various quarters to review its economic policy. As Raj has pointed out, because of the class composition of intermediate regimes, and their inability to ensure policies that can generate surpluses, 'not only is the growth of state capitalism itself blunted, but it helps more to promote the development of private capitalism . . . Once the forces of private capitalism gain strength, the bureaucratic and military apparatus of the state may well be used, like the instrument of state capitalism itself, to shift the balance of power further in their favour'.[57]

This is exactly what happened in Bangladesh. The mercantile class, which had made huge profits in domestic and foreign trade (including illegal trade and smuggling) was pressing for an upward revision or elimination of the ceiling on private investment and for the government to commit itself to a more prominent role for private enterprise in the economy of Bangladesh. This pressure was supported strongly by members of the bureaucracy as well as foreign-aid agencies and foreign investors wanting to collaborate with private enterprise in Bangladesh.[58]

Under the combined domestic and foreign pressures the government in July 1974 announced a new investment policy which comprised the raising of the ceiling on domestic private investment to Taka 30 million, and the allowance of foreign investment without any ceiling at all. In addition, there was a moratorium on nationalization of private industries for a period of 15 years as well as incentives to private investment, including a seven-year tax holiday.[59]

Given the simultaneous occurrence of events in the economic sphere in the latter half of 1974, there are reasons to believe that outside pressure on the government was considerable. The World Bank had recommended raising the ceiling on private investment, and along with donor countries it had long insisted on the setting up of a formal aid-consortium. The Bangladesh government had been against such a measure, and it had hesitated to draw on the second credit tranche from the International Monetary Fund, as the tranche was subject to Bangladesh agreeing to meet specific conditions regarding her monetary and fiscal policies. However, by the middle of 1974 Bangladesh had no choice but to accept credit from the IMF, and at the same time it requested the donors to form an Aid Consortium and to increase its aid to Bangladesh.[60]

The Aid-to-Bangladesh Consortium had its first meeting in October 1974, where an additional 600 million dollars worth of aid was pledged. Between August and November the country had already received 400 million dollars as emergency assistance and 145 million dollars as loans.[61]

In October the government signed contracts with seven foreign oil companies (including three American) for offshore oil explorations, but otherwise there was no great response from Western entrepreneurs for investment in Bangladesh.[62]

In view of the economic policies pursued, one cannot but agree with the following assessment: 'In the final analysis the concept of socialism institutionalised by Sheikh Mujib as state policy may have served a purely rhetorical purpose'.[63] The ambiguous commitment to socialism turned out to be no commitment at all. As the first chairman of the planning commission has observed, 'what was crucial was that the government reverted, gradually, if not immediately, to the pre-liberation policy of "sponsored capitalism" where the state would provide concessional financial and fiscal facilities to allow the private investors to invest, to reap large gains, to gain initial experience, if necessary with government subsidies, and then to grow in size and power'.[64]

As mentioned in the introduction to this chapter, Sheikh Mujib's initial socialist policy was a concession to the radical demands within and outside the party. Its limited implementation reflected Mujib's attempt to balance between the 'progressive' and 'conservative' factions within his own party and the groups on which the party depended for survival. Under pressure, 'when the economic situation reached crisis proportions and massive foreign aid was required, Mujib "tilted the balance" in favour of the "rightist faction" of the A.L.'.[65] At that time the concession to the conservative forces appeared appropriate 'to stem the rising tide of criticism against the government's economic performance'.[66]

As was the case for Pakistan, the role of the state in the Bangladesh economy soon came to fit the pattern outlined for peripheral states by Ziemann and Lanzendörfer, according to whom the state acts as the 'midwife' of the capitalist mode of production.[67] Bangladesh also came to conform to the aspects of statehood characterized for peripheral states by the same authors, the results of which are permanent economic and political crises.

(5) Mounting political crisis

The economic and political problems facing the Awami League government were interrelated. The rising economic crisis was compounded by a mounting political crisis. As mentioned above, during 1974 and 1975 the government introduced various repressive measures. These were in response to the rising political opposition both from open political parties as well as from the underground political groups. In early 1974 the JSD Party had launched a mass movement against the Awami League, in which they demonstrated against higher prices, corruption and the government's inability to arrest the smuggling of jute and food grains to India. Several of the JSD's leaders were arrested, but this did not prevent the party from arranging two big public meetings in October and November in which they demanded the resignation of the corrupt Awami League government. The popular response to these meetings was considerable, and again several party leaders were arrested, as were many other party workers throughout the country.

Also, other political parties demonstrated against the government. Several of these parties joined together in a United Front under the leadership of Bhashani and formulated a four-point demand: (1) release of political prisoners and repeal of the Special Powers Act, (2) introduction of a rationing system of food grains throughout the country, (3) eradication of corruption, smuggling and profiteering, and (4) cancellation of all unequal pacts, particularly those with India.[68] When the Front decided to launch a mass movement in early July, Bhashani was interned at his home.

The government's economic policies also accentuated the crisis within the Awami League. When the government announced its new investment policy in July, six of the more 'radical' ministers resigned from the government, and when Tajuddin (leader of the 'socialist' faction within the party) openly stated that the government's policy was responsible for the famine, he was asked to resign in October.

In the Awami League serious conflicts also mounted among the younger cadres, especially between the leader of the Jubo League, Sheikh Moni, and the leaders of the other affiliated party organizations. Sheikh Moni in fact declared that the Jubo League was no longer connected to the Awami League and was loyal only to Sheikh Mujib. During the autumn of 1974 Sheikh Moni started advocating a change in the political system, as the parliamentary system had failed. He argued that Bangladesh needed a Second Revolution which should also be led by Sheikh Mujib.[69] In addition he advocated the adoption of a single-party system.[70]

The mounting political opposition, coupled with increased violence on the part of the leftist underground parties, made Sheikh Mujib adopt the suggestions of Sheikh Moni. The first step was the proclamation of a State of

Emergency at the end of December, which suspended all fundamental rights conferred by the constitution for an indefinite period. This step was followed by a constitutional amendment changing the form of government to a presidential system. The amendment provided that Sheikh Mujib would be president for a five-year period, and the president was authorized to form one National Party and to suspend the activities of all political groups which did not join the 'new' party. In introducing the new system (or his constitutional coup), Sheikh Mujib referred to it as the Second Revolution to bring about the democracy of the exploited masses.

If it had not been evident before, this leftist ideology—or rhetoric—could certainly be termed 'a vague, even opportunistic, populism—one more ploy of building a broader popular constituency' as Saul has reported on regarding so-called leftist factions within the African petty bourgeoisie.[71] Besides, it was not quite clear whether the 'shift in policies would have been carried towards the right or the left'.[72]

As was the case regarding the leadership's commitment to socialism, its commitment to parliamentary democracy was dubious. As has been pointed out, 'the élite rejected parliamentary democracy and turned to an alternative system which promised it a longer stay in power. Thus both the adoption as well as the repudiation of constitutional democracy as a model of government and politics were due to power (tactical) considerations'.[73]

In order to ensure a longer stay in power, Sheikh Mujib within a month after the constitutional amendment introduced the National Party, under the name of BAKSAL (Bangladesh Peasants and Workers Awami League), and all other political parties were dissolved. The new party was nothing but the old Awami League under a different name. However, members of other previous political parties were asked to join, a call which was only followed by the pro-Moscow parties.

As mentioned above, the bureaucracy had already come under the political control of the government. This control was significantly increased under the new system, which included a reorganization of the administration. The districts[74] were to be ruled by governors, and these were to be appointed by the president. In addition, the district councils would include representatives from the party, the civil bureaucracy, the army as well as the Rakkhi Bahini.

In its policies regarding the rural sector, the new system introduced measures which, at least superficially, appeared radical. The major innovation was the decision to introduce compulsory multipurpose co-operatives in all the villages of Bangladesh. In these co-operatives the produce would be divided equally among the actual tillers of the land, the owners of the land, and the government. However, in introducing the compulsory co-operatives scheme, Mujib was careful to mention that private landownership would be left intact.[75] Nevertheless, the landowning farmers were suspicious of the new scheme, and coupled with the other measures introduced during the short-lived Second Revolution, Mujib in fact managed to threaten the major social groups in the country.[76]

(6)   The downfall of Sheikh Mujib

In analysing the developments during the last year of Mujib's rule one is struck by the ironies arising from the attempt to solve the contradictions within the entire system. When the economic situation during the middle of 1974 forced Sheikh Mujib to tilt the balance in favour of the rightist faction within the Awami League, the advocates of a socialist economy resigned, or were forced to resign. At the same time, at the political level the government increasingly followed the advice of the sections within the party who had close connections with the Soviet Union, as witnessed, e.g., by the decision to adopt the one-party system. As the revolutionary rhetoric mounted during the Second Revolution, the country became increasingly dependent on foreign aid, and thus on the western nations. But given the government's preoccupation with staying in power, these ironies are not surprising, and ss has been observed, 'it seemed obvious that the new system of "copying the Soviet methods but rejecting its ideology" was designed to suppress every vestige of opposition and perpetuate the corrupt rule of the "Sheikh Mujib Tribe" in the "softest" state in the world'.[77]

In analysing the Uganda state which was initially also ruled by the petty bourgeoisie and which had many characteristics similar to Bangladesh—as referred to above—Saul characterizes that country as the 'unsteady state' *par excellence*.[78] Given the political developments during the first years of independence, Bangladesh certainly also fits that characterization. As Ziemann and Lanzendörfer point out, the permanent economic and political imbalances in the peripheral states increasingly force their governments to intervene, and in fact these states are characterized by permanent intervention. And—as they point out—in the long run, such intervention 'can only be based on a paternalistic regime of military-bureaucratic-technocratic type'.[79] Also Wertheim has argued that populist regimes are often followed by military regimes because of the former's weakness and inability to solve the economic situation, as well as their linkage to neo-colonialism.[80]

It was such a military/bureaucratic regime which was to follow the Awami League petty bourgeois, populist, government in Bangladesh.

As mentioned above, most within the armed forces were very anti-Indian. The upgrading of the Rakkhi Bahini at the expense of the army as well as the greater allocations to the former soon gave the anti-Indian sentiment on the part of the armed forces an anti-Mujib orientation. This was further accentuated when in 1975 the government decided to increase the strength of the Rakkhi Bahini from 25,000 to 310,000 within a five-year period, without increasing the recruitment to the regular forces (which were at the time about 55,000 strong). It is therefore not surprising that the impetus to the coup against Mujib came from the army. It was carried out by three dismissed officers of the army in collaboration with 20 to 30 majors and captains, supported by about 1,400 soldiers. In the early hours of 15 August these attacked the residence of Sheikh Mujib, Sheikh Moni and Mujib's brother-in-law, killing most of their family members. The forces also occupied the radio station of Dacca and surrounded the Rakkhi Bahini headquarters. Before noon the Foreign Trade Minister in the Mujib cabinet, Khondokhar Mushtaq Ahmed, was installed as President by the army. The reaction in the country was one of shock but there was no public fury against the leaders of the coup.[81]

Khondokhar Mushtaq Ahmed was known for his pro-American sympathies, and there is circumstantial evidence to suggest that the coup was preplanned, and that Mushtaq had collaborated with the army to bring about the coup with the knowledge and support of certain foreign powers.[82] Although there is no firm evidence regarding the actual planning and involvement of civilians, there is no reason to deny the correctness of the following assessment: 'The real issue was now apparent. It was a situation where vying factions among Bangladesh's ruling class, each with its own distinct international alignment, were engaged in a struggle for control of Bangladesh'.[83]

The groups which came to power after the August coup consisted of a coalition of forces, viz. the rump of the Awami League,[84] the civil bureaucracy and the group of junior officers who had carried out the coup.[85] This coalition, however, was not to last long, as the struggle for control of Bangladesh had not been resolved, especially among the upper echelons of the army.

At the overt political level the period of the Awami League government had witnessed serious factional struggles within the government party. As will be shown below, the following period was to witness struggles for power within the armed forces.

C. Military rule

(1) Struggle for power

In the short-lived government of Khondokhar Mushtaq Ahmed, some changes took place in policy, not least as regards foreign relations. As mentioned, Khondokhar belonged to the pro-American faction within the Awami League, and during his period as president the so-called Dacca-Delhi-Moscow axis became less prominent. Although the regime proclaimed that it would continue the foreign policy of the country, it also made it clear that it would establish friendly relations with countries 'who had not been friends before', an obvious reference to Pakistan and China. Pakistan was the first country to recognize the new regime.[86] There had been negotiations with China for diplomatic recognition of Bangladesh before the August coup, but China only recognized Bangladesh just after the coup.

Internally the Mushtaq government took steps to purge the rival factions of the Awami League. The BAKSAL leaders, including six ministers, were arrested, and 'much time of the new regime was taken in by the "ins" and "outs" game. Those who were very much "in" with the Mujib regime (pro-Soviet and pro-India forces) were out and those who were against Mujib (pro-Peking left and Islamic forces) were "in" with the new regime'.[87] The BAKSAL was dissolved and political activities banned for a period of one year, but elections were promised for February 1977. Moveover, the government cancelled the district reorganization scheme, and the Deputy Commissioners were kept as heads of the original 19 districts.[88]

However, the Mushtaq Ahmed civilian cabinet only served as a facade, since the real power remained with the army. But the army was not united, and a fierce struggle for control took place. Major-General Ziaur Rahman (who was then Deputy Chief of Staff) was promoted to Chief of Staff of the Army, and several senior and junior officers were also promoted. A revolutionary council consisting of the majors who had led the coup and senior officers of the defence forces was formed. Within the army high command there was, however, disagreement regarding the fate of those who had participated in the killing of Mujib. The officers and their troops refused to return to their barracks, and the chain of command was unclear. The Chief of General Staff, Brigadier Khaled Musharraf, insisted on their return, but Zia refused to support any action against them.

On 3 November a new coup took place. This was led by Khaled Musharraf with the support of the Dacca brigade. Zia was arrested and Khaled Musharraf promoted himself to Army Chief-of-Staff.

On the day after the coup a procession led by leaders and students of the pro-Moscow parties went to Sheikh Mujib's house, but it did not draw any crowds.[89]

The 3 November coup, or *putsch*, was primarily a result of the struggle for power within the army. The Musharraf regime was short-lived, so no trends in change of policy could be discerned. However, given the support of the pro-Moscow parties, there are reasons to believe that the regime would have reverted to the close collaboration with India and the Soviet Union. This hypothesis is corroborated by the strong support given to the new regime by India.[90] Before Musharraf was replaced, Khondakhar Mushtaq and his cabinet was forced to resign and the Chief Justice of the Supreme Court, A. M. Sayem, was made President.

Immediately after 3 November coup groups within the army started to plan a revolt. Most of these groups were under the leadership of the Biplobi Gono Bahini, the Revolutionary People's Army, which had till then been a secret organization headed by Colonel Taher and affiliated with the JSD. Leaflets were circulating among the soldiers urging them to revolt against Khaled Musharraf who was accused of being a paid agent of India. According to available evidence,[91] instructions for the first stage of the revolt—to overthrow Musharraf—were issued by Taher on 6 November. The revolt took place on 7 November, when fighting broke out within the Dacca cantonment. Khaled Musharraf was killed while attempting to flee, and Zia was released and reinstalled as Chief-of-Staff of the army.

The second stage of the revolt was to be a real insurrection by the soldiers who issued a set of Twelve Demands, including the establishment of a revolutionary army to supersede the traditional army. The second stage of the revolt was planned as a social revolution.

(2)   The rise to power of Ziaur Rahman (indirect military rule)

a.   Consolidation of power

Immediately after the 7 November coup the JSD leaders who had been imprisoned by Mujib were released. The party leaders, however, continued to press for an uninterrupted revolution under the leadership of the Biplobi Gono Bahini. Meanwhile a Martial Law Administration was set up with Justice Sayem as Chief Martial Law Administrator, and the chiefs of the three services as deputy Martial Law Administrators.[92] The most powerful person was Zia, who immediately started to restore discipline within the army.[93]

The continued pressure from the JSD soon turned against Zia, who was accused of being led in an anti-revolutionary direction by the 'rightist reactionaries and pro-U.S.A. elements'. On 25 November Major Jalil, Colonel Taher and 17 other party leaders were arrested for subversive and anti-state activities.[94]

Besides the threat from the JSD, the government also had to fight the pro-Mujib guerilla activities under the leadership of one of the 1971 guerilla leaders most loyal to Mujib. Throughout 1976 there was constant firing in the northern part of the country. In order to counter these challenges the military government decided to strengthen internal security and the armed forces. The budget of Sheikh Mujib for 1974 – 5 had set aside 13 per cent of the total revenue budget for Devence and Internal Security. This allocation was revised and raised to 32 per cent of the budget. Recruitment to all forces was stepped up, especially the police force which was almost doubled. The increased police strength included a combat-ready Special Force, trained to counteract guerilla raids.[95]

Within the army, the struggle for power had many dimensions, one of which was the factional infights between those who had fought in the war of liberation and those senior officers who had been repatriated from Pakistan in 1973. Zia obviously belonged to the former category, but at the same time it was clear that he dissociated himself from the radical groups, led by Colonel Taher, who were suppressed. The influence of the 'repatriates' was on the increase, as witnessed particularly by the fact that when Colonel Taher was tried (and later executed) in July 1976, the Special Tribunal was headed by Colonel Haider, who had been in Pakistan all during 1971, and who was known to belong to the hawks within the army.

During 1976 there were two serious threats to the military leadership. One was carried out by a group loyal to Khaled Musharaff, and another was an attempted coup by the chief of the Air Force.[96] Both threats were met, and in order to avoid concentration of potentially dissident elements within the services, a regrouping and replacement of troops was carried out during the middle of 1976, a procedure which was to be repeated when the government again felt threatened.

Despite challenges from outside as well as within the army, the army faction loyal to Zia initially gained actual control of political power in Bangladesh.

The other major power group is the civil bureaucracy whose decision-making powers had steadily increased since the overthrow of Mujib, especially as regards economic policies. A few weeks after the 7 November coup President Sayem set up a seven-member Council of Advisers with the rank of ministers. Besides the president and the three deputy martial-law administrators, the Council included four civilians, of whom at least two had held important posts during the Pakistan regime, one as a minister and the other as a civil servant. Also other advisers, who were nominated later, had held important posts during the Pakistan regime, as had many of the top civil servants who were reinstalled (many top civil servants not agreeable to the Mujib government had been dismissed or left voluntarily).

In fact the regime which came to power after the downfall of Sheikh Mujib had many of the characteristics of the Pakistan regime, which was governed by a bureaucratic-military oligarchy. As will be shown below, the policies pursued by the new regime were also reminiscent of that period.

As regards foreign policy, the new military government continued the policy of the Mushtaq government. Relationships were improved with China and Pakistan, as well as with other Muslim countries. The United States continued to increase its economic assistance to Bangladesh, not least its food aid under P.L. 480,[97] and during 1976 the country obtained a record total of about 1,450 million dollars worth of foreign aid, of which 40 per cent came from the United States.[98]

Relationships with India were more strained. While that country did not disguise its enthusiasm after the 3 November coup, neither did it disguise its anxieties after the 7 November coup. Ever since the independence of Bangladesh the two governments had negotiated over the division of the water of the Ganges river. Contrary to an agreement reached in 1974, the Indian government in the autumn and winter of 1975/76 began to divert the water at Farakka, adversely affecting the situation within Bangladesh.[99] This accentuated the anti-Indian sentiments in Bangladesh.[100]

The government sought negotiations with India over the Farakka issue, negotiations which were to last for years. Furthermore, it appealed to other nations for support, and finally it took the issue to the United Nations. Internally, the issue was used to rally public support to the government in order to defend the sovereignty and independence of the country. Also the government's appeal for national unity became very pronounced during this period, and those opposing the government were accused of anti-state activities.[101]

While the ideology of Mujibism had been based—verbally at least—on nationalism, democracy, socialism and secularism, the predominant ideology of the military regime was based on Bangladesh nationalism, where the issue of national unity in defence of sovereignty and independence was the major ingredient.

b. Establishment of legitimacy

(i) Ideological issues

In the framework of Laclau referred to in Chapter II, the basic function of ideology is to interpellate individuals as subjects.[102] As pointed out above, during the political mobilization of the 1960s and the liberation struggle, the people were interpellated primarily as Bengali nationals. Being the unchallenged leader of the Bengali nationalist movement, the legitimacy of Sheikh Mujib was not questioned: he was the Father of the Nation. As a counterpoint value against Pakistan, Bengali nationalism could thus serve as an ideology for the maintenance of hegemony, once the Awami League came into power. The military regime of Zia, however, had no unquestioned claim to legitimacy on the basis of nationalism, as it was still shared with the Awami League and other groups which had participated in the liberation struggle (including Colonel Taher and other radical freedom fighters). It is for these reasons that the relationship with India came to play a dominant role in the definition of nationalism, with its stress on the defence of sovereignty and independence.[103] So by stressing the issue of national unity, the government sought to neutralize potential antagonisms among the different groups in society. (As pointed out above, political repression was used when ideology failed.)

As Bengali nationalism in the mid- and late seventies was still associated primarily with the independence movement, the role of Zia in that movement was stressed. As mentioned above, it was Zia who had announced the independence of Bangladesh from Chittagong in March 1971, and he had been the commander of the northern section during the fight for independence.[104]

During the liberation movement the issue of secularism had also been used as a popular interpellation, both as a counterpoint value against the Islam of Pakistan, and as a strategy by the Awami League to get the support of radical groups as well as Hindus. But after independence secularism figured less prominently, although it was incorporated as one of the basic principles in the constitution. There are several explanations for this development. One relates to the problem of defining the identity of the new nation, in this context the relationship to the Hindu Bengalis living in West Bengal, including the issue of territorial boundaries. The constitution defined identity in terms of ethnicity and language and termed the citizens 'Bengali',[105] but as has been pointed out, such interpellations have a restricted emotional appeal—at least when the values are not in jeopardy.[106] Also, although the Bengali Muslims had always been less orthodox than the Muslims of West Pakistan, one is tempted to question the extent to which the issue of secularism had in fact taken root among the broad masses.

As, among others, O'Connell has pointed out, the Muslims tend to view political and social affairs as religiously significant, and before the constitution was in fact changed with respect to the issue of secularism, he suggested that '. . . it is also possible that the constitution . . . may have gone beyond what the typical Bengali Muslim will eventually find acceptable'.[107] In terms of national identity, the issue of religion in a traditional society thus cannot but play a prominent role. As one observer pointed out regarding this issue just after the independence of Pakistan: 'Given the fact that it is a democracy (formally) and that the great majority of its citizens are Muslims, it must, virtually, pursue Islamic ideals or no ideals at all. For practical purposes, the alternative to the Islamic state is complacency or corruption'.[108]

Besides the lack of commitment to secularism on the part of the masses, as postulated above, there were other factors working against secularism. One was the increasing anti-Indian sentiments, which led the people in Bangladesh to identify themselves as Bengali Muslims, a development which was not without communal overtones. Also at other levels, the foreign policy of the country encouraged greater emphasis on Islam, as it improved the relationship with other Muslim countries, not least the oil-rich Arab countries, from whence economic assistance increased.[109]

As far as internal politics was concerned, secularism was played down when Mujib in 1973 granted amnesty to collaborators in order to co-opt the Islamic nationalists in the effort to broaden the support base of the government. This tendency was accentuated after the military take-over; and when Zia took over the office of president in April 1977, the constitution was simultaneously amended, deleting the word 'secularism' which was replaced by 'Absolute trust and faith in the Almighty Allah'. In addition the following sentence was added: 'The state shall endeavour to consolidate, preserve, and strengthen fraternal relations among Muslim countries based on Islamic solidarity'.[110]

With reference to the issue of nationalism, the constitution was amended from 'a historic struggle for national liberation' to 'a historic war for national independence', stressing the role of the military. Also the word 'Bengali' was substituted for 'Bangladeshis'.[111]

As regards the remaining two basic ideological principles of the constitution, viz. democracy and socialism, these were retained. When the amendments were announced, Zia promised to hold national elections by the end of 1978, but given the fact that the country was ruled by the military, the commitment to democracy was of less relevance than it had been to the previous regime. The concept of socialism was redefined to mean 'economic and social justice', and—as will be shown in the following sections—the regime's commitment to socialism was no commitment at all. In this respect the military regime was less ambiguous than the Awami League with whom the rhetorical value of socialism continued to the very end. This was dropped, and only the reference to economic and social justice remained.

(ii)   Economic issues

As pointed out in Chapter IV, one of the purposes of the economic policy under Ayub Khan was a legitimating one, i.e. if he could demonstrate the regime's ability to secure economic development, the seizure of power would be justified. Also Zia sought to justify his seizure of power by emphasizing economic development; as has been pointed out: 'He put the powerful ideology of Bengali nationalism to immediate use in the service of the development effort. The nationalist ideology thus produced a concomitant "development ideology", whose major tenet was to develop or perish'.[112]

The government's economic policy was proclaimed in the spring of 1977 as part of a 19-point policy package. The emphasis was on self-reliance and self-sufficiency in food, and the agricultural sector was given top priority. Measures to check the population explosion were stepped up, and the role of the private sector was encouraged.[113]

As mentioned above, the reference to socialism was dropped as official ideology. This happened already in December 1975, when the Government issued the 'Revised Industrial Policy' which stated that the 'Government is of the view that while industries of basic and strategic importance or in the nature of public utility service, should remain in the public sector, for reaching the goal of mobilization of investment funds and rapid industrialization, the private entrepreneurs should be afforded adequate scope and facilities for setting up industrial enterprises within the broad framework of a planned economy'. (In the 1974 Industrial Policy statement, the government was still committed 'to the establishment of a socialist economy', while the private entrepreneurs were to 'play an expanded role within the framework of a planned economy'.[114])

Immediately after the government had issued its revised industrial policy statement, it was followed up by several measures in favour of private entrepreneurs. Within a few days of the policy statement, the government announced its decision to pay compensation to the former shareholders of the industrial enterprises which had been nationalized, and the ceiling on private investment was again raised, from Tk. 30 million to Tk. 100 million.[115] This was followed a month later by an amendment to the Nationalization Order enabling the government to transfer nationalized enterprises to its original Bengali owners. Originally 150 industrial units were to be disinvested (excluding 'hard core' industries such as jute and textile as well as defence industries and public utilities), but the number was later revised upwards.[116]

The effect of the new policy was a marked improvement in the private sector, and private investment more than quadrupled during the financial year 1975 – 6. Also the nationalized sector improved, including the jute industry which went up by about 7 per cent. This favourably improved the export sector, which increased by almost 50 per cent.[117] Also foreign reactions were favourable; as early as January 1976 a German delegation declared that the 'recent decisions taken by the government had helped to create a climate for foreign investment in Bangladesh';[118] and foreign investment was reported to have accelerated already during 1976 – 7.[119]

One of the government's major achievements during the first year was to check the smuggling across the border. This, coupled with an exceptionally good harvest due to favourable weather conditions, increased the availability of food grains. The production of food grains rose by 14 per cent over the previous year, while the gross domestic product rose by 11 per cent, as compared to 2 per cent the preceding year.[120] The good performance of the economy had the effect that the cost of living index declined by 20 per cent, as against a rise of 31 per cent during the preceding year.

The successful results of the government's economic policies greatly contributed to legitimize the military's seizure of power, and during the first year support for the government was broad.[121]

However, although the initial performance of the Bangladesh economy during the military regime was better than during the Awami League regime, the government was not able to keep up the progress of the first year. Because of the predominance of agriculture in the country's economy, the performance of this sector is vital. One problem is the dependence on favourable weather conditions, which is beyond the control of any government. Another problem was the government's dependence on the surplus farmers. Like previous regimes, the government was careful not to alienate this group of farmers;[122] and secondly the government's economic development policy was very much a growth policy, the major aim of which was not only to increase agricultural production but especially to increase the surplus available for consumption in the cities. This is a political necessity in order to keep the price of rice low for the politically conscious urban population (the allocation for food subsidy amounted to 10 per cent of the central government's expenditures during 1977 – 8).[123] In order to ensure the transfer of agricultural surplus from the rural to the urban areas, the government had to rely primarily on the rich farmers. Therefore the government was as little inclined as previous regimes to introduce land reforms and land distribution, as it was politically and economically dependent on the rich landowning farmers. As will be discussed in Chapters VI and VII, such an agricultural policy cannot ensure agricultural growth in the long run, and it accentuates the trend towards pauperization among the mass of the agricultural population.

Even in years with good harvest Bangladesh still has to import food grains to supplement internal procurement. The government's target was to achieve self-sufficiency in food by 1985, a target which is unlikely to be reached. As self-sufficiency in food is a major pre-condition for the achievement of a self-reliant economy, it is far from surprising that the prospect of reaching this goal is poor, at best. In commenting on the Two-Year Plan for 1978 – 80 one observer pointed out: 'The planners in the objective of the TYP stated "greater reliance on domestic resources and reduced dependence on foreign aid". But the actual position in the plan outlay is quite reverse to what is stated in the objective'.[124] In a similar vein, commenting on the fact that 77 per cent of the development budget for 1979 – 80 was calculated to come from foreign sources, the Bengali weekly *Holiday* coined it a 'budget to foil self-reliance'.[125] During 1973 – 4 foreign aid financed 75 per cent of the government's development expenditure. The percentage rose to 84 per cent in 1974 – 5, and for the succeeding years the figures are as follows: 1975 – 6: 74 per cent; 1976 – 7: 80 per cent; 1977 – 8: 74 per cent; and 1978 – 9: 78 per cent.[126] The figures certainly do not indicate a trend towards reduced dependence on foreign aid.

(iii) Political issues

As shown in Chapter IV, Alavi's observation that the bureaucratic military oligarchy prefers to rule through politicians as long as the latter do not impinge upon its own relative autonomy and power aptly characterized the policy of Ayub Khan—at whom the observation was aimed in the first place. As will be shown below, it is equally valid in characterizing the political development pursued by the military government which came to power in Bangladesh in November 1975. Just as General Ayub Khan decided to remain as president in a civilian government, it soon appeared that Major-General Zia had similar ambitions. A transformation of power to a 'civilian' government had many advantages for Zia. Internally, such a step would have a legitimizing function, as a vote of confidence would strengthen the government, and also externally a 'civilian' government would be viewed favourably by western countries on whom the government, as mentioned above, was dependent for aid. Further, because of the continued internal struggles for power within the army (another coup was attempted in the autumn of 1977), Zia's personal strength *vis-à-vis* other factions within the army would be enhanced by broadening the power base outside the army—thus making it more difficult for a rival faction to assume power through a military coup.

After the resumption of power in November 1975 the military government reaffirmed the pledge of the Mushtaq government to hold national elections in early 1977, and political activities were allowed to resume in August 1976. In the autumn of 1976 there were fierce debates in Bangladesh on whether or not to hold the elections. Interestingly, the pro-Peking left parties were against the elections, which they thought would weaken the policy of national unity against 'Indian expansionism and hegemonism abetted by. Social Imperialism'.[127] On this and many other issues, this section of the left strongly supported Zia's definition of Bangladesh nationalism. On the other hand the emergent Islamic rightist parties as well as the Awami League and the pro-Moscow parties were in favour of holding elections. It seems that the President was insistent on holding elections, while the military hesitated. In November the President, however, announced the postponement of the elections, and a few days later, Zia took over the post as Chief Martial Law Administrator.

It seems clear that Zia wanted to consolidate his position and to build up a party before he wanted to test his strength through a vote. At the time when the national elections were postponed, the date of the Union Parishad (local council) elections was moved forward—to early 1977. When Zia finally took over the office of president in April of 1977, his strategy became clear. On assuming the office of president, he announced that he would seek a vote of confidence in a national referendum in May, and at the same time he declared: 'As a matter of principle we think it is reasonable to pave the way for general elections in phases through other elections. Hence I make the announcement that the elections to the Pourashavas (municipal councils) will be held in August this year to be followed by elections to the Zilla (district) Parishads in December. Therefore, arrangements will be made for holding general elections on the basis of adult franchise in the month of December of 1978 . . .'[128]

At that time the Union Parishad elections had already taken place,[129] and Zia used the time before the national referendum to win the support of the newly-elected local leaders through training, increased channelling of development funds through the local councils and patronage.

Although the political formula adopted by Ayub Khan in the early sixties constituted a more limited or 'guided' form of democracy, not least through the institution of an electoral college (indirect elections), the strategy of the two military leaders had many similarities. Zia's strategy of 'paving the way for general elections' is reminiscent of Ayub Khan's strategy of 'an unhindered evolution' of a new constitutional system. And also Zia's use of the local leaders in building up a support base in the rural areas parallels Ayub Khan's strategy of building up the Basic Democrats as a loyal rural power base. Finally, both military leaders sought a vote of confidence once the local power base had been built up.

The strategy of paving the way for general elections in phases through other elections can also be regarded as a measure to gauge the political situation before proceeding with the next step. Here the results were not too favourable as—according to one analysis—77 per cent of the Union Parishad members and chairmen were politically aligned to the right and centre, and about 47 per cent of them had had at least some form of association with the Awami League.[130] Otherwise the strategy paid off, as Zia got an overwhelming vote of confidence in the national referendum (99 per cent voted 'yes' to him and his 19-point policy programme). The successful result of the referendum has been attributed to the active participation of the bureaucracy in mobilizing public support (comparable to the role of the bureaucracy during the elections of Basic Democrats), the unqualified support of most of the newly-elected Union Parishad leaders, active support from the moderate and right-wing forces, the influence of the officially controlled mass media, and the absence of any other candidate.[131]

The municipal elections took place as scheduled in August 1977, and the outcome was quite similar to the results of the Union Parishad elections, viz. persons affiliated with the Muslim League as well as the Awami League got elected. Maybe for this reason—coupled with the fact of an attempted coup in November—the district council elections were cancelled, and instead the government devoted its efforts to build up a new party. In an attempt to recruit new leaders, some of the members of the Advisory Council were replaced, and the new members included persons known for their pro-Peking and anti-Indian views.[132]

In late February 1978 the new party, the National Democratic Party (JAGODAL) was convened by the Vice-president with ten presidential advisers in the executive body. About one month later Zia decided to hold a presidential election. He, however, did not directly join the new party, but contested the election with the support of a National Front, which consisted of six parties, including the JAGODAL and the Muslim League. The sudden decision to hold a presidential election before proceeding with the promised elections to parliament fits into the strategy of paving the way in phases, and it provided one more opportunity to gauge the strength of the opposition.[133] The one serious contender in the presidential election was General Usmani, who was supported by the United Democratic Alliance (GOJ) consisting of seven parties, the Awami League and the pro-Moscow parties being the major ones.

In the presidential election which was held in June, Zia got 76 per cent of the votes cast, while Usmani got 21 per cent, the remainder going to independent candidates.[134]

The result was sufficiently favourable for Zia to prepare for the final step in setting up a 'civilian' government elected by the people. However, the JAGODAL was not a viable party, so before the parliamentary elections could take place, a new strong party had to be created.

In launching the new party Zia got the support from factions of some of the parties who had been active in the National Front, including the pro-Peking NAP and the Muslim League. The party, the Bangladesh National Party (BNP),[135] was formed in September, and in February 1979 the long-promised parliamentary elections took place.

When the party was launched, 'all believing in Bangladeshi nationalism' were invited to join[136] and, as mentioned, factions from the NAP and the Muslim League were supporting the party. This led to splits in these two parties, as well as in other parties which some members decided to join. Also the opposition was split, including the Awami League, where the dispute was focused on the claim of leadership within the party, one faction urging for the continuation of the BAKSAL line, while the other argued that the real Awami League should dissociate itself from the legacy of the dictatorship of Sheikh Mujib.[137]

Despite the predominance of factionalism in all old parties during the period preceding the election, the major fronts were the same as during the presidential election, viz. the government BNP versus the opposition, where the Awami League was the most serious contender. The results gave 207 seats out of a house of 300 to the BNP. The second-largest party was the Awami League which secured 39 seats.[138]

One of the major issues during the election had been the constitutional question, where Zia favoured a strong executive presidential type of constitution, while the opposition wanted to reintroduce a British type of parliamentary system. With a clear two-thirds majority in the National Assembly the BNP under the leadership of Zia did not face any serious opposition on the constitutional issue.

An indication of the new form of 'democracy' was witnessed by one of the bills passed by the National Assembly during its first session in April 1979. The bill (the Fifth Amendment bill) ratified and confirmed all proclamations, martial law regulations and orders and other laws made during martial law (from 15 August 1975). Subsequent to the passing of the bill martial law was withdrawn, and the government-controlled newspapers could inform the nation that democracy was restored. In announcing the withdrawal of martial law, Zia repeated his strategy: 'We naturally had to proceed gradually in the process of transition to democracy. The process was successfully completed by first holding the elections to the Union Parishads, then the municipalities, next the presidential elections and finally the parliamentary elections'.[139]

The strategy proved successful. After building up a power base, the army under Zia no longer had to rule directly, but could rule indirectly through politicians.

There is no analysis available on the characteristics of the members elected to parliament in early 1979. Data from the Bogra district show that of the nine persons elected, at least five had been influential Muslim League leaders during the Pakistan period and had held important posts at the district level as Basic Democrats, and all were influential in their own localities.[140]

Although the situation in Bogra was not necessarily repeated all over Bangladesh (Bogra is known as conservative, Muslim League district), the data—supplemented with incidental information—do support the hypothesis that by and large Bangladesh in the late seventies was ruled by the same forces which were in power at the provincial level during the Pakistan regime. The political, social and economic policies of the government analysed in the above pages further substantiate this hypothesis.

(3)   Re-emergence of direct military rule

Although President Ziaur Rahman managed to establish a facade of democracy through the presidential and parliamentary elections, the political system remained unstable. As Jahan has pointed out, 'Similar to other military rulers, Ziaur Rahman tried to legitimize his regime by "civilianizing" and "democratizing" his rule, and similar to other such "civilianized" and "democratized" regimes, Zia's too remained essentially a personal rule. As power continued to remain concentrated in his hands, the multiple political institutions Ziaur Rahman created as part of his grand design of democratization, became mere facades'.[141]

His personal style was witnessed in foreign affairs, where Zia during 1979 and 1980 paid numerous visits both to the United Nations and other international bodies, as well as to several foreign countries. Although his diplomatic achievements increased the image of Bangladesh abroad, many critics felt this placed a heavy burden on the economy of the country.[142]

It was, however, primarily as regards internal politics that his personal rule was resented. Not only did the opposition contend that 'Zia's system was neither parliamentary nor presidential nor an amalgam of both, but rather an authoritarian one, in the Ayub style, under the garb of presidential democracy',[143] but also within the government party, the BNP, the members were discontented and demanded the scrapping of undemocratic clauses in the party constitution.[144] The problem within the party was, however, that it was a heterogeneous one, made up of various groups with opposing beliefs and interests. As has been pointed out, such a government party 'generally attracts members who are not at all concerned about party ideology and programs, rather they are there simply to share government patronage and power'.[145] The party was split in internal conflicts, and as a 'party of parties (it had) two focal points—Zia and power'.[146]

Zia, as president, devoted much of his energy to expand and strengthen his power basis, viz. the army, the private sector and the rural population.[147] The army was given better privileges and positions within the top administration as well as within the cabinet. The free enterprise system was encouraged, as exemplified in the Second Five-Year Plan which was launched in 1980. The private sector was allocated 22 per cent of the plan outlay, compared to 11 per cent in the First Five-Year Plan, and 16 per cent in the Two-Year Plan for 1978 – 80.[148]

His policies towards the rural population primarily distinguished themselves at the rhetorical level. Just after the parliamentary elections in 1979, Zia announced that the party's election pledges would be redeemed through a Revolution,[149] a statement which confused party members as well as the opposition. Zia's definition of 'Revolution' was rather nebulous. It was to be carried out in two phases and involved excavation of canals and attempts at eradicating illiteracy.

Zia's village-oriented politics also included the establishment of village governments (*gram sarkars*), which were elected during the end of 1980. The few studies undertaken show that the leaders elected to the *gram sarkars* came from traditional rural families of the rich and influential.[150]

Many of Zia's rhetorical statements, most notably the stress on the 'Revolution', formed part of a strategy to preempt the left. The fact remains that Ziaur Rahman's policies were consistently centrist, but he 'coopted leftist rhetoric and slogans to blunt the real issues'.[151]

The most serious resentment against Zia came from within the army. It was argued above[152] that Zia wanted to strengthen his position *vis-à-vis* other factions within the army by a popular mandate through elections. This strategy was resented by the military, where army leaders 'were wary of Zia's attempts to build a political base independent of the military'.[153]

Until the very end of Zia's rule, the army remained split between the repatriates and those who had fought in the liberation struggle in 1971. By 1980, the former faction dominated the army, partly because of Zia's promotion policy—reflecting his strategy to build up a strong, disciplined army—and partly because many who had fought in the liberation had been killed in connection with the many coups (one Bengali newspaper recorded as many as 26 coup attempts upon Zia by the end of 1980).[154]

On 20 May 1981, several major generals met with Zia and criticized him for over-democratizing the political system and for tolerating the rampant corruption within the BNP. They demanded a reimposition of martial law. On the night between 29 and 30 May, Ziaur Rahman was killed by a group of twenty officers while visiting Chittagong. While there are different theories as to who was in fact behind the coup,[155] the government's version has—as at 1982—not been disproved. According to the government's White Paper, the person behind the killing was Major General Manzoor, a leftist army officer who had managed to flee from Pakistan in 1971 to participate in the liberation war. Initially he had been a protégé of Zia's, but later the two had fallen out, as Manzoor was considered 'too independent, arrogant, ambitious and revolutionary to warrant Zia's complete trust'.[156] Two days prior to the killing of Zia, Manzoor had received orders to transfer. This fact, coupled with the fact that the officers who killed Zia were in the command of Manzoor, lends credence to the government's version; although these facts do not prove it. (The circumstances surrounding Manzoor's killing a few days later remain a mystery.)

With the killing of Zia and Manzoor, the liberation army leadership was completely destroyed, and 'the repatriates (had) emerged as a viable politico-military force under the leadership of Lt.-General Ershad',[157] whom Zia had nominated to be Army Chief of Staff in 1977.

Immediately after Zia's assassination the military chose not to take over direct control of the country. Instead it chose to ensure the continuation of the system and the domination by the military over the policy-making process.[158] The constitutional provisions were followed, whereby the Vice-President, Justice Sattar, became Acting President, and a presidential election took place in November 1981. Justice Sattar fought the election on the BNP ticket, and with the active support of the military he won 66 per cent of the votes.[159]

Although the army leadership had backed Sattar and the BNP, it was far from satisfied with the party, and it put pressure on the president to dismiss corrupt ministers. Shortly after the presidential election, Lt. General Ershad issued a statement in which he outlined his view of the army's role in government. With reference to the army's discipoine and efficiency, he pointed out that 'Potentials of such an excellent force in a poor country like (Bangladesh) can be effectively utilized for productive and nation-building purposes in addition to its role of national defence'. According to him, the concept of the army requires a departure 'from the conventional western ideas of the role of the armed forces. It calls for combining the role of nation-building and national defence into one concept of total national defence'. In such a national military, 'there will be very little or no difference between civil and military'. He finally argued for constitutional provisions and administrative measures to define clearly the role of the military in Bangladesh society.[160]

Before any constitutional provisions could be made, the army, under the leadership of Lt. General Ershad, on 24 March 1982 took over direct and complete control of the country. The bloodless coup was not unexpected, as the civilian government's ability to stop corruption and manage the economy and the law and order situation had steadily deteriorated. Ershad justified the action by stating that 'national security, independence and sovereignty were threatened by social and political indiscipline, unprecedented corruption, a devastated economy, administrative stalemate, extreme deterioration of law and order, and frightening economic and food crises'. Like other military coup leaders he promised economic recovery, a corruption- and exploitation-free society as well as restoration of democracy by holding fair elections as soon as possible.[161]

It is premature[162] to speculate on future political developments in Bangladesh, except to predict a decisive role for the military-bureaucratic oligarchy for a time to come. In this context, the following observations, written after the assassination of Zia, seem very much to the point: 'The dilemmas confronting the Bangladesh military now are the same as those faced by Ziaur Rahman. Rule by the military-bureaucratic élite may produce a political process that looks quite orderly, but it tends to cover up problems and suppress discontent . . . while the military has historically been able to suppress the opposition, it has not been able to inspire the population to produce more or to distribute it more equitably, both of these being necessary if problems are to be solved in the future'.[163]

Synthesis

Given the absence of change in the economic and social structures of Bangladesh since independence, it is not surprising that the country should be ruled by the same social forces as those which were in power during the Pakistan period. The Bengali nationalist movement was, among other things, a movement against vested interests, i.e. the vested interests of the West Pakistan power bloc. However, the leadership of the movement was not interested in changing the social structure of Bengal society. While the nationalist interpellations were based both on the élitist and the rural populist traditions in Bengal political culture, once in power the élitist leadership soon became preoccupied with keeping the revolutionary potential of the people within limits.

While the Mujib regime took some steps to 'facilitate the transition to socialism' through the nationalization of major industries, its commitment to socialism turned out to be no commitment at all. As pointed out above, the Awami League government soon reverted to the pre-liberation policy of 'sponsored capitalism', which eventually gave rise to the growth in size and power of private investors.[164]

The policy of 'sponsored capitalism' through government subsidies was continued and strengthened by the military governments which succeeded the Awami League, and this economic policy parallels the one pursued by the Pakistan regime during the early years following partition, when Pakistan did not have an indigenous national bourgeoisie.

As shown in this and the preceding chapter, at the time of independence an indigenous national bourgeoisie was also absent in Bangladesh, and—as was the case in Pakistan—the state in Bangladesh has taken on the role as 'mid-wife' of the capitalist mode of production.[165] However, given the 'sponsored' nature of capitalism, capitalist relations of production are not likely to become dominant. Instead traditional modes of production are preserved and are being reproduced.

As agriculture is the most important sector in the economy of Bangladesh, the social formation is largely characterized by the dominant mode of production in agriculture. The agricultural sector will be analysed in the following three chapters where it will be argued that capitalist relations of production are not dominant. The mode of production prevailing is referred to as 'colonial', in the sense this concept is used by Alavi, and which implies the integration of the small peasant farming econony into capitalism.[166]

The integration of the Bangladesh economy into capitalism following European capitalist expansion is continuing, and Bangladesh remains a peripheral society with a structurally distorted and dependent economic development, as well as heterogeneous relations of production.[167] Because of the nature of the peripheral economic structure, economic crises recur, forcing the state to make constant interventions in the economic and political processes. As was the case during the Pakistan period, such a situation necessitates a 'paternalistic regime of military-bureaucratic-technocratic type'.[168]

As was the case with the populist Awami League regime, the military-bureaucratic 'civilian' regime of Zia was not based on political mobilization of the people. Like the former regime, the government sought to keep the revolutionary potential of the people within limits. Because of its 'civilian' nature, however, the BNP government was forced to maintain its hegemony through interpellations which served to neutralize potential antagonisms.[169] It is in this context that the ideology of Bangladesh nationalism and national unity was given a central role by Ziaur Rahman.

It may be argued that Zia was to some extent able to neutralize potential antagonisms. However, his survival in power for five years may also be explained by what Jahan has observed as the changed mood of the 'volatile Bengali masses'.[170] She points out that the nationalist movement bridged the gap between the élite and the masses, whereas the great expectations from independence turned into frustrations, and class differences 'became a significant factor of social differentiation'. Independence meant suffering for the poor, and 'the masses were no longer as enthusiastic about political struggle as they were before independence, when they believed that a political change would necessarily bring about the betterment of their socio-economic conditions'. Another Bengali observer has referred to this process as depoliticization.[171]

Based on his own ideology, Ziaur Rahman's regime may be judged by the extent to which the economic development aspects of Bangladesh nationalism was a success. Here the record shows that contrary to the regime's emphasis on self-reliance, the country became increasingly dependent on foreign aid. By 1980 Bangladesh had become dependent on foreign aid to fund 60 per cent of its investment, 85 per cent of its development budget and 63 per cent of its commodity imports.[172] Thus, instead of sovereignty and independence, Bangladesh under Zia, as well as under the military regime which followed him, may be characterized by its aid-dependence. As Sobhan has pointed out, 'the leverage of a regime whose survival, both as a regime and as a class, is dependent on external donors is nominal and must remain subservient to those who keep it alive'. And, in a terminology reminiscent of that used in the analytical framework pursued in this study,[173] he concludes: '. . . the incapacity of the dominant groups in Bangladesh to sustain a productive and stable social order is likely to make Bangladesh into another crisis state during the remaining years of this century'.[174]

<h1 style="text-align:center">VI</h1>

<h1 style="text-align:center">BANGLADESH RURAL SOCIETY</h1>

A. General trends

By all criteria, Bangladesh is a rural society. According to the latest (1974) population census 91 per cent of the population live in the rural areas, and 77 per cent of the civilian labour force is engaged in agriculture.[1] Agriculture is the most important sector, contributing 57 per cent of gross domestic product (1977 – 8), compared to 13 per cent for industry and 30 per cent for services. This proportion has changed slightly during the last decade, due to the increase in services which contributed 26 per cent of g.n.p. in 1969 – 70, while industry's contribution has fluctuated, but has not increased significantly.[2] Furthermore, agriculture contributes 90 – 95 per cent of export earnings.

Despite the dominance and importance of agriculture in Bangladesh's economy, only a little less than one-quarter of the government's development expenditure is allotted to this sector (1978 – 9).[3] Thus, although the various governments have verbally stressed the importance of improving agriculture, Bangladesh seems to follow a pattern observed in many other countries of the Third World, a pattern which Michael Lipton has characterized as follows: 'Priority to agriculture, funds to industry and urban infrastructure'.[4]

This neglect of the agricultural sector has made several analysts point at an 'urban bias' in development planning.[5] There are other indices of an urban bias in the economic development of Bangladesh. During most of the Pakistan period, the terms of trade between industry and agriculture were against agriculture, although there was an upward shift in favour of agriculture in the early sixties.[6] During the period since independence, the terms of trade have again moved against agriculture (with the exception of 1974 – 5 when food prices soared, cf. Chapter V).[7] Moreover, the availability of institutional credit is much less for the rural sector which receives only about 10 per cent of total bank credit. In fact, much of the savings made by the rural population is used in the urban sector, resulting in a 'relentless transfer of resources from rural to urban areas . . . spearheaded by the national banking services'.[8]

The overall result of this development has been not only a wide disparity between urban and rural income[9] but also—and more importantly—to discourage investment in agriculture. This tendency has been further accentuated by the government's food policy, where the combination of food import and procurement at low prices has depressed prices paid to the producers.[10]

Because of the factors discussed above, and despite various development programmes aiming at agricultural growth, agricultural production in Bangladesh has not increased very much. Rice is the most important crop, and during most of the Pakistan period, production as well as yield per acre was

103

stagnant. During the latter half of the sixties a slight increase took place, but this increase has not continued. Bangladesh agriculture is still very much dependent on availability of rain, so yearly production figures vary. But, the overall development trend reveals yearly production as well as average yields in the latter half of the seventies to be only slightly above the figures of the late sixties. With a yearly population increase of about 3 per cent this means that Bangladesh continues to be dependent on import of foodgrains from abroad. Even in the good year for Bangladesh agriculture, 1977–8, the country had to import more than 10 per cent of its foodgrain consumption. Despite this import, per capita availability of foodgrain remains low and has deteriorated since pre-independence.[11]

The inability of the agricultural sector to match the increase in population has led to a situation of increased poverty. As regards the rural population, a study has shown that while only five per cent of the rural population could be categorized as extremely poor in 1963–4, the proportion has risen to over 40 per cent in the seventies.[12] This situation has led one analyst to point out that as a result of the historical processes, the majority of the population is caught in a 'Below Poverty Level Equilibrium Trap' between the poverty line and the famine line, where the 'former is indicated by a level of per capita expenditure adequate to purchase a bundle of food and related items which is considered adequate to satisfy a minimum need of a person' and 'the latter is given by the level of consumption below which the probability of death is close to unity'.[13]

While the rural sector in general is faced with adverse terms of trade *vis-à-vis* industry, and while the majority of the population is caught between the poverty line and the famine line, this urban bias and increased poverty is not affecting all sections of the rural population equally. One of the major determinants for the standard of living of the rural population is the access to land, which is the major factor of production.

The most recent information on the distribution of land-ownership is available from the 1977 Land Occupancy Survey of Rural Bangladesh, as shown in Table 6.1.

If one considers only landowning households, the small peasants owning between zero and 2 acres constitute 67 per cent. While it is difficult to compare

Table 6.1. Distribution of landownership (other than homestead land) in rural Bangladesh, 1977.

No. of acres owned	Percentage of households	Percentage of land owned
Zero	33	–
0 — 2.0	45	25
2.1 — 10.0	21	56
over 10	2	19

Source: calculated from Summary Report of the 1977 Land Occupancy Survey of rural Bangladesh, table II.

different surveys, as definitions tend to vary, there seems to be a tendency towards a greater concentration of smaller holdings. Wood has noted that between 1960 and 1968, holdings below 2.5 acres increased from 51 per cent to 57 per cent of total holdings.[14] This is in conformity with the fact that between 1960 and 1974 the average size of farms in Bangladesh decreased from 3.5 to 2.8 acres.[15]

Not only are farms getting smaller and smaller, but the trend is also towards increased landlessness. The data provided from the 1977 Survey list 33 per cent of rural households as landless. The same report indicates that an additional 15 per cent of rural households—those owning below half an acre—should be listed in this category, giving a total of 48 per cent, or almost half of all rural households, as functionally landless.[16] Earlier reports give the percentage of landless households to total households in the rural areas at 14 per cent in 1951, 18 per cent in 1961 and 38 per cent in 1973 – 4.[17]

The data from the 1977 Survey also show that 39 per cent of all farm households are involved in some form of tenancy relationship, either as owner-cum-tenants (32%) or as pure tenants (7%). In commenting on the change in tenancy between 1960 and 1967 – 8, Abdullah found a decrease in the category of owner-cum-tenants and an increase in pure tenancy. In 1967 – 8 the category of owner-cum-tenants was found to be 21 per cent, and pure tenants were found to constitute 2 per cent of all rural households.[18] Alamgir has also commented on the increase in pure tenancy and suggested that the trend may be due to a 'substitution of landless tenants for landed ones'. The suggestion is based on the hypothesis that 'transfer of assets in distress situations has weakened the staying power of a large number of families and perhaps this makes them more exploitable, thus more desirable, as tenants than those families having some land-holding of their own'.[19] More data are needed in order to prove the validity of this statement, as information from e.g. India suggests that landowners in general tend to give land to tenants who own some land themselves, as these are usually better cultivators.

The increase in landlessness as well as the concentration of holdings in the small-farm size category is due to many factors, one being the population growth, and another the Muslim inheritance laws causing subdivision and fragmentation of landholdings. Moreover, there are other factors inherent in the poverty situation. As one observer has noted, 'in order to survive most of the small farmers (perhaps up to 50 per cent of the total if 2 acres is accepted as the limit for self-sufficiency) must have been forced to borrow and to sell assets. Since most of them already were heavily indebted, distress sales of assets (including land) must have occurred very frequently'.[20] This observation is confirmed by several surveys indicating an increase in distress sale of land during the post-liberation period; and among sellers, small farmers constitute the major proportion. The buyers of land are primarily big farmers, followed by medium farmers and businessmen.[21]

The change in the ownership pattern of land outlined above certainly supports the characterization of Below Poverty Level Equilibrium Trap for an increasing majority of the rural population. Distribution of landownership is becoming more unequal, a process which may best be described as polarization. This process will be discussed in more detail in the chapter on the mode of production in Bangladesh (Chapter VIII).

B. *Rural development programmes*

In order to increase agricultural production and to help the small farmers, the government has launched an Integrated Rural Development Programme (IRDP) which is based on a two-tier co-operative system with primary co-operatives at the village level and a federation of co-operatives at the thana level. All inputs (in the form of irrigation, new high-yielding seeds, fertilizers, management training, etc.) are to be channelled by the government through this system.

The co-operative system was first introduced as an experiment in one thana in the Comilla district in the early 1960s. In 1968 it was expanded to cover the entire Comilla district, and at the same time it was introduced in a few other areas in the country. After the independence of Bangladesh, the programme was further expanded; and it is the aim that ultimately all thanas in the country shall be covered by the IRDP programme.

The aim of the programme is to encourage development and mobilization from below and to benefit especially the small peasants. The general approach of the programme has been criticized from many quarters as being inadequate, in particular due to its neglect of institutional changes, including land reforms.[22] Thus, Faaland and Parkinson have observed that 'if the problems of income distribution and access to work are to be solved, communal cultivation systems will have to be introduced'. These economists point out that available information 'strongly suggests that the present system of ownership of land within a market-orientated economy would not function . . . the analysis stems not from any doctrinaire view but from the difficulty of seeing how, given acute scarcity of land, incomes can be assured for those without it'.[23]

Available evidence on the co-operative programme's ability to help the poorer sections of the rural population is not very encouraging. A recurrent theme in writings and discussions regarding the programme is that the societies are dominated by large and medium farmers, and that the leadership is in the hands of the large farmers who derive most of the benefits.[24] The findings of an evaluation from the whole of Comilla district show that whereas the small peasants are well represented in the co-operatives as regards formal membership, the leadership of the primary co-operatives is dominated by the medium and large peasants, and that both categories are substantially overrepresented in the leadership compared to their numbers in the population. At the thana level the co-operative system is dominated by the large peasants. Regarding benefits derived through the co-operatives, the evaluation shows that in the villages where irrigation facilities were available, the size of the leaders' irrigated land was substantially bigger than that of the ordinary members.[25]

The Comilla evaluation further shows that the leaders of the co-operative system were more engaged in subsidiary activities outside agriculture than the ordinary members. As has been pointed out elsewhere, if a family is able to diversify its economic activities and is involved in for instance business or professional activities, then these may 'provide connections and access to the various resources and items of patronage which are being distributed'.[26]

The overall effect of the IRDP has been increased agricultural production in selected areas, and by—primarily—the big farmers who have access to the subsidized inputs. At the same time the programme has further strengthened the economic and political position of this group of farmers on whom the government—as pointed out in the previous chapter—is dependent for the supply of foodgrains to the cities and for political support.

C. Regional variations

Most of Bangladesh consists of a low-lying deltaic plain and a monsoon climate with high population densities. Most of this plain consists of new alluvium with highly fertile soils. In a few pockets, including the Barind tract, the soil consists of old alluvium which is less fertile. Besides, along two parts on the eastern border there are hills. In the hilly area in the north, tea is grown.[27]

Because of the differences in ecology, with consequent variations in fertility, population densities differ from region to region. Thus, while the average density for Bangladesh as a whole was recorded to be 1,286 persons per square mile at the time of the 1974 Population Census, it was found to be 2,245 in the fertile Comilla district and 1,486 in Bogra district, which is located in the Barind tract.[28]

With higher soil fertility it is possible to survive on smaller areas of land, and in the fertile, densely populated areas it is found that the average size of farm is smaller, and there is a higher percentage of small farms than in the less fertile areas.[29]

Rice is by far the most important crop in Bangladesh. It is grown on 80 per cent of total cultivated land. In some parts of Bangladesh it is possible to cultivate three crops of rice a year. The biggest crop is the *aman* crop (harvested in December/January), and in most places it is possible also to grow *aus* (summer crop). Both these are cultivated during the monsoon period, whereas the third crop, *boro*, is grown during the dry season and requires irrigation. It is especially the *boro* crop which has increased in recent years, as regulated water supplies and new needs have made higher yields possible. However, only a little less than one-tenth of the rice area is cultivated by *boro*.

Because of different soil fertilities and the fact that some areas are only suitable for one yearly rice crop, the division of farmers into small, medium and big (surplus) farmers obviously cannot follow a uniform pattern, based on acreage owned or cultivated, for the whole of Bangladesh. On the contrary, divisions for each ecological area must be made on the basis of careful analysis. Thus it is generally found that in the Comilla area households with above two acres are above subsistence level,[30] while in the Bogra district a household requires 8 – 10 acres to be classified as surplus peasants.[31]

The different ecological characteristics and the resultant variation in population densities have also given rise to different settlement patterns. While the villages in the east and south are dispersed to the extent that it is difficult to differentiate one village from another, the villages in the north tend to be nucleated, and they constitute much more of a social entity than villages elsewhere in Bangladesh.[32]

A further difference is found in land tenure patterns, with a much higher degree of tenancy in the north than elsewhere in the country. This difference has led Wood to advance the hypothesis that exploitation of the poor takes on different forms, with 'more petty leasing in the North and West, more usury and petty commodity exchange in the East'.[33] This problematic will be discussed in detail in Chapter VIII.

While jute is only grown on about two per cent of the cultivated land, it is very important to the economy of Bangladesh, as it provides the bulk of export earnings. Of more importance in the present context is the fact that in the jute-producing districts the peasants are very much aware of fluctuations in market prices, viz. the relative price paid to producers of rice and jute. Thus during periods of high prices for rice, the cultivation of jute decreased, as was witnessed e.g. in 1974 and 1975. It is argued here that this orientation towards market prices also makes the villagers more conscious in other matters, and it is hypothesized that this outward orientation provides some of the explanation for the greater political awareness found in a village studied in the jute belt, as compared to the local area studied in Bogra district, which is characterized by rice monoculture.[34]

The data provided on the above pages point towards great caution in generalizing about rural Bangladesh from any study of a local area. Until recently most research has been undertaken in the Comilla area, where most of the government's development efforts started. This area is the 'minifundist case' *par excellence*.[35]

The information presented in the following chapter is from a local area in the Barind tract, and the generalizations which may be drawn from the study only hold for villages with the same ecological characteristics.[36]

After the presentation of general trends in the Bogra study area, the data will be compared to information available from studies in other parts of Bangladesh, and it will be discussed within the framework of the mode of production in Bangladesh (Chapter VIII).

Finally, it should be pointed out that also politically Bangladesh can be divided into two areas. The eastern part is economically and politically more advanced, whereas the north is less industrially developed and politically less advanced. During the Pakistan period, political leaders from the north complained that the provincial government neglected the region, and most of them were not in favour of parliamentary democracy but 'preferred the presidential system under which a strong President could allocate larger resources to the northern areas than the parliamentary regimes had done'.[37] This difference showed up in the 1965 presidential election, where the eastern and central regions voted for Miss Jinnah, whereas Ayub Khan won a substantial majority in the northern districts. Thus, the highest vote for Ayub Khan came from Bogra district, where he got 70 per cent of the votes cast (compared to 53 per cent for the whole of East Bengal).[38]

Administratively Bangladesh is divided into 4 divisions, 19 districts, 415 thanas and about 4,500 unions. There are approximately 63,000 villages.

VII
LOCAL-LEVEL CASE-STUDY[1]

A. Village description

The village described in the following pages has been given the name *Boringram*. Literally this means 'red soil village'. The fictitious name is used to protect the anonymity of the inhabitants of the village. The choice of name implies that in most respects the village is regarded as representative of villages in Bangladesh with the same ecological characteristics.

Boringram is located in Sherpur thana in Bogra district. The thana is divided into two district topographical areas by the Karatoa River which runs north/south. To the east of the river the land is level with silty ridges and perennially flooded depressions, and the soil is relatively recent deltaic alluvium. Boringram lies west of the river where the land rises to an elevated terrace which is known as the Barind tract which covers a large area in the north-western part of Bangladesh. The soil of the Barind tract is red clay of old alluvium. The productivity of the soil is lower than in the deltaic alluvium, but the land is free from floods.

Unlike other villages in some other areas of Bangladesh, e.g. the densely populated Comilla area, the villages in the Barind tract have distinct geographical and social boundaries.[2] Boringram is clearly separated from the surrounding villages by paddy fields.

Sherpur thana is situated about 100 miles north of Dacca, from whence there is regular bus connection by ferries and a paved road. The thana covers 115 square miles, and at the time of the 1974 population Census there were 134,220 persons, giving a population density of 1,167 persons per square mile. This is a population density a little lower than the average for the district, but much lower than e.g. the densely populated districts in the south.[3] As part of the thana is comprised of the fertile land east of the river, it is not surprising that the population density for Boringram is lower than the average for the thana, viz. about 1,000 persons per square mile.

Ninety-five per cent of the population in the thana live in the rural area distributed among the 237 villages, most of which are rather small with an average of a little less than 100 households. There are 9 unions in the thana, and Boringham is located in Madhyapur Union[4] which is fairly big with about 40 villages. The population of Boringram was 704 in the beginning of 1976, distributed among 122 households.

The majority of the population in Sherpur is Muslim. There are no exact figures of the Hindu minority which probably constitutes between 10 and 20 per cent of the population. Both in the small towns and in some villages the Hindus may live in separate living quarters, and they are often engaged in specific trades. However, in some villages the Hindus are engaged in agriculture just like the Muslims, and in the villages with Hindu populations near Boringram, these are engaged in ordinary farming activities. Among landless Hindus it is common that the women also hire themselves out to work in the field, especially at the time of transplanting rice. This is never seen among Muslim landless families, where the women will seek work within the households of more well-to-do families.

The Biharis[5] of the area tend to be settled in specific areas. In one of the villages neighbouring Boringram there is a Bihari colony, where the population was settled after partition on individual pieces of land given to them by the government. Unlike some areas in Bangladesh the people in the Bogra area do not tend to migrate out of the area in search of work. However, among the Biharis it was found that during the Pakistan period many had gone as far as Dacca in search of work.

In Boringram the entire population is Muslim.

Boringram is located about 3 miles south-west of the thana headquarters, from whence it is accessible by a dirt road. It is not possible to drive to the village in an ordinary car, but an occasional jeep or motor cycle is seen on the road. The villagers transport their rice and other products to the bi-weekly markets (*hats*) in Sherpur and Madhyapur either on ox-carts or they carry them on their shoulders. The Madhyapur market is sited near the union council offices about 3 miles to the south-west.

From the thana headquarters Boringram is entered from the north by the dirt road which cuts through the village, and on *hat* days people from the villages south of Boringram pass through on their way to the market.

At the entrance to the village from the north a combined primary and high-school is located to the east. This school caters to the children (boys and girls) from the village as well as from neighbouring villages.

Inside the village the road bends, and most of the houses are located on either side, grouped in three *paras* (neighbourhoods), viz. south para which is the biggest with 54 households, north para with 47 households, and middle para comprising 21 households.

The most influential family in the village lives in middle para, where it has built the village mosque on land which it has donated. This mosque is frequented by households from all three paras.

Many of the houses are grouped in clusters, or *baris* which are homesteads of patrilineal kin groups. A bari is usually composed of several extended family generations, broken down further into household units.

B. *Economic activity*

In the locality there are few job opportunities outside agriculture. The landless may find occasional short-term employment (1 – 5 days) outside the village, but most of the time they are dependent on the landowners for employment. Only among the carpenters is it customary to go outside the district for work, and two of the three carpenters in the village are often employed outside. The most common occupation outside agriculture is teaching, and in 7 households in the village a son is employed as a school teacher, either in the school in the village (which is a primary and high school which also caters for the neighbouring villages) or in one of the surrounding villages. Three households get supplementary income by working as assistants to shop-keepers in the local markets. Two of the richer landowning households are themselves owners of small cloth-shops in the local markets, and one rich farmer is engaged in lucrative buying and selling (rice and buffaloes). A few households get—primarily supplementary—income from petty business.

In the village itself two households get supplementary income from selling cigarettes and a few other items, and two from working as tailors. Besides there are two homeopathic doctors and the carpenters and teachers mentioned above.

Most of the landless are unemployed outside the peak season of agriculture. While some landless labourers have settled in the village after marriage and others have moved to neighbouring villages, labour migration in search of work outside the area is very limited. This situation is quite unlike many other places in Bangladesh, especially in the densely populated areas, where it is common to move far away in search of work. The absence of labour migration was noted also in the 1940s by Mukherjee who wrote that 'the scope of migration is very limited in the whole village . . . persons were found to have moved from one village to another for work, but this sort of migration of labourers is restricted within the locality and so the form of labour does not undergo change'.[6]

In terms of actual employment the villagers thus have very few economic relations with the outside world. The great majority of the population in Boringram is engaged in agriculture, from which they get not only their daily food but also the means to buy their necessary requirements. It is this integration in the market economy which constitutes the basic economic relation outwards.

The most distinct characteristic as regards agricultural production in Boringram is the complete dominance of rice cultivation. In some areas of Bangladesh it is possible to cultivate cash crops, notably jute, but the soil of the Barind tract and the absence of water (other than rain) does not allow for such cultivation in the Barind Tract. Some vegetables are grown, but with the exception of water melon and—on a small scale—potatoes, these are for home consumption only. There are no rivers or canals, and most of the ponds dry out during the dry season. In few of the bigger ponds (which are privately owned) it is possible to grow fish which are sold in the market. Quite a few households are able to supplement their income either by selling juice from their own date trees or by converting date juice into *ghur* (a kind of sugar) which is sold in the market.

Traditionally it has only been possible to irrigate from the few big ponds. Now one farmer has bought a small power pump, and a few have taken to use small hand irrigation pumps. There are no jointly-owned power pumps or other artificial irrigation facilities in the village, and *boro* cultivation is therefore negligible in Boringram.

The soil in Boringram is only well suited for the *aman* crop, and all the farmers cultivate this crop on all their cultivable land (about 80 per cent—some is taken up for homestead, some is waste land and some are ponds, among other things). The yield varies, with a tendency for higher yields among the bigger farmers who can afford to use fertilizers. The 1975 – 6 *aman* harvest was considered fairly normal for the area, and the average yield among the individual economic units was about 15 maunds per acre[7] (ranging between 12 and 24 maunds). This is only slightly higher than the 14 maunds reported by Mukherjee in 1942, but lower than the average reported for Bangladesh which is usually estimated at around 18 maunds per acre.[8]

On about one-third of their cultivable land the farmers in Boringram grow *aus* paddy. Because of the unsuitability of the soil for this crop the yield is low, averaging about 9 maunds per acre (the range is between 5 and 15 maunds). This is well below the average estimated for the country at 15 maunds.[9] Only a small fraction of the land is cultivated with *boro*, but as it is possible to use the high yielding varieties, the yield is much higher than for the other crops, about 40 maunds per acre. It is, however, much more expensive to cultivate the high-yielding varieties, and the grain is not as good as those of the traditional varieties.

As Boringram is characterized by monoculture, rice is then not only cultivated for home consumption but is also regarded as a cash crop; the cultivators are dependent on the income from sale of rice in order to buy bare necessities (e.g. fertilizer, kerosene oil and clothes). All cultivators without supplementary income sell off their rice production, also those who are not able to meet their families' consumption requirement. It is generally estimated that rice constitutes about one-half of the rural population's basic needs.[10] In order to meet the daily requirement of about 1 pound of rice per person, 8.5 maunds of paddy are needed per year.[11] In order to provide the population of 704 persons with their daily rice requirement, about 6,000 maunds of paddy are needed a year. In addition, another 6,000 maunds are needed a year to produce the cash income necessary to provide for the basic needs of the population. In 1975 the land cultivated by the inhabitants of Boringram produced about 7,000 maunds of paddy,[12] somewhat above the consumption requirement. As mentioned above, however, all the rice is not consumed in the village, and the produce is not equally distributed. Thus, for a substantial proportion of the population the daily rice requirement is not met, not to speak of the basic needs. The majority of the population lives below subsistence level (defined as non-fulfilment of basic needs). Only about one-fifth of the households live at or above the subsistence level, and a few of these have a surplus. This will be discussed in more detail in the following sections.

C. *Relations of production*

(1) *Tenurial arrangements*

The differences in the standard of living among the population is due to the relations of production which regulates the access to the factors of production. Since the economy of Boringram is almost exclusively dominated by agricultural production, access to land is the most important factor (access to irrigation and inputs are also important but by and large derived from the access to land).

There are three types of relationship between man and land. Man may be related to land in terms of ownership, cultivation, and work. In principle the State is the ultimate owner of the land, but in practice ownership rights rest with the registered owner. The landowner may either cultivate his own land, mortgage it, or rent it out to others.

In Boringram most of the landowners cultivate their own land. Traditionally the big landowners rented out all or a large portion of their land to others, but this has become less common. None of the big farmers rent out all their land, but some rent out a small proportion. However, some (six) of the poorest land-owners who do not possess any tools themselves rent out their land and work as day-labourers for others. In addition, one small farmer is engaged full-time in petty trade and also rents out all his land.

It is increasingly difficult to obtain land for cultivation, and the proportion of land rented in the total acreage of cultivated land is small. There are two different ways of obtainng access to the cultivation of other people's land. The most common is through the share-cropping system, where a landowner gives a portion of his land in cultivation to another person, and the crop is divided among the two, usually on a fifty-fifty basis. Another is the so-called *khai khalasi* (literally 'I eat free') which is a usufructuary mortgage where a person gets the use of another person's land in return for paying him some money. In Boringram the usufruct is usually for 7 years, but it is possible—but not common—to redeem one's own land before the stipulated period by paying a proportion of the money back, depending on the time elapsed since the usufruct was given. Land is usually given in *khai khalasi* in times of stress, i.e. a landowner gives a proportion of his land in *khai khalasi* to another in order to borrow money to meet the daily expenses. This means that it is primarily the better-off peasants who have the usufruct of other people's land through mortgage.[13]

However, due to the difficulty of obtaining land on a share-cropping basis, it is not uncommon for poorer households to buy the usufruct of land for money saved from working for others. This is possible when in land-poor households there are several grown-up sons who manage to get all-year employment in other persons' households. Finally, it is very common for the person who has given his land in *khai khalasi* to cultivate the land himself on lease from the money-lender. If a peasant has given his land in *khai khalasi* to a relative and cultivates the land himself, he usually pays half the crop to the related money-lender. If the transaction is between two unrelated persons, it is common to pay a lease in kind at a fixed amount of paddy per acre (generally more than half the yield).

In relation to the total number of acres cultivated by the inhabitants of Boringram the actual number of acres cultivated but not owned is not very high. In total the population of Boringram own 423 acres and cultivate 458 acres. Not counting own land mortgaged out and cultivated by the actual owner, a total of 53 acres are cultivated on a share-crop basis. This constitutes 11 per cent of the land cultivated. Thirteen of the share-cropped acres belong to landowners in the village. These share-crop out of a total of 20 acres (5 per cent of the total land owned), the rest to people in neighbouring villages. Eleven of the share-cropped acres belong to people in neighbouring villages, and 29 to persons outside the local area, who can be classified as absentee landowners. The 29 acres belonging to these persons constitute 6 per cent of the cultivated land. For the individual land-poor household, however, the access to land owned by other persons is important. As many as 42 per cent of the cultivating households rent in land. (Compared to the national average, the percentage of households taking in land is about the same, the national average being 39 per cent. But the percentage of land cultivated on a share-crop basis is considerably lower than the national average of 23 per cent.[14])

Land may be bought and sold in the open market, but such land transactions are not very frequent. Since the independence of Bangladesh in late 1971 only a little less than 5 acres were sold by the landowners in Boringram in 1976, and a little over 5 acres bought. (The increase in land sales in the post-independence period noted from other areas in Bangladesh did not seem to have taken place in the study area.[15]) With the exception of one cultivator-cum-businessman, who has bought between 2 and 3 acres, nobody has bought more than one-half acre in that period. From the land transactions for which data are available it appears that land is bought and sold among people who live either in the village or in neighbouring villages, i.e. absentee landowners have not bought up land in the Bangladesh period. From the above data on share-cropping it appears that such people did buy up land previously. It is interesting to note that whereas town people do not buy up land at present, they still act as money-lenders in the village.

The vast majority of land transactions take place through inheritance. According to Muslim inheritance law the land is inherited by all children, in such a way that all sons get an equal share and the daughters half the share of the sons. It is, however, quite common for the daughters to forgo their part of the inherited land—primarily to remain on good terms with their brothers on whom they may depend for help in case of divorce or widowhood.

As mentioned above, the landowners cultivate most of their land themselves. A few of the better-off households do not take active part in the production, but as cultivators they supervise others. The work on the land is done either by family labour, i.e. persons working on land cultivated by their own household, or by hired labour, i.e. persons working on land cultivated by others. With the exception of the few persons mentioned above who are engaged outside agriculture, all adult males (and bigger children) in the cultivating households are engaged as family labourers. The employment of hired labour is widespread; except for the poorest, all cultivating households hire outside labourers in the peak agricultural seasons, and in addition it is quite common to engage hired labourers on a year-round basis. For the households possessing no land, the employment as hired labourers in the cultivating households constitutes their main source of livelihood, as there are few outside job opportunities. Also households with little land have to hire themselves out as labourers in order to meet their basic needs.

Although in some cases there is a more permanent relationship between landless households and cultivating households using hired labour on a year-round basis, in the sense that the labourer's contract is renewed year after year, it is just as common that the labourer changes his employer every year. Most labourers cannot count on year-round contracts, and employment on a day-to-day basis is the most common. In the peak agricultural seasons there is work for all, but for three or four months of the year there is hardly any work offered, and many are unemployed. The remuneration for hired labourers is extremely low and is paid both in cash and in kind. For day-labourers the cash payment depends on the season, but fluctuates around Tk. 3.00 per day.[16] In addition the day-labourers are usually served two to three meals during work.[17] Labourers on a yearly contract get all their meals, and the cash payment for an adult labourer is on the average around 1,000 takas.

The women do not work in the field,[18] but females from poor households often help with household work and rice processing in the rich baris. In such cases the female labourers do not receive any cash payment but are only given food, either for themselves or to be shared with their children.

(2) Distribution of land

As mentioned above, the access to land is the most important factor determining the standard of living of the population. Since relatively little land is rented out, it is most relevant to examine the distribution of *landownership* among the 122 households in the village.[19]

If we look at the individual households' ability to maintain their families on the basis of their landownership, the population falls into four distinct groups: (1) landless, (2) marginal peasants, (3) subsistence peasants (small and medium), and (4) surplus peasants. The division is made on the basis of the following criteria: (a) whether family members are forced to take outside employment or to rent in land, (b) whether households can produce enough from their land to maintain their families with rice, (c) whether households can produce enough from their land to maintain their families with basic needs, and (d) whether households can produce a surplus over and above their basic needs.[20]

As will be seen from Table 7.1,[21] besides landownership per household, landownership per capita is an important factor, and there is a tendency for size of household to increase with the size of landownership.

Of course, it is not possible to place all households in one of these categories on the basis of landownership alone. The boundaries are not absolute, they are rough groupings of the households on the basis of their ability to maintain their families.

If we look at the ability of the landowning categories to maintain their families according to the criteria listed under (a) to (d) above, the pattern emerges as shown in Table 7.2. The ability of the households to maintain their families does not depend on ownership of land alone. It was mentioned above that 11 per cent of the land is cultivated on a share-crop basis, and 42 per cent of the cultivating households have taken in land on share-cropping. On the other hand, 36 per cent of the landholding households (31 out of the 86 landowners) have given land in *khai khalasi*. Together they have given a total of 21

Table 7.1. Distribution of households according to landholding and population

Classification according to landownership (acres)	No. HH.	% HH.	No. of persons	% of persons	Average family size	Acres owned	% of land owned	Acres owned per cap.	Acres cultivated	% of land cultivated	Acres cultivated per cap.
Landless	36	30	156	22	4.3	–	–	–	10	2	0.06
Marginal peasants 0.1 – 2.9	42	35	205	29	4.8	59	14	0.3	76	17	0.4
Small peasants 3.0 – 6.9	24	20	157	22	6.5	111	26	0.7	125	27	0.8
Medium peasants 7.0 – 10.9	15	12	142	20	9.5	136	32	1.0	132	28	0.9
Subsistence peasants 3.0 – 10.9	(39)	(32)	(299)	(42)	(7.5)	(247)	(58)	(0.8)	(257)	(55)	(0.9)
Surplus peasants 15 + acres	5	4	44	6	8.8	117	28	2.7	115	25	2.6
TOTAL	122	101	704	99	5.8	423	100	0.6	458	99	0.7

Note: There are no households owning between 11 and 15 acres, thus the jump between Subsistence and Surplus category.

Table 7.2. Landowning households' ability to maintain their families from their land

Peasant category	(a) Family members forced to sell their labour		(b) HH who can provide family with rice[23]		(c) HH who can provide family with basic needs[23]		(d) HH who produce surplus[24]	
Total No.	No. HH	% HH	No. HH	% HH	No. HH	% HH	No. HH	% HH
Marginal 42	29	69[22]	2	n.s.	0	0	0	0
Small 24	1	n.s.	22	92	14	58	(5)	(21)
Medium 15	1	n.s.	14	93	4	27	(3)	(20)
Surplus 5	0	0	5	100	5	100	4	80

(46% next to the 58/27 figures in column (c))

Table 7.3. Share-cropping and mortgaging patterns among the households in Boringram

Peasant category	No. HH.	HH share-cropping in land		HH share-cropping out land	HH mortgaging in land	HH mortgaging out land		HH cultivating own mortgaged land
		No.	%	No.	No.	No.	%	No.
Landless	36	4	11	–	–	–	–	–
Marginal	42	16	38	3	4	14	33	4
Small	24	11	46	2	6	9	38	5
Medium	15	4	27	2	2	8	53	1
Surplus	5	0	0	3 (60%)	5 (100%)	0	0	0
Total	122	35	28	10	17	31	–	10

Table 7.4. Distribution of peasant categories according to tenurial status

Peasant category	No. HH.	owner cultivator		owner-cum-tenant		pure tenant		non-cultivator	
		No.	%	No.	%	No.	%	No.	%
Landless	36	0	0	0	0	4	11	32	89
Marginal	42	20	48	16	38	0	–	6	14
Small	24	12	50	11	46	0	–	1	–
Medium	15	11	73	4	27	0	–	0	–
Surplus	5	5	100	0	0	0	–	0	–
Total	122	48	39	31	25	4	3	39	32

acres in *khai khalasi*, about one-half to landowners in the village, the other half to persons in the neighbouring villages, or (a few) in the nearest town. Thus, the share-cropping and mortgaging patterns among the villagers very much influence—and reflect—their economic position. The details are given in Tables 7.3 and 7.4.

As is shown in Tables 7.3 and 7.4, with the exception of the surplus peasants, there are households in all landowning categories giving land in mortgage and renting in land from others. Mortgage of land is most widespread among the medium peasants, whereas renting-in land is most common for small and marginal peasants who are very dependent on the cultivation of other people's land in order to meet their rice and basic needs requirements.

The use of hired labour was found to be quite high, as is shown in Table 7.5.

Table 7.5. The use of hired labour among different landowning groups

Peasant category	HH hiring labour on all-year contract		HH hiring labour on contract for season		HH hiring labour on day basis in season	
	No.	%	No.	%	No.	%
Marginal	0	0	0	0	10	24
Small	8	33	5	21	24	100
Medium	5	33	4	27	15	100
Surplus	5*	100	–	–	5	100

Note: *All surplus households hire more than 1 permanent servant on all-year contract (3 – 4 each).

It is noteworthy that even among the marginal peasants as much as one-quarter employ persons outside the family to help in the peak season. Among the other categories all households hire seasonal day-labourers. It is also noteworthy that among the subsistence (small and medium) peasants as many as one-third hire labourers on a year-round basis, and another quarter on contract for the season. This despite the fact that about one-half are unable to meet their basic needs from the cultivation of their land (see Table 7.2). (The use of hired labour seems to be higher than that recorded from other areas. A sample survey undertaken from villages in different areas of Bangladesh shows that 43 per cent of total households used hired labour.[25] The data provided in Table 7.5 indicate that 65 per cent of the 83 cultivating households[26] in Boringram used hired labour.)

On the basis of the information given in the tables it is now possible to characterize in more detail the categories of households listed above:

Landless: Households owning no cultivable land. With the exception of 4 pure tenants these are not cultivating households but entirely dependent on working for others.

Marginal peasants: Households owning and cultivating insufficient land to maintain their families with rice. They are forced to take either outside employment or to rent in land for cultivation, or both (about 70 per cent have outside employment and 38 per cent rent in land).

Subsistence peasants: On the basis of acres owned per capita it is possible to subdivide this group into *small peasants* (with an average of 0.7 acres owned per capita) and *medium peasants* (with an average of 1.0 acres owned per capita). However, on the basis of acres cultivated per capita alone, the difference becomes minimal, the acreage being 0.8 and 0.9 respectively, and on the basis of the criteria listed under (a) to (d) their ability to maintain their families from their land shows a similar pattern. *Subsistence peasants* are thus characterized as peasants with sufficient land not to be forced to take outside employment but without a surplus over and above their basic needs. Some 38 per cent of the subsistence peasants have taken in land on a share-cropping basis, and 44 per cent have given part of their land in *khai khalasi*. According to their own estimate, about 80 per cent have a surplus, but for the majority of these this is primarily because of supplementary income. Two-thirds of the small and one-third of the medium peasants own below 0.9 acres per capita—the acreage necessary to meet basic needs.

Surplus peasants: Households with land sufficient to provide a surplus over and above their basic needs. Three of these five households rent out a small portion of their land to others on a share-cropping basis, and they all take land in mortgage (i.e. act as money-lenders).

In the above pages the peasant households have been characterized with respect to landholding, and on the basis of this factor they have been divided into what has been described as groups or categories. Purposely, they have not been described as belonging to different classes. As Bernstein has pointed out, in differentiating the peasantry one has to distinguish between differentiation in the sociological sense—where the indicators are differences in the accumulation and consumption of use-values, not necessarily indicating socially significant differences at the level of production—and differentiation in the materialist sense which poses class in terms of the social relations of production.[27]

Differentiation in the materialist sense is 'tied to the conditions in which wealth becomes capital, when it is not consumed individually but productively through investment in the means of production'. As will be shown in the following two sections there are few instances of productive investment among the peasants in Boringram. Nevertheless, the classification used above does allow for differentiation in terms of class, based on the relation of production. The tripartite class classification of peasants as 'poor', 'middle', and 'rich' used in classical Marxist writings[28] is based on the same criteria as those used in the present analysis. 'Poor' peasants are those unable to reproduce themselves by household production and who exchange their labour-power on a regular basis (landless and marginal peasants). 'Middle' peasants are able to reproduce themselves through family labour and land (subsistence peasants), and 'rich' peasants or 'kulaks' (surplus peasants) accumulate sufficiently to invest in production ('insofar as they initiate and maintain a cycle of extended reproduction based on accumulation they come to form a category of capitalist farmers').[29]

The problematic relating to productive investment is discussed in detail in the following chapter on the mode of production. In the present context it suffices to point out that the 'surplus' peasants of Boringram—and other areas of Bangladesh—act in a manner similar to those peasants which in the Russian context were described by Lenin as 'kulaks', i.e. they are not only farmers employing labour-power, they also act as local merchants and money-lenders.[30] As in the African context discussed by Bernstein, capital accumulated in agriculture in Bangladesh is often invested in mercantile and transport activities which yield a better rate of return than reinvestment in production.

While it is argued above that the criteria used in differentiating the peasant households do justify a classification in terms of class in the materialist sense, a caveat should be added. As Bertocci has pointed out, 'It is still possible to argue that we are dealing with differences between ranked, but open status groups of fluctuating, internally competitive membership within the peasantry taken as a class in itself'.[31] In his discussion of peasant class in Bangladesh Bertocci refers to Béteille's observations from India where, the latter points out, the differences between big landlords and landless labourers as classes are obvious, but 'when . . . we consider large, medium and small landowners, we find the differences between them to be fewer and less clear [and] the lines we draw between them are bound to be subjective and to that extent arbitrary'. Béteille emphasizes the minor differences in the size of landholdings which 'may be mitigated by a variety of other factors such as family size, efficiency of cultivation, availability of credit, and so on'.[32]

D. *Relations between production and poverty*

It was mentioned above that 42 per cent of the cultivating households cultivate land belonging to others. If we look at the tenurial arrangements in detail the following pattern emerges: of the 83 cultivating households, 58 per cent are owner-cultivators (cultivating their own land only), 37 per cent are owners-cum-tenants (cultivating own land *and* land belonging to others), and 5 per cent are pure tenants (cultivators with no land of their own).[33]

However, the access to the cultivation of other people's land is limited. It was mentioned above that only 11 per cent of the total cultivated land is cultivated on a share-crop basis. This means that the individual tenants only rent in small pieces of land, and that the access to rented-in land is insufficient for the tenants to support their families from land alone.

Although over one-third of the marginal households rent in land (Table 7.3, column 2), none of these are able to maintain their families with basic needs, and only a few with rice from the cultivation of land (Table 7.2, columns b and c). However, these statistics only provide information on income based on cultivation. As appears from Table 7.2, column a, a little over two-thirds of the marginal peasants have outside occupations, primarily as day-labourers.

Although no detailed household consumption survey was conducted, some information is available on the peasants' food consumption. One-half of the marginal peasants stated that even with supplementary income they were unable to provide their families with rice. Some of these (20 per cent of all marginal peasants) stated that they often starve, others (30%) that they managed through the help of relatives or by borrowing.

The ability of the landless to provide their families with rice is worse. In this category 70 per cent of the households had insufficient income; 44 per cent of the landless families stated they often starve, and 26 per cent that they managed to provide their families with rice through the help of relatives or by borrowing. Less than one-third (29%) of the landless families had sufficient employment to enable them to feed their families.

The total number of landless and marginal peasant households who are unable to provide their families with rice is 24 and 20, respectively, and together they account for 36 per cent of the households in the village. These households can be considered to live at or below the famine line.[34] With a few exceptions (such as some carpenters and petty traders) none of the remaining households in these two categories have sufficient money to provide their families with basic needs (food, clothing, etc.), and these 34 households (28 per cent of all households in the village) live somewhere between the famine line and the poverty line.

Among the subsistence (small and medium) peasants almost all households can provide their families with rice, and they can thus be considered to live above the famine line. Hardly any of the households in this category sell their labour, a few are engaged in trade or other occupations, but by and large the subsistence peasants maintain their families from the income from cultivation only. It is seen from Table 7.2, column c, that a little less than half (46%) of the subsistence households are able to provide their families with basic needs; these 18 households live at or above the poverty line, whereas the remaining households in this category (21 households in all, 17 per cent of all households) live between the famine and the poverty line.

All surplus peasants can provide their families with basic needs and most of them (4 out of 5) have a surplus.

To sum up, 36 per cent of all households live at or below the famine line, 45 per cent (12 landless, 22 marginal and 21 subsistence households) between the famine line and the poverty line and 19 per cent (18 subsistence and 5 surplus peasant households) live above the poverty line. The data thus confirm the argument made by Alamgir that the majority of the population in the rural areas are caught in a Below Poverty Line Equilibrium Trap.[35]

Although the above figures certainly reveal a dismal picture, the people in Boringram seem to be better off than most people in rural Bangladesh. A recent sample survey concluded that 'a majority of the people in Bangladesh, mostly rural, were found to consume less than the minimum level required'. In this survey it was found that only 10 per cent of cultivating households could just maintain their families with food; 62 per cent of the cultivating households could meet their families' food requirements for 3 months only, and 23 per cent from four to nine months.[36]

The fact that a big proportion of the peasants are unable to meet their basic needs means that there is not much money for investment in agricultural production. Due to lack of irrigation facilities only a small portion of the land is cultivated with *boro* paddy. For the other paddy crops mostly local varieties are used, and the yields are low, especially for the *aus* crop. Although the data do not reveal a clear correlation between yield per acre and farm size, there is a tendency for higher yields among the bigger farmers. This is primarily due to the use of chemical fertilizers. All surplus and medium peasants use chemical fertilizers. Among the small peasants the proportion is about two-thirds, and among the marginal peasants about one-quarter only use small amounts of chemical fertilizers sometimes.

Among the 12 peasant households (Table 7.2, column d) who indicated that they were able to produce a surplus over and above their basic needs, only one household used this surplus for investment in capital equipment for agricultural production, viz. for the purchase of a power-pump, for which a government loan was also obtained. The most common use of accumulated surplus was money-lending which was engaged in by seven households. Besides, the accumulated surplus was found to be spent on purchase of land, business, and education of sons. For half of the peasants in the subsistence category the surplus was so little that virtually no investment took place. For those who did invest, it was most common to invest in more than one activity, and for almost all it was found that money was spent on the higher education of sons where there were children at the appropriate age. Five households had bought land in the Bangladesh period, but only one surplus peasant household on a relatively large scale. Three households had used their accumulated surplus for investment in business.

In addition six of the households with surplus were in possession of either a watch or a bicycle (both are rare), and at the time of marriage and other ceremonies considerable amounts were spent on gifts and feasts.

From the little information available this use of accumulated surplus seems to be general for the area. If we look at the investment pattern of the 37 persons who stood for election as members of the Union Parishad in 1977 we find that money-lending and investment in business were the most common use of accumulated surplus, 14 persons being engaged in both activites. Five of the candidates had bought land in the Bangladesh period, and only 6 stated that they cultivate *boro* (which may be—but is not necessarily—an indicator of investment in agricultural production through the purchase of a power pump).

The virtual absence of long-term investment in agricultural production among the pesants who do have an investible surplus seems to indicate that the gain in income from increased productivity brought about by technological change is less than income from money-lending activities or investment outside the agricultural sector.

The relations of production thus perpetuates poverty and agricultural backwardness.[37] This argument will be further elaborated in the following chapter.

E.   *Man and land in an historic perspective*

In order to relate the above data on production relations and poverty to the dynamics of the structure, it is necessary to examine the information in an historic perspective. Unfortunately no comparable data are available from the village so we shall have to suffice with a comparison with the data obtained from the villages studied by Mukherjee in 1942 from the same ecological area.

The first thing which can be observed is that the population density is much higher in Boringram in 1975 than in the five interior villages studied by Mukherjee.[38] The population density with respect to total land owned by the villagers was 668 persons per square mile for the five villages in 1942, and 1,066 in Boringram at the time of study in 1975. The average size of owned holding was 6.2 acres in the five villages, and is 4.9 acres in the present village studied.[39]

With regard to distribution of landownership there are also noticeable differences, as will be seen from Table 7.6.

Table 7.6. Distribution of landownership in 6 villages in 1942 and in Boringram 1975.

Land owned in acres	6 villages in 1942		Boringram 1975	
	No. HH	%	No. HH	%
No land	10	4	36	30
0.01 – 5	157	68	56	47
5.01 – 10	28	12	19	15
10.01 – 20	24	10	11	9
Above 20	13	6		
	232	100	122	101

Source: adopted from Mukherjee, p. 189 and own data.

The most striking difference between the two sets of data is found at the extreme ends of the scale, viz. in the proportion of landless and of big farms (over 10 acres). This trend corresponds to the trend for Bangladesh as a whole, where the scanty data available indicate a slight decrease in the number of large farms and a considerable increase in the number of landless agricultural labourers.[40] As regards the proportion of land controlled by the top 20 per cent of the big peasants, there is no change between the 1942 Mukherjee data and the 1975 Boringram data, the proportion of land controlled by the category being 70 per cent in both sets of data. (In the Mukherjee data the top 10 per cent control 45 per cent of the land, and the next 10 per cent control 25 per cent. The proportions for Boringram are 50 per cent and 20 per cent, respectively.)

As the 1942 study took place prior to the land-reform act in 1950,[41] the data on tenancy may be less comparable than other data, but they nevertheless indicate a trend. At the time of the early study, 63 per cent of the cultivators were share-croppers, and as much as 19 per cent of the land was cultivated on a share-crop basis.[42] These figures certainly are considerably higher than those given for Boringram above, viz. 42 per cent (owners-cum-tenants and pure tenants) and 11 per cent, respectively.

As pointed out in the previous chapter, in Bangladesh as a whole there is a trend towards increase in the incidence of pure tenancy. Unfortunately, detailed data are not available on the extent and kind of tenancy in operation one or two generations ago in Boringram, but the information available from interviews does not indicate such as a trend, as it appears that it is especially among the landless, who do not have access to draft animals and tools, that it has become increasingly difficult to get land on a share-crop basis.

Finally we can compare the ability of the individual households to maintain their families. In the 6 villages studied in 1942, 17 per cent of the owner-cultivators, 38 per cent of the owners-cum-tenants, and 42 per cent of the agricultural labourers and share-croppers lived at or below the famine line, and below the poverty line the respective figures were 37 per cent, 64 per cent and 70 per cent.[43] If we compare these data to the 70 per cent of landless households living below the famine line and the 81 per cent of all households at or below the poverty line, a noticeable deterioration seems to have taken place.

Mukherjee was able to revisit the area in 1945 after the Great Famine, and he found that the differentiation in the economic structure had 'been further accentuated, leading to sharp polarization. The slightly inflated group at the top, which controls the vast mass of the people at the bottom, is being swelled more and more and is having a gradually weaker link through the middle layer . . .'. At the bottom, he found 'a significant trend towards further deterioration leading to destitution'. From these observations he concluded that 'an economy of this nature is likely to collapse in the near future, if the process of transition is not an accidental phenomenon but an inherent feature of the economy'.[44]

In order to examine the underlying structure of the economy, Mukherjee set out to collect data (from peasants' memory) on landownership at the time of the 1922 land settlement. From a comparison of the 1922 and 1942 data he concluded that 'the concentration of income in the hands of a few as a result of property inequality (concentration of land) is further enhanced by the concentration of agricultural income in the same group. The cumulative effect of the operation of these factors is expressed in the changing economic structure. The operation of these factors is that poverty due to uneconomic holdings, being coupled with the concentration of agricultural wealth (conditioned by the same property-relations), leads to further inequality which in its turn results in greater concentration of agricultural wealth. In consequence, share-cropping and cultivation by hired labour grow at the expense of self-cultivation and this is expressed in the form of transition of the economic structure, which, as noted earlier, means the depletion of (the middle layer), a slight gain in (the top layer), and a considerable inflation (at the bottom). The vicious circle thus moved on, leading to further and further disintegration of the peasantry, which gathers momentum at every stage of the transition'.[45]

The implications of Mukherjee's analysis will be discussed in the following chapter. In the present context it should be pointed out that a continued trend towards deterioration does not necessarily imply the collapse of the economic system. The data on landownership in Boringram from two generations show that the process of deterioration has continued, but there are no indications that the system will not continue to function.

A comparison was made between the data on landownership among the present inhabitants of Boringram and the same families one generation ago. Looking at the position of the 36 landless households one generation ago, it was found that 13 of them come from families who possessed land in the previous generation, another 12 units consist of families partly originating outside the village (most often an outside male married into a poor peasant household), and the remaining 11 households come from families which were already landless in the previous generation. If one considers only the households originating in the village the ranks of the landless have been more than doubled.

The data on the 86 landowning households are given in Table 7.7.

Table 7.7. Landownership of present landowning households compared to landownership in the previous generation.

Present units	No. of respondents	No. HH. moved down	No. HH. moved up	No. HH with no change	Unknown
Marginal	33	24	3	6	9
Small	22	12	4	6	2
Medium	14	7	6	1	1
Surplus	5	2	1	2	0
Total	74	45	14	15	12

Of the respondents who are all landowners in the present generation, 45 come from economic units which owned more land in the previous generation, 14 households have been able to improve their landownership since the previous generation, and for 15 there has been no change. Looking at the cyclical movements within the individual peasant categories, it is noticeable that especially within the category of marginal peasants downward mobility is very strong. Also for the small peasants more households have moved down than have been able to hold their own or move up. Only for the medium peasants have half of the households either moved up or been able to hold their own. This might be interpreted as an indication of 'cyclical kulakism', a notion which was first advanced by Bertocci and later questioned by Wood.[46] The available data from Boringram are too scanty to say anything definite on this matter. All the middle peasant households which possess more land in the present generation consist of big families, and the families are likely to decline in the next generation; two of the families have already started giving land in mortgage.

It was mentioned above that in the Bangladesh period only a little over 5 acres had been bought, and a little less than 5 acres sold. Among the 5 surplus peasants 3 have bought land in this period, two of them small amounts and one between 2 and 3 acres, about half of the land bought by the villagers in that period. One surplus peasant has sold land in the post-independence period. Among the medium peasants, 4 have bought and 2 have sold some land during the period; and among the small peasants the numbers are 3 and 1, respectively. Of the marginal peasants 1 has bought and 3 have sold land.

With the exception of the amount of land purchased by the one surplus peasant and 1½ acres sold by one marginal peasant, the peasants have bought or sold less than 1 acre each during the period, and most less than half an acre.

However, if we add the data on land transaction in Bangladesh since 1971 to the generational data presented in Table 7.7 (most of which reflect land transactions prior to 1971), the process of deterioration among the poor becomes clearer than appears from recent land transactions. As mentioned above, 13 of the landless households come from families possessing land in the previous generation. In other words, a little over 10 per cent of all households became landless within one generation.

The biggest patrilineage in the village consists of 9 landowning households which together possess 27 per cent of the land. Four of the households are surplus peasants, two of whom have been able to hold their own through supplementary income, while two have smaller landholdings than their fathers due to the division of land at the time of inheritance. Two households from this patrilineage are now classified as subsistence peasants, and three as marginal, and all five have smaller landholdings than their fathers due to the inheritance laws. This trend confirms an earlier observation from Comilla by Bertocci, viz. 'unless accumulation of land is kept up, a lineage's wealth stands to be dissipated'.[47]

Admittedly, data from two generations only do not suffice to show any process, but on the basis of the data available, households from all categories seem to have experienced deterioration as far as landownership, and thus standard of living, is concerned. This process is best described as general pauperization. The process of deterioration has also been observed from Comilla where, it was pointed out, 'the workings of the "system" under current ecological pressures seem continuously to force people out at the bottom'.[48]

Also, surplus peasants have less land in the present generation, but some of them have been able to retain or improve their economic positions. For most of them, however, this has only been possible through a diversification of their economic activities, either through the education of their sons or through investment outside agriculture. The implications of this trend—which is also observed elsewhere in Bangladesh—will be discussed in the following chapter.

F.   Village power structure

In traditional rural Muslim Bengali society the social organization is the *samaj*, meaning society, which is a symbolic and organizational reference for the political and religious community. A *samaj* may be coterminus with the village or extend it,[49] and it is under the leadership of a council of elders who have the function of moral arbiters of community life and who play an important role in dispute settlements.

Until 10 years ago there was one such *samaj* in Boringram under the leadership of the village headman who was also the head of the richest household in the village. This person was powerful even outside the village and had been chairman of the union council in the British period. His second son was a member of the union council in the Pakistan period, and his youngest son was the chairman of the Union Parishad from 1973 to 1977. After the death of the old village headman the second son wanted to continue as head of the entire village, but a dispute arose and the village became divided into two factions.[50]

The two leaders of the rival factions belong to the subsistence peasant category and are thus not as economically powerful as the old headman's family. However, one had a son and the other a nephew who had studied in college, which is one indication that they belong to families who want to assert their positions. Besides, one of the families is related by marriage to a local politician who had for long been a rival of the old village headman at the union council level.

Until a few years ago there were just the two factions in the village, but then a new dispute arose within the original *samaj*, which was again split, and at the time of the study there were four factions in the village. Three of the sons of the old village headman (all surplus peasants) constituted the leadership of the biggest faction. As mentioned above, the leadership of the first rival faction was made up of two rising subsistence peasants. One faction was under the leadership of the fourth son of the old village headman, while the fourth faction was led by the one surplus peasant not belonging to the old headman's patrilineage.

The fact that the village was split in four factions meant that there was no longer any body to deal with village affairs, to settle local disputes or to facilitate joint undertakings.

The disputes within the village as they come to light through the factions do by no means run along class lines. They are more akin to the factional disputes which are known primarily from studies of Indian villages, where it is often found that 'the important cleavage runs through the category of big men, not between it and the category of small men'.[51] In other words they represent struggles for power among the upper peasantry.

The impact of the many factions—and thus of the power struggle—clearly came to light within the village co-operative which was formed in connection with the introduction of the government IRDP programme. The co-operative was formed in 1972, and the son of one of the leaders of the first rival *samaj* was made manager. A managing committee consisting of six persons was formed, and with the exception of the model farmer they all belonged to families which dominate faction politics; the vice-chairman was the grandson of the old village headman, and one of the directors was the son of the surplus peasant outside the dominant patrilineage who leads one faction.

Soon after the formation of the co-operative the other members of the managing committee became dissatisfied with the manager, but because they were all struggling for power, they were unable to elect a new manager. The result is that the co-operative did not function at all, and nobody in the village was able to partake of any of the benefits offered by the government's development programme. Before the friction in the co-operative came into the open, the members had been promised a power-pump from the IRDP office. However, they were unable to agree where to put the pump, as all the members (and especially the managing committee members) wanted it installed next to their fields. As a matter of fact, it may be the dispute over the installation of the power-pump which made the power struggle come to light.

Apart from the fact that the factional system in the village militated against joint undertakings, the split-up of the *samaj* comes most clearly to light at the times of ceremonies. At the time of Eid each *samaj* celebrates separately. It is within the *samaj* that the animals are killed on this occasion, and it is likewise within the *samaj* that the distribution of money obtained from the sale of the skins of the slaughtered animals takes place among the poor. People from different *samaj* are not supposed to take meals in each others' houses. As a matter of fact, some of the *samaj* were overtly split consequent to the violation of this rule. At the time of marriage and other family ceremonies only members of the *samaj* are, as a rule, invited.

Economically, it is difficult to discern a clear pattern as regards the importance of the various factions. Among the persons who worked on all-year contracts it was quite common to change masters from one year to the next, and often the masters would belong to different factions. Certainly, there are instances of a servant working for years for the same master and being in a dependency relationship to his faction leaders.

As it is difficult to obtain land for share-cropping, the share-croppers have to remain on good terms with the landowners. The little information available indicates that share-cropped land is obtained either from a relative or from a rich person, with whom there are many-stranded relationships, and one of these is often membership of the landowner's *samaj*.

As regards the access to loans, these are often obtained from relatives. When money is borrowed outside the family, it is most often obtained from a rich person within the faction; but too little data are available to make any definite statements.

Generally members of one *gosthi* (lineal segment of a patrilineage) belong to the same faction; but there are several instances where this does not hold, and in most cases this is due to marriage alliances undertaken prior to the split up of the original *samaj*. As was shown above, factionalism in the village has also split up the brothers of the most influential family, one brother being the leader of one of the rival factions which broke away from the original *samaj* headed by the family.

The bulk of the data on *samaj* and factions were gathered during the extended stay in Boringram during 1975 – 6 and during the Union Parishad elections in 1977. As pointed out in Chapter V, the government in 1980 introduced the institution of *gram sarkar* (village government). During a visit to the village in 1981 it was learned that the villagers had agreed to elect members from all the different *samaj* factions. In fact it was mentioned that following *gram sarkar* there was only one *samaj* in the village. This was symbolized during the first Eid which the entire village celebrated together. It has not been possible to ascertain whether this reconciliation is a lasting phenomenon, or whether rivalries have re-emerged.

As pointed out above, factions represent struggles for power among the upper peasantry, and they do not run along class lines. In fact, none of the disputes recorded in the village were of a class nature, and class consciousness was low. On commenting on this phenomenon from other parts of rural Bangladesh, Bertocci has suggested that the 'multiplicity of dyadic relationships' (e.g. owner-tenant, creditor-debtor, patron-client relationships) contributing to structural fragmentation makes 'too narrow an approach to the analysis of class stratification take on an air of the unreal'.[52]

Bertocci argues that the problematic of class consciousness must be analysed within the framework of the 'political culture' of rural Bangladesh. Within this culture, 'individuals' relative social ranks and prestige are seen as outcomes measures by and flowing from their own efforts, i.e. the receipt of 'just deserts', as it were. Allied to this ethic is the equally widely-accepted belief that one's capacity to maximize attainment of one's (especially economic) goals is intimately linked to the degree one is successful in attaching oneself to persons who are powerful and prestigious'. He goes on to suggest that given these key elements of 'the Bengali Muslim peasant ideology of social rank', it takes no great leap of analysis to see the consistency of such an ethos with the generally reported inter-personal and inter-group conflict in rural Bangladesh and the primacy of factionalism in the rural social process, as opposed to 'class conflict'.[53]

As will be shown in Chapter IX, the factional conflicts within the village also play an important role in issues relating to politics above the village level.

G.   *Relations outside the village*

As was pointed out in Section B on 'Economic activity', it is the villagers' integration in the market economy which constitutes their basic economic relations outwards. As mentioned above, all cultivators sell of their rice in the market. Unfortunately, it is not possible to obtain data on the quantity of produce marketed by the survey method, as the peasants 'sell a little every week'. It was mentioned above that a total of about 7,000 maunds of paddy is produced by the cultivators a year, which is a little more than the amount necessary to meet the rice consumption requirement (6,000 maunds) of all the inhabitants, but far below the amount necessary to meet the basic needs. However, as pointed out above, all the rice is not consumed in the village, as all the cultivators have to buy their daily necessities in the market, notably kerosene oil, vegetables, cloth and fertilizers, etc.

After meeting their rice consumption requirements the five surplus households have an excess of about 1,000 maunds, which is more than enough to meet their basic needs. The vast majority of the cultivators, however, are forced to sell of their rice although their basic needs are not met. Thus, a considerable part of the harvest is siphoned out of the village to the local markets.

No exact figures are available on rice export from the area, but it is estimated that about 20 – 25 per cent of the rice produced in the thana is exported, primarily to Pabna, the district south of Bogra, from whence some is transported to Dacca.[54]

It is the area associated with the local market-place and the Union Parishad which constitutes the villagers' local community. It is within this narrow radius that their needs are met and contacts made. As mentioned, the villagers (i.e. the men) come to the bi-weekly *hats* regularly, but with the exception of the few households engaged in business, few of the villagers have any need to go outside the thana. Members of the surplus peasant households visit Bogra town (about 15 miles away) about once a week, and four of them have been to Dacca. Among the other households, only one person has been to Dacca, and on an average they visit Bogra once or twice a year, or less.

At time of land transactions and other official business the peasants visit the Union Parishad headquarters. This local government plays a role in the villagers' life. The local representatives are known to the people, and administratively it is important, not least through the collection of local government tax. Also, at times of stress, relief is administered through the Union Parishad, as are rural works programmes.

When the villagers visit the market-place and the Union Parishad headquarters, they not only carry out their various business, they also exchange information with people from other villages. Few of the villagers ever read a newspaper or listen to the radio, and these local meeting-places in fact serve as the main vehicle through which news is transmitted. Local affairs are uppermost in their minds, and at the time when the study was carried out very few knew the name of the President of Bangladesh.[55]

The local offices of the various national development programmes are located at the thana headquarters. At the time of study, no officer from any of these programmes was ever seen in the village. As mentioned above, there was an attempt to establish a co-operative in the village under the government sponsored Integrated Rural Development Programme, but due to a conflict in the village, this did not work well in Boringram.[56]

To sum up, the villagers' daily world is by and large circumscribed by the local community defined as the group of villages surrounding a market-place and belonging to the same Union Parishad. It is here their daily needs are met, where they get news, and it is within this radius most family alliances are made through marriage.

As will be shown in Chapter IX, it is also at this level that local struggle for power takes place.

Table 7.8. Distribution of Households according to Ownership of Land (Acres)

Size of land owned	No. acres owned	% acres owned	No. acres cultivated	% acres cultivated	No. HH.	% HH
No land	0	0	10	2	36	30
0.1 − 0.9	6	1	9	2	12	10
1.0 − 1.9	24	6	38	8	19	16
2.0 − 2.9	29	7	29	6	11	9
3.0 − 3.9	26	6	29	6	8	7
4.0 − 4.9	25	6	22	5	6	5
5.0 − 5.9	15	4	21	4	3	2
6.0 − 6.9	45	11	53	12	7	6
7.0 − 7.9	23	5	16	3	3	2
8.0 − 8.9	42	10	42	9	5	4
9.0 − 9.9	9	2	8	2	1	1
10.0 − 10.9	62	15	66	14	6	5
11.0 − 14.9	0	−	−	−	0	−
15.0 − 19.9	33	8	35	8	2	2
20.0 − 26.9	0	−	−	−	−	−
27.0 − 30.0	84	20	80	17	3	2
	423	101	458	98	122	101

VIII

THEORETICAL DISCUSSION OF FIELD DATA (MODE OF PRODUCTION PROBLEMATIC)[1]

A. *Structural change in rural Bangladesh*

The current debate about the development and trends in Bangladesh agriculture involves two questions, one largely empirical and the other theoretical. The empirical question is whether or not capitalist relations of production are becoming dominant at the expense of pre-capitalist production relations within agriculture. The conclusions to be drawn from the data provided in the preceding chapter as well as from the analysis below do not support this thesis. The more theoretical question is whether the development of capitalism in agriculture is antagonistic to the reproduction of pre-capitalist relations. This is really a debate about the way in which the subsistence requirements of a village society are subordinated to world market forces, and about the indices relevant to the study of changing trends within agriculture.

As pointed out in the previous chapter, the integration of the peasants in the market economy constitutes their basic economic relations outwards. These relations have an important impact on peasant society, for as Saul and Woods have pointed out within the African context, both the creation and differentiation among the peasantry should be viewed as the 'result of the interaction between an international capitalist economic system and traditional socio-economic systems, within the context of territorially defined colonial political systems'.[2] These authors define peasants as 'those whose ultimate security and subsistence lies in their having certain rights in land and in the labour of family members on the land, but who are involved, through rights and obligations, in a wider economic system which includes the participation of non-peasants'.[3] The involvement in a wider economic system is thus one important dimension in analysing peasantries. Another is a conceptualization of 'peasant' economic behaviour. As Shanin has pointed out, peasantry can be defined 'as a process, a historical entity within the broader framework of society yet with a structure, consistency and momentum of its own'.[4]

In the literature concerning special 'peasant' economic behaviour it is stressed, among other things, that the peasant farm should be considered both as a production and as a consumption unit. The aim of the family farm is production for consumption rather than for accumulation. Most of the work is done by family labour which is considered as 'of no cost'. At times of increasing consumption pressures or e.g. tax burdens, the family labour wil be intensified, but farming will not be given up altogether—often because there are no alternative means of surviving.[5] Chayanov has termed this intensification of family labour 'self-exploitation'.[6]

In their analysis of rural Bengal under colonial rule the Rays give a lucid account of the interaction between the traditional socio-economic system and

133

the wider economic system. They show that it was possible to extract a surplus from agriculture and to market commercial crops from agricultural producers for export without a great expansion of production forces. The peasant methods of production were found to be really efficient in terms of costs and cheaper than modern scientific methods. As the peasant economy showed itself perfectly responsive to the pull of the world market, there were no problems in securing an adequate quantity of commercial crops from small peasant farms.[7] Most of the peasants were heavily indebted, and through the combined pressures of rent, interest and taxes they were forced to sell just after harvest when prices were low. Thus, an expanding volume of exports could be secured by 'holding down the level of domestic consumption in the rural sector'.[8]

The thrust of the Rays' argument is that the forces working upon rural society during colonial rule 'ensured continuity rather than change for two centuries'.[9] In fact, in their analysis they question some of the interpretations Mukherjee makes of his own data—cf. the analysis Section E of Chapter VII. While they agree that subsequent to the deepening crisis of agriculture in Bengal since 1920 a number of cultivating families were reduced each year to share-croppers and agricultural labourers, they argue that 'such a trend has not brought about a radical alteration in the proportion of the classes in village society'.[10] Mukherjee's own data show that between 1920 and 1942 no family altogether lost land. The Rays' conclusion is opposite to the one reached by Mukherjee, viz. 'while there was considerable mobility within this class structure . . . the structure itself remained seemingly unchanged'.[11]

Contrary to the assumptions in the Mukherjee study and on the basis of detailed analyses of historical accounts and statistics the Rays show that before the establishment of British rule in Bengal, cash-crop cultivation, organized money markets, and internal trade had substantially modified the self-sufficient subsistence economy of the villages. Monetized commerical transactions had brought about considerable exploitation and concentration of wealth within the village society as a result of money-lending and grain-dealing.[12]

This concentration of wealth had resulted in the emergence of a class of rich *jotedars*, who during British rule became legal tenants of the zamindars, but who were in fact 'the real landlords in effective possession of land and labour within the village'.[13] It was this class which acted as money-lenders, and they held the political power and economic control over the village.

At the political level the interests of the British export-import firms and the interests of the dominant village groups were compatible.[14] The British firms were able to acquire a plentiful supply of export products at low prices, and the dominant village groups were able to maintain their economic and political power in the countryside. The land-revenue burden on the peasants increased their need for cash which led to a considerable indebtedness, which in turn increased the power of the money-lenders. Over time the peasants were forced to incur debts also for the purchase of agricultural inputs and maintenance of their families until the next harvest.

The drain from agriculture operated through a complicated financial superstructure of the rural credit system with the village money-lenders and traders as the primary units of rural credit. A majority of these village money-lenders were rich cultivators who depended on urban money-lenders for funds. These in turn borrowed from indigenous bankers and commercial banks. In this way a large part of the interest paid by the producers was transferred to the towns.[15] Thus, the whole structure of government taxation became 'squarely dependent on the rural credit system', while 'the whole mechanism of local indigenous exploitation was made subservient to the wider process of colonial exploitation'.[16]

The socio-economic structure created by colonial rule acted as a built-in depressor within the village economy. The outflow of agricultural products was made possible by the depressed level of consumption of the peasants who were forced to sell at low prices. At the same time the capital which was accumulated in the rural areas went into money-lending and not to investment in agriculture, because of the much greater margins of profit to be earned by the former. For persons with an investable surplus, upon purely economic considerations of the balance of profit, risk and labour, collection of rent from landed properties and interest from usurious loans were usually more attractive than agricultural production for the market. At the local political level the influence and economic control of the dominant village groups depended upon an unchanging mode of production, as it largely rested on usury and crop sharing.[17]

From his observations in the 1940s Mukherjee concluded that 'an economy of this nature is likely to collapse in the near future, if the process of transition is not an accidental phenomenon, but an inherent feature of the economy'.[18] However, the analysis provided by the Rays shows how the traditional social structure in the village combined with unchanging methods of production was compatible with the advanced market integration during the colonial period.

The conclusions reached by Mukherjee also pointed towards a distinct process of disintegration as well as polarization. The same conclusion was reached by Abdullah *et al.* in their analysis of the change in tenurial patterns between 1960 and 1967−8. The same authors pointed out that 'it certainly looks like the development of a minuscule but dynamic capitalist sector within agriculture, accompanied by the alienation of the small and marginal farmers from their land'.[19]

Commenting on the same sets of data Wood has focused on the fact that land was being concentrated in the small-holding (less than 2.5 acres) category, while at the same time there was a reduction of holdings in the 7.5 acres and more category as well as a reduction in the share of land belonging to the latter big farmer category. Rather than polarization, Wood interpreted the data as indicating 'a slight movement towards equalization in the distribution of landholding' and he further maintained that 'the existence of a significant "kulak" class employing labourers, renting to share-croppers and appropriating a marketable surplus is denied'.[20] In fact, the thrust of Wood's argument is that 'the formal destruction of the landlord tenant system did not bring about the development of capitalist relations of production in the countryside'.[21]

Wood's argument is to a large extent based on an analysis of a village in the Comilla District, an area which is densely populated and where the impact of government programmes in agriculture has been particularly strong. Here he found that class differentiation did take place, but that it was dominated by usurious capital.[22] In the village studied, money-lending and mortgage transactions played a major role, and 'the cumulative impact of these mortgage transactions functions to increase and stabilize the gap between the classes'. Besides accumulating land through mortgage transactions, the richer peasant families 'diversify their economic activity into the sphere of exchange and professional employment',[23] i.e. there is no shift towards capitalist relations of production in agriculture.

In a recent study of two villages in Sawar thana of Dacca District, Jahangir found some of the same trends as those noted by Wood. Here also there was a clear process of differentiation which 'led to the formation of a rich peasant layer on the one hand, and a depressed layer of impoverished peasants composed of middle and poor peasants on the other'.[24]

Jahangir notes an increase in the use of wage labour and mechanization.[25] He does not discuss this trend in terms of a development towards capitalist relations of production in the countryside, but rather in terms of agriculture's role within the national economy: 'Capitalist development in the post-colonial period was uneven and produced two interlinked but contradictory effects in the rural areas. Firstly, it generated class differentiation within the peasantry and shaped the polarization process. Secondly, it determined the placing of the different peasant classes within the wider social structures . . .'[26]

In their analysis of a village studied in Kushtia District in the West, Arens and van Beurden compare their data to those presented from Comilla by Wood. While share-cropping is on the decline in the Kushtia village, it is still more important than in Comilla. In the Kushtia village fewer households have mortgaged their land than in the Comilla village. Arens and van Beurden argue that the difference between the two areas is mainly due to the greater impact of modernization in Comilla. They describe their area as more traditional with more feudal traits; and the rich landowners do not use their surplus for investing in agricultural innovations, but rather for their personal wealth and status. However, class differentiation is also proceeding in Kushtia, albeit not so fast as in Comilla, due to the smaller degree of modernization in agriculture.[27]

As pointed out in Chapter VI, on the basis of the higher degree of tenancy in the North than elsewhere in the country, Wood has advanced the hypothesis that exploitation of the poor takes on different forms with 'more petty leasing in the North and West, more usury and petty commodity exchange in the East'.

If we compare the data from Boringram regarding control over land with those presented from Bandakgram (Comilla village) and Jhagrapur (Kushtia village), it is found that with respect to the two important aspects mentioned by Wood, viz. petty leasing and usury, the Boringram data reveal a closer similarity to the Comilla case than to the one from Kushtia, as shown in Table 8.1.

While the fertility of the soil and population density is quite similar in the Bogra and Kushtia areas, the degree of landlessness is much higher in the Bogra village. At the same time, a smaller percentage of the households are

Table 8.1. Landlessness, share-cropping and mortgaging patterns in 3 villages in Bogra, Comilla and Kushtia Districts, respectively.

Village	% of landless HH	% of all HH share-cropping in	% landowning HH share-cropping out	% landowning HH giving land in mortgage
Boringram	30	28	12	36
Bandakgram	18	22	12	44
Jhagrapur	21	38	15	14

able to obtain land on a share-cropping basis in the Bogra village. This points towards a higher degree of pauperization among the rural poor in Boringram. If mortgaging is taken as an indicator of indebtedness and thus exploitation through usury, it is found that the degree of usurious exploitation in Boringram is not that much lower than what was reported from Bandakgram.

The conclusion to be drawn from the Boringram data is that the regional variation is less than expected by Wood. At the same time the data confirm Wood's argument concerning the importance of usurious exploitation.

Also as regards the use of surplus the Boringram data show a pattern similar to the one in Bandakgram. Twelve of the households in Boringram indicated that they had a surplus over and above their basic needs. Of these, only one had invested in capital equipment for agricultural production. The most common use of accumulated surplus was money-lending. Moreover, the accumulated surplus was found to be spent on purchase of land, business, and education of sons, and it was most common to invest in more than one activity. Five households had bought a little land in independent Bangladesh, the biggest buyer being a surplus peasant who had bought between 2 and 3 acres. He and two other households had invested in business.

The degree of land accumulation in recent time is relatively low in Boringram, but otherwise the rich households repeat the investment pattern found in Bandakram, viz. diversification of economic activities into the sphere of exchange and professional employment.[28]

Thus, the above analysis of the Comilla and the Boringram data shows that, like the situation during colonial rule, the traditional social structure in the village combined with unchanging methods of production is compatible with the advanced market integration. The economic system does not show signs of collapsing, nor do the data point towards a trend where capitalist relations of production dominate in agriculture.

On the basis of analyses of rural development programmes which have benefited the rich peasants and with reference to the increase of land sales in post-independence Bangladesh, as well as to the rapid swelling of the ranks of the landless rural families, many observers have referred to the increasing polarization within the Bangladesh social structure, thus reinforcing the early conclusions drawn by Mukherjee.[29] Based on the predominant trend towards deterioration for all categories of peasants in terms of land-holding, the process was characterized in the previous chapter as one of pauperization. This does not preclude a simultaneous process of polarization; but to the extent that one can talk about a process of polarization from the Boringram data, it is not due to considerable land accumulation by a small inflated group as noted by Mukherjee. Rather, through the employment of their educated sons as well as through money-lending and investment in non-agricultural activities, a rich peasant layer is able to stabilize its position, while at the bottom increasing numbers are forced off their land.

In Boringram only one family can be termed as a rural entrepreneur. This is the family which is both buying up land and investing in various business activities. Besides, this family held the union council chairmanship from 1973 to 1977. Looking at the local power structure for the area as a whole, it is this group of rich farmers-cum-entrepreneurs which dominates: in the 1977 union parishad election seven out of nine winning chairmen were rich farmers who had diversified their economic activity into business.[30]

At the political level, this economic diversification contributes to a merging of interests between rural and urban entrepreneurs, a trend which is also emphasized in the analyses provided by Jahangir and Wood, both of whom point out that the policies of the state have led to the rise of rural entrepreneurs whose interests merge with those of their urban counterparts.[31] Also at this level, the situation is characterized by continuity rather than change. The Rays noted how at the political level the interests of the British and the dominant village groups merged. In a recent article Broomfield has shown how during the colonial period the interests of the rich peasants became merged with those of the local rural towns, thus 'bringing village and rural town together in one system'.[32]

To sum up, the self-perpetuating nature of the socio-economic relations within the villages which were reinforced during colonial rule remain as strong as ever. Agriculture remains backward and usury continues to be more profitable than agricultural investment. At the same time, the continued emergence of small-town entrepreneurs from among the ranks of the rich peasants determines the relationships that are established through structures of power and economic structures that encapsulate the village community.[33]

With the continued urban bias in economic development planning this trend is likely to continue. Thus the relationship between state and rural society determines the development within agriculture. This theme will be further discussed in Chapter X.

B. *The mode of production debate*

In their analysis of colonial exploitation in Bengal during British rule the Rays argue that the integration of the peasant economy in the world market economy took place without any change in the mode of production. Their study thus provides a thorough empirical analysis of the impact of capitalist penetration on traditional social and economic structures, a process which has recently given rise to a theoretical debate among Marxists. Much of this debate has focused on the determination of the mode of production in the peripheral societies as a result of this penetration.[34] Ziemann and Lanzendörfer have pointed out that 'the type and structure of the peripheral production relations have to be seen as a product of the encounter of the worldwide economic system with technologically and socially backward societies, in which elements of the original society interlock with elements of the dominant society'.[35]

One way of analysing the interlocking of the elements of the two societies is based on theories concerning the articulation of pre-capitalist and capitalist modes of production, where the pre-capitalist social relations are reproduced, subject to the domination of capital. According to those theoretical arguments, the particular way in which the two modes of production are articulated is through an unequal exchange, where the commodities produced by the pre-capitalist sector are systematically exchanged below their value. This unequal exchange derives from the different conditions of production and reproduction of labour-power in the two modes of production, articulated to the benefit of imperialism. One of the proponents of this theory, Meillassoux, points out that agricultural production based on pre-capitalist relations continues because through its integration with capitalist commodity circuits, it provides capital with a flow value independently of any investment or intervention in production, and thus the reproduction of the peasantry in the Third World should be regarded as an intrinsic element of capitalist development rather than a single, initial phase.[36] A somewhat similar conclusion is reached by Ziemann and Lanzendörfer who argue that peripheral societies are marked by a dynamic element of development as well as a static element of stagnation where 'through the spread of capitalist production relations the non-capitalists are themselves produced and reproduced'.[37]

The notion of articulation of modes of production as regards the peripheral societies has been rejected by several critics. One of these is Hamza Alavi who points out that it is wrong to describe colonial economics as those in which pre-capitalist relations 'co-exist' with 'capitalist' relations. He argues that the essential nature and significance of the relationship between the producer and his master is radically transformed by the colonial impact and can thus no longer be characterized as 'pre-capitalist'.[38] Secondly, he argues that if there were two 'separate modes of production in a single social formation, a Marxist conception would postulate a contradiction between the two'. But, as he points out, the reality in the countries of the Third World is 'that the "feudal mode of production" in agriculture is precisely at the service of imperialism rather than antagonistically in contradiction with it'. Instead of contradiction between the two modes of production there is a unity which 'expresses a hierarchical structural relationship within a single mode of production',[39] a mode which is capitalist and which he refers to as the colonial mode of production.

The concept of colonial modes of production has also been advanced by Banaji who points out that they are 'specific entities with their own coherence and laws of development' which can only arise within the sphere of capitalist production, viz. 'within the sphere of reproduction of the capitalist mode of production on an even larger scale'.[40]

Thus, while the 'articulation' theories argue for the continued production and reproduction of pre-capitalist modes of production subject to the domination of capital, Alavi and Banaji stress the complete transformation of the previous modes.[41] As Alavi has argued, 'the small peasant farming economy . . ., transformed from its pre-capitalist "natural economy" drawn into the orbit of capitalist commodity production and exploitation through its subordination to (usurer's and) merchant capital as well as through its new found role in the reproduction of labour power for capitalist enterprise, is integrally a part of capitalist mode of production and does not constitute by itself a distinct mode of production whose structural characteristics could be defined without reference to its integration into capitalism'.[42]

The debate on how to characterize the mode of production in agriculture in the peripheral societies is of a more than semantic interest, as it also relates to how to analyse class conflicts. As Alavi has pointed out, the increasing militancy in rural India 'cannot be explained in terms of contradiction between a "feudal" mode of production and a "capitalist" mode . . . the wage labourers (are not) aligned differently from the other subordinate classes in the countryside, viz. the share-croppers and the smallholding "middle peasants". The alignments are structural alignments and conflicts of the colonial mode of production'.[43] However, while the arguments regarding the radical transformation of pre-existing modes and their complete integration in the capitalist mode constitute important contributions to the debate, the concept of a specific colonial mode of production leaves some problems unresolved. As Foster-Carter has pointed out, one problem is to specify its precise relationship to capitalism. He also points out that it is not clear whether it should be considered as a transitional mode.[44] McEacherm has solved the problem by referring to 'colonial forms of capitalist mode of production'.[45] This deflates the semantic aspect of the discussion, but it does not solve the fundamental analytical problem.

On the basis of the analysis of the Bangladesh data provided in the preceding section, the theoretical analysis provided by Alavi remains the most adequate so far in characterizing Bangladesh agriculture, even if one does not accept the semantics, i.e. the terminology of the 'colonial mode of production'.[46]

However, also in a Bangladesh context, this analysis has been rejected by Alamgir, for instance, who points out, among other things, that it does not provide a 'clear basis for identifying the dominant production relation and the antagonistic classes that are related to it'.[47] This and similar objections raised by Alamgir seem to be based on a misunderstanding of some of the basic arguments advanced by Alavi, who specifically relates his analysis to structural alignments and conflicts in class terms.

Alamgir suggests that the mode of production in contemporary Bangladesh is best described as semi-feudal, (see Chapter IV).[48] The manifestations of the semi-feudal mode aptly describe rural Bangladesh—and parts of India[49]—and, as shown in Chapters VI and VII, the analysis provided by Alamgir has supported the conclusions drawn from the local area-study. However, the analysis does not contradict the structural analysis provided by Alavi, and the concept of a 'semi-feudal mode of production' does not advance the analysis of the structural relationships.

C. Mode of production in Bangladesh

The arguments referred to above by Alavi and Banaji were advanced as contributions to an ongoing debate regarding the proper characterization of Indian agriculture. Similarly, the arguments by Wood referred to in the introduction to this chapter relate to various issues raised in the Indian debate; and in fact, Wood uses some of the criteria from that debate in his analysis of Bangladesh agriculture. Given the joint economic history of those two countries and the relevance to Bangladesh of some of the issues raised concerning Indian agriculture, it is relevant to outline the major points and to adopt Wood's approach of relating them to an analysis of Bangladesh agriculture.

The Indian debate has centred around defining the characteristics of capitalism and feudalism as modes of production and how these characteristics are manifested in agrarian relations in the colonial context. As summarized by McEachern, the following points have been used as indicators for assessing the passage from feudalism to capitalism under conditions of colonial imposition: '(1) the extent to which commodity production was generalized, (2) the extent to which landless labourers constituted a force of free wage-labourers . . ., (3) the extent to which capital in the countryside remained in the the sphere of circulation and did not actively affect the production relations in agriculture, and (4) the significance of tenancy relations in agrarian production'.[50]

McEachern adds that 'often it would seem that the main reason for describing the agricultural situation as semi-feudal rested on the belief that tenancy and sharecropping were incompatible with capitalism'. Similarly, there has been a tendency to equate wage-labour with capitalism. Against this view, Patnaik has argued that wage-labour is a necessary, but not a sufficient condition of capitalist organization. In her analysis she points out that 'given the Indian experience of the break-up of petty production in the colonial period without simultaneous or sufficient growth of capitalist production in agriculture . . . it seems more realistic to regard the labourers as being the outcome of a process of pauperization, rather than proletarianization'.[51-2] A similar position is advanced by Banaji who argues that 'wage labour and the capitalist mode of production are concepts based at different levels, even though the latter presupposes the former. Thus capitalism cannot be defined in terms of the existence or non-existence of wage-labour . . .'[53] In analysing the development in Bangladesh, Wood comes to the same conclusion, viz. that 'the extension of wage-labour cannot be interpreted as a sign of advancing capitalist relations'.[54]

In a succinct fashion Alavi has discussed the existence of share-cropping under capitalism in terms of labour process. In discussing the transformation in India under colonial rule he argues that 'the key to that transformation was the fact that the direct producer was dispossessed . . . and having been dispossessed appeared before the owner of the land . . . to sell his labour power in the form of a share-cropping relationship'.[55] He adds that share-cropping 'was a convenient *form* of capitalist exploitation of dispossessed rural labour at one stage, especially because it minimized the tasks of supervision and control of the labour process from day to day . . .'

Whether exploitation takes the form of share-cropping or wage-labour may also depend on the relative price between labour and agricultural output. As Mukherjee pointed out in his follow-up study in 1945: 'during 1943 and early 1944 the wage level of the agricultural labourers did not rise at the same rate as the price of paddy and so cultivation by hired labour became more profitable to the non-cultivating owner than by share-cropping'.[56] Describing the reverse process Banaji argues that 'if a big peasant chooses to substitute tenant labour for wage labour, then this could relate to a permanent shortage of labour in the area, or to the fact that wage costs have been rising . . . the particular form of tenancy a big peasant or landowner decides to organize does not affect the social character or content of the production-relations that these labour-arrangements embody'.[57]

The conclusions to be drawn from the above statements are that an increase in the use of wage-labour in agriculture does not by itself constitute a development towards capitalist relations of production. In the Kushtia study, share-cropping was reported to be on the decline. Also, in Boringram it is becoming increasingly difficult to obtain land for share-cropping, and the land-poor and landless are instead forced to work as wage-labourers. This is not due to development of capitalism in agriculture, but rather to the increased pressure on land 'forcing people out at the bottom'.[58] The swelling in the ranks of the landless depresses agricultural wages, and thus the use of wage-labour becomes the cheapest form of exploitation of the dispossessed rural poor.

As regards the existence of generalized commodity production Patnaik argues that this was imposed from outside by imperialist exploitation. It thus did not lead to capitalist relations in *production* in agriculture, but to development of capital in the sphere of *exchange*. In order to examine whether a capitalist mode of production exists in agriculture, she further argues that the criterion of accumulation and reinvestment must be specified as well, and that it must take place in the sphere of agricultural production itself.[59] It was in particular this line of argument which was followed by Wood in his analysis of the Comilla case,[60] and it also provided the framework for the analysis of the investment pattern among the surplus peasants in the Boringram case presented in this study. On the basis of the investment criterion neither the Comilla nor the Boringram case points towards development of a capitalist mode in the sphere of agricultural production.

In their historical analysis the Rays show that imperialism not only reinforced socio-economic relations within the villages, but it also acted as a built-in depressor within the village economy. In fact their empirical analysis centres around the criterion regarding accumulation and reinvestment outlined above. They point out that the rich peasants-cum-money-lenders would be interested in improving agriculture only if the increase in income would outweigh the loss of interest from money-lending. But, as they argue, 'the fact was that in Bengal the conditions for such a big jump in productivity were ruled out by the inexpansive character of the domestic market for agricultural products'.[61] At the theoretical level Patnaik has argued much along the same line. She points out that capitalist production in agriculture cannot emerge as long as it is surrounded by petty production 'unless the level of capitalist rent (surplus profits over and above "normal profit") at least equals that of pre-capitalist rent (surplus of output value over necessary cost for petty producers). As long as a majority of the producers are poor peasants who are enforced to rely for a livelihood on those who monopolize landed property, pre-capitalist rent remains high, and in such a situation capitalist production would make sense only if it is associated with substantial technical progress which gives a discrete increase in surplus per acre, i.e. a discrete "jump" in land productivity must take place compared to the same level of labour productivity as in the petty production'.[62]

The data presented from Boringram show that no 'jump' in land productivity has taken place. As mentioned, the government IRDP programme in the area has not taken root in the village.

In their analysis of the Agrarian Structure and the IRDP, Abdullah *et al.* point out that 'the advent of HYV and small-scale irrigation transformed the situation by introducing a higher level of productivity and dynamic economic forces', and they conclude that the IRDP provides a strong organizational basis for the promotion of increased growth of agricultural production with all the dynamism inherent in modern agricultural technology. They consider that the co-operatives are 'destined . . . to serve as vehicles for the growth of capitalism in agriculture . . .'[63]

In view of the analysis of the IRDP programme referred to above, the conclusions reached by Wood from the Comilla case are somewhat surprising, as Comilla is the area where the programme has had the greatest impact and for the longest period.[64] Based on his field material Wood argues that 'even where resources were allocated to agriculture through the specific experimental circumstances of the Comilla programme . . ., it was precisely these minifundist characteristics of the regional social formation which prompted the local emergence of specific antediluvian forms—namely mortgaging and money-lending . . .'[65] His data convincingly substantiate his argument regarding the continuation of usurious exploitation and its determination of the form of class differentiation. However, data from the Comilla area show that considerable investment has taken place in agricultural production, not least in connection with the expanding acreage under HYV *boro* rice cultivation.[66] In fact, in his study of Bandakgram, Wood himself points out that 'offholding employment can actually facilitate innovation in agriculture, since capital for agricultural investment and access to information, credit and inputs has been acquired. This extends the willingness to invest in high-yielding varieties of seed on a greater proportion of the holdings . . .'[67] As mentioned above, Jahangir also reports on investment by the rich in agricultural innovations, including tractors and power pumps, in the Dacca area.

So far, few studies have been published regarding development trends in Bangladesh agriculture. At the empirical level more analyses are required than those undertaken so far, while at the theoretical level, many issues remain unresolved. One can agree with Alavi that the transformed small peasant farming economy does not by itself constitute a distinct mode of production whose structural characteristics could be defined without reference to its integration into capitalism. But analysis of the continuing process of this integration needs to be further refined.

As argued above, the structural analysis inherent in the concept of the 'colonial mode of production' advanced by Alavi remains the most adequate so far for characterizing the mode of production in Bangladesh agriculture. In Chapter X the mode of production in agriculture will be discussed in the context of the Bangladesh social formation.

IX

LOCAL-LEVEL POWER STRUCTURE AND ITS RELATION TO NATIONAL POLITICS[1]

A. *Village power structure and local-level politics*

As mentioned in Chapter VII the old village headman in Boringram was very powerful also outside the village. He himself had been chairman of the Union Board during the British period, and through family connections the influence of the family was increased during the Ayub government in the Pakistan period. This was the time when the Muslim League became influential in the rural areas through the institution of the Basic Democrats. The old village headman and his sons were influential in the local Muslim League and, as mentioned, his second son was member of the union council during the Ayub period. During the end of that same period the father-in-law of his youngest son was chairman of the union council, and from 1973 to 1977 his youngest son was himself chairman. Until the 1977 Union Parishad election the vice-chairman was the husband of the old village headman's daughter. Furthermore, the daughter of the second son (who used to be member of the union council in the Pakistan period) was married to the manager of the Union Multipurpose Co-operative.

The power position in the local area of the traditional and influential family is shown on Fig. 9.1.

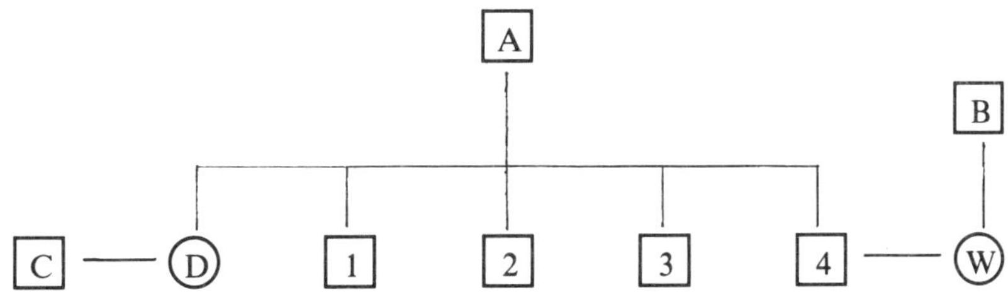

Legend:

(A)	— old head of traditional family, chairman of U.B. in British period
(B)	— father-in-law of (4), chairman of U.C. 1969 and of Peace Committee 1971, candidate in 1977, failed
(C)	— married to (D), vice-chairman of U.P. 1973 – 7
(D)	— daughter of (A)
(W)	— wife of (4)
(1) – (4)	— sons of (A)
(2)	— member of U.C. in Pakistan time and Peace Committee 1971
(4)	— chairman of U.P. 1973 – 77

145

Through marriage connections the family was also related to influential families outside the local area (in the district of Rajshahi through the wife of 2, and in the district of Patna through the second son of 2).

The political power of the old village headman and his family, however, did not go unchallenged at the union council level. Another influential member of the local Muslim League had long competed for power against the old village headman, and in the beginning of the Ayub period this rival managed to become elected as union council chairman. As mentioned above, however, towards the end of the period the chairmanship again passed to the old village headman's family when the father of his daughter-in-law became chairman.

The competition for power among the two influential families at the union level was also influenced by the political situation in Bangladesh (then East Pakistan) at the time, and so was the power struggle within the village.

As mentioned in Chapter VII, the village was split into two factions just after the death of the old village headman. This was just before the 1970 national election in Pakistan, when the Awami League came out as the all-powerful party in East Pakistan. The family of the old village headman remained loyal to the Muslim League, but the leaders of the rival faction supported the Awami League. As mentioned, one of the leaders of this faction was related by marriage to the rival influential person who had long challenged the old village headman at the union level. This person, however, still supported the Muslim League at the time of the 1970 election, although he was to switch allegiance later.

During the war for the national liberation of Bangladesh in 1971 and immediately afterwards, national politics had an impact on the local power struggle both in the village and at the union level. The leader of the original *samaj* (the second son of the old village headman) became chairman of the peace committee set up by the Pakistan government. Although nobody in the village joined the Mukti Bahini, the educated sons of the leaders of the rival faction were members of the Awami League, and towards the end of the war they came out in open support of the Mukti Bahini.

At the union level the rival of the old village headman changed allegiance during the liberation struggle, and after Liberation he was nominated Relief Chairman by the Awami League government.

At the time of the national elections in March 1973 all the persons who were elected Members of Parliament from Bogra District were Awami League members (as were 99 per cent in the whole of Bangladesh). When election took place for the Union Parishad towards the end of that year, people were already tired of the Awami League politicians,[2] and fierce competition took place for the post of Union Parishad chairman. Before the election, with the help of influential Awami League members in the district, the old rival of the influential Boringram family filed a petition against the youngest son of the old village headman, who was contesting the chairmanship on a neutral ticket (the Muslim League party was then banned). However, nothing came of this, and the son was allowed to fight the election which he won by 13 votes over the old family rival (who had actually held the chairmanship post, being nominated Relief chairman).

The case history shows that national issues tend to reinforce struggles for power among the upper peasantry at the local level.

As far as national political issues are concerned, the failure of the Relief Chairman (and former union council chairman) to win the Union Parishad election in 1973 can be best interpreted as a popular vote against the Awami League; and as mentioned in Chapter V, the reaction against the Relief chairmen and the government was repeated in many places of the country.

Given the fact that the Union Parishad elections took place barely two years after the Liberation war, it is remarkable that the traditional family managed to obtain the chairmanship. It was mentioned above that the family set up Peace Committees as ordered by the Pakistan regime. However, it should be mentioned that interviews conducted in the area left the impression that—at least as the villagers perceived the situation in 1975 – 6—the Liberation war did not have the impact that has been reported from other parts of Bangladesh. Many of the interior villages were not attacked by or entered into by the Pakistan army, and the local freedom fighters were from the towns, not the villages. In this connection it is noteworthy that the traditional family put up as candidate for chairman not the older brother who had been member of the Union Council during the Pakistan period, but the youngest brother who had no previous experience in local politics.

As mentioned in Chapter VI, the northern part of Bangladesh is less politically conscious than other areas, and the village study referred to below from Mymensingh does indicate more political consciousness from other areas, than the one reported here. However, more comparative studies are needed on political consciousness in the local areas of Bangladesh. In view of the trends towards repeating the policies (economic, political and ideological) of the Pakistan regime,[3] the data from this case-study may not be unique. As pointed out in Chapter VII, the villager's daily world is to a large extent circumscribed by the local community, and ideological issues by and large do not play a dominant role in their political decisions. As O'Connell has suggested, 'Faced with staggering problems in economic, social, political and religious life, the typical peasants and laborers of Bangladesh cannot live by language and culture alone. They need rice, and a palpable focus of solidarity, trust and direction'.[4]

B.   The 1977 Union Parishad chairman election

(1)   Madhyapur Union

As mentioned in Chapter V, the 1977 Union Parishad elections were moved forward in time, when the government decided to postpone the national elections. It was suggested that the local elections should also serve as a means to gauge the political situation in the country. However, nobody contested on a party ticket, but the party affiliation of the three candidates were well known among the people, and all three had been deeply involved in local politics for a long time.

One candidate was the former Relief Chairman who had also been union council chairman from 1964 – 8. As mentioned above, he contested the 1973 Union Parishad chairmanship which he lost by a narrow margin. The second candidate was the father-in-law of the sitting chairman who did not contest the election—the latter was not well liked, he had 'done nothing for the people', and probably he knew that he had no chance of re-election.[5] The second candidate came from a family which had been influential already during the British period. Like the family of his son-in-law this traditional family had also been on the Union Board at that time, and he had himself been chairman of the union council from 1969 until the Civil War. As mentioned above, he was chairman of the Union Peace Committee during the Pakistan period, and he did not contest the 1973 elections. The third candidate also came from an old influential family. The brother had been member of the Union Board during the British period, and he himself had been member of the union council during the Pakistan period. During the Civil War he had formed a Peace Committee in his village, and he did not contest the election in 1973, neither as chairman nor as member.

The candidates fell in two categories, one consisting of the two candidates from the old traditional families. These had been influential both during the British and the Pakistani periods. Both were ardent Muslim League supporters and supported the Pakistani government in 1971. These two candidates were both big landowners, possessing 20 and 45 acres, respectively, Neither was engaged in any occupation outside agriculture.[6] Both were headmen of their respective villages.

The other category was made up of the previous Relief Chairman. He did not belong to the traditional élite but to the rich peasantry category which rose during the Ayub era. Like the two other candidates he was the headman of his village. He was also a big landowner owning around 20 acres, but unlike the others he was engaged outside agriculture, owning a cloth shop in the local market place. He was known to have been a good chairman during the Pakistan era, when he got an award of Tk. 6,000 for his union council work.

The three candidates contested the election fiercely, all playing very much on their past record during the Pakistan period. Ideology did not play a role, except that the two traditional candidates were playing on the religious issues, with the result that all the Hindus in the area voted for the former Relief Committee chairman who to them represented the secular aspect of the Awami League. Also, many of the poor voted for the former Relief chairman believing he would do most for them. In an interview before the election he himself told that the Ayub chairmen had a good reputation among the people, and that he thought he had a good chance to win because of this good records during that period.

The election turned out to be an overwhelming victory for the former Relief Chairman. Having lost the previous Union Parishad election by a narrow margin, he won over 50 per cent of the votes cast for chairman in 1977, viz. 3,122 out of 5,538 votes cast. The two other candidates won 1,373 and 1,043 votes respectively.

It is noteworthy that the former Relief Chairman failed in the 1973 Union Parishad election, despite the Awami League backing. In 1977 the Awami League was out of office, and it is suggested that the chairman's short affiliation with the Awami League was not as significant as his previous record as a 'good' chairman during the Ayub Khan period. The results may be interpreted as a vote for the candidate who was believed to be best able to 'deliver the goods'. This interpretation is consistent with the interview data from the local area at the time. As the villagers believed he would do most for them, the interpretation is also consistent with Bertocci's observation regarding political culture, referred to in Chapter VIII. He points to the villages' 'widely accepted belief that one's capacity to maximise attainment of one's . . . goals is intimately linked to the degree one is successful in attaching oneself to persons who are powerful and prestigious'.

(2) Sherpur thana

If we look at the candidates who contested for the post of chairman in the other eight unions in the thana, available information indicates that it is by and large the same category of persons who put up their candidacy. Some information is available on 31 out of the 34 candidates who fought the election in these unions (the average number of candidates in each union varied between three and five). Of these, 23 candidates had had previous affiliations with the Muslim League and six with the Awami League, only two being without party affiliation. It is interesting to note that of the six members who had had affiliation with the Awami League, five got elected as chairman. Two of these had also been returned as chairmen in 1973, and for the last one no information is available regarding the 1973 election. Fourteen of the candidates had been members of the union councils during the Pakistan period, but only two of these got elected in 1977.

Only little information is available on the family history background of the candidates from the eight unions. However, the overwhelming majority of them came from families who are headmen in their respective villages and from the upper peasantry, about half of them (48%) owning above 15 acres.

About one half of the candidates were engaged in other occupations besides agriculture, and of the eight candidates who won the chairmanship in their respective unions, six had such other occupations.

Without detailed information on the local power struggles in a historic perspective in these eight unions, it is difficult to interpret the result of this 1977 Union Parishad election. However, the results do confirm the major conclusion from the union studied in detail, viz. that families who have managed to diversify their economy, by branching into occupations outside agriculture, stand a good chance of becoming elected to the local councils. Economic diversification not only gives these families a chance of higher incomes, it also provides them with avenues for access to persons beyond their own locality. Many of these farmers-cum-entrepreneurs often reside in the local towns and act as brokers between the villagers and the state.

It is of interest that many of the chairman elected in Sherpur thana in 1977 had party affiliations with the Awami League. This confirms a trend in the country.[7] This issue will be discussed in further detail at the end of this chapter.

C.   Election of Union Parishad members (1977)

Whereas the chairmen were elected by adult franchise by voters in the entire union (the post of vice-chairman had been abolished in 1977), the members were elected from their respective wards. There were three wards in each union, and from each ward three members were elected. Each voter could cast three votes, which means that it was not uncommon for member candidates to form electoral alliances. The most common alliance was between candidates from different villages

In the union studied (Madhyapur) 37 candidates stood for election as members during the 1977 election, 14 from Ward No. 1, 10 from Ward No. 2, and 13 from Ward No. 3. Of these, six were members of the Union Parishad elected in 1973, two from each ward. The remaining three sitting members did not fight the election.

About one-half of the candidates had had previous affiliation with party politics, 18 having been members of the Muslim League and one of the Awami League during the Pakistan period. Eight of the candidates came from families who had been members of the Union Board under British rule, and six of them had themselves been union council members during the Pakistan regime. The majority of them came from village headmen families and from the upper peasantry, 27 per cent of them owning above 15 acres and another 38 per cent between 7 and 15 acres. None of them were landless, and the candidates with little land all had other occupations besides agriculture. Among all the candidates about one-half (18) had occupations outside agriculture.

None of the six candidates who had been elected to the Union Parishad in 1973 were re-elected in 1977. On the surface of it, this result may be interpreted as a massive vote against the previous leadership in the union, i.e. against the leadership aligned with the old influential family which also lost the chairmanship. This factor most probably accounts for much of the explanation. However, two of the newly-elected members were supporters of one of the traditional chairman candidates. Another three did not support any of the chairman candidates but were powerful persons in their own locality, two having been members of the union council during the Pakistan regime and one coming from an influential family who had members on the local councils during the Pakistan and British periods. Four of the new members were supporters of the newly-elected chairman.

The election to the Union Parishad in Madhyapur Union in 1977 seems to follow the pattern observed in the Pakistan era. Here also new members were voted in at times of election, but—as was observed—'the class composition of the elected members remained unchanged, only the faces changed'.[8] As a group the new members were not different from the persons elected in 1973, or during the Pakistan period for that matter. As regards landownership, five of the old and seven of the new members came from the upper peasantry, their landholdings being bigger than the average for all member candidates. With the exception of one old and one new member, all belonged to headman families in their respective villages.

Five of the members elected in 1977 had fought the 1973 election and lost, and of these, two—like the new chairman—had been on the Relief Committees formed by the Awami League just after Liberation. The party affiliation of the members is shown in Table 9.1.

Table 9.1. Party Affiliation of old and new Members of the Union Parishad

	Muslim League	Awami League	No party affiliation	Unknown
Old members	5	0	1	3
New members	5	1	3	—

D.   Local-level data in a wider perspective

In the absence of studies of the Union Parishad elections from several other local areas in Bangladesh it is not possible to generalize from this one case-study. It was mentioned above that the Liberation war did not seem to have left the impact that has been reported from other parts of Bangladesh. Data are available from one other detailed study of the 1977 Union Parishad election, and as this study was conducted in an area where the local population was more actively involved in the Liberation struggle and which has a history of political involvement, it may serve as a comparison.

The other study was conducted in the Kishoreganj Subdivision of Mymensingh District.[9] The person who got elected as Union Parishad chairman in the Mymensingh Union had a long history of political involvement, but unlike the candidates in the Bogra Union he had been an opposition leader, first against the British and later against the Pakistan regime. He had been active in the language movement of the early 1950s, the popular uprising against Ayub in 1968–9, and during the Liberation struggle he was influential in organizing the freedom fighters in the area. He was a small peasant owning only a little over one acre of land, and he got elected partly because of his past political record and partly because he was a representative of the poor.

The election campaigns in the two areas show a higher degree of political awareness in the Mymensingh area, where the candidates had actual pro-grammes for what they would do when they became elected, and at least one poor peasant got elected as member to the Union Parishad because he was regarded as the poor's own candidate.

In this Mymensingh area the influence of the orthodox and powerful Muslim families had been controlled already during the Ayub regime, when in 1964 a non-Muslim League chairman got elected, albeit from an influential family. He was supported and controlled by the progressive elements in the area.

It is, however, noteworthy that the poor peasant who got elected in 1977 also contested the chairmanship in 1973. Prior to the Liberation struggle he had joined the Awami League party, and there are reasons to believe that his affiliation with that party proved to be an obstacle in 1973, as was the case in the Bogra union.

The results recorded from the Mymensingh area are much more in line with what one would expect. However, survey data from other areas indicate that a majority of those elected to the local bodies in 1977 had affiliation with either the Muslim league or the Awami League.[10] Although data on the socio-economic background of these persons are not known on a national scale, earlier studies have shown that the local leadership of these two parties are recruited from among the upper peasantry (see Chapters IV and V). Given the absence of mass mobilization, it is not to be expected that a new leadership will emerge, at least not in the more traditional areas.

The results from the municipal elections held in August 1977 also show that persons with political affiliations to old political parties played a dominant role. In the Municipal Council election in the area studied, 20 of 27 candidates for the posts of chairmen and councillors had had previous party affiliations (8 National Awami Party, 6 Awami League, 5 Muslim League, and 1 Jamaat-Islam). Of the ten successful candidates all but two had had previous party affiliations (3 National Awami Party, 3 Muslim League and 2 Awami League).

Although no studies of the municipal council elections are available from other areas, accounts tend to indicate that the situation was repeated elsewhere in Bangladesh. Both the Muslim League and the Awami League claimed success after the municipal council elections, and the account in the Bengali weekly *Holiday* shows that the union council election and the Municipal Council elections in the Bogra area studied was not a unique case: 'Thus, by all accounts, the last union council and municipal elections were mostly an anti-people exercise of the corrupt corps of Pakistan days and Awami-Baksal days . . . .'[11]

The results of the union parishad and municipal elections in 1977 showed that the traditional parties were still very influential in the local areas. As suggested in Chapter V, this may be one reason why the government decided not to hold the scheduled elections for district councils. Instead, the government started to build up a new party, the JAGODAL, and later the BNP. At the same time efforts were devoted to gain the confidence of the newly-elected local leaders and of the rural population in general. The efforts paid off, as shown by the victory to Zia both in the national referendum, as well as in the presidential and national elections in 1978 and 1979, respectively.

However, despite the victory to Zia and his party, the elections show that a solid group of voters (including especially the Hindu population) still supported the Awami League and its allied aprties, with 21 per cent of the votes going to the United Democratic Alliance during the presidential election. The Awami League remained the biggest opposition party.

Data collected from Sherpur thana during the 1979 general elections furthermore indicate that the support for the government among the voters was much stronger than that of the leaders. Of eight union parishad chairmen from the thana,[12] four supported the Awami League, and four the government party, the BNP. Only the chairman from Madhyapur had changed affiliation from the Awami League to the BNP (he had been Relief Chairman in 1972, but otherwise his record was primarily associated with his chairmanship of the union council during Ayub—see above).

Although it is impossible to generalize from this one case-study, the data suggest that the villagers did not follow the advice of the local leaders to the degree one would have expected. In the traditional Muslim League area, they voted for the government party which had secured an economic situation which was better than during the previous, Awami League, government.

On the basis of the local political study it is hypothesized that in the absence of institutional changes, in the rural areas struggles for power will remain among the upper peasantry—and increasingly among those who have diversified their economic activities and have become engaged also in semi-urban entrepreneurial enterprises. Similarly, the interplay between local factional rivalries and national issues will continue to dominate local-level politics.

X

THE RELATIONSHIP BETWEEN THE STATE
AND RURAL SOCIETY

A. *The persistent power of the dominant village groups*

A recurrent theme throughout Chapters III – IX has been the economic power and political dominance of the upper peasantry in the rural areas throughout the period covered by the study. The compatibility of interests between the British and the dominant village groups observed by Raj for the colonial period parallels the compatibility of interests between these same village groups and the forces in power at the state level during the Pakistan period as well as in independent Bangladesh.

During colonial times the British were able to acquire a supply of export products at low prices, and in independent Bangladesh the agricultural products are siphoned out of the rural areas to supply food grains for the politically conscious urban population at low cost. The outflow of agricultural products from the countryside continues to be possible because of the depressed level of consumption of the majority of the peasants who are forced to sell at low prices. As a result of this historical process, pauperization of the rural masses has been a predominant trait, and the majority of the population has been caught in what Alamgir has referred to as a 'Below Poverty Level Equilibrium Trap'.

The economic structure serves the political and economic interests of the dominant village groups. The capital accumulated in the countryside continues to be invested primarily in non-agricultural activities, including money-lending, petty trade and rural entrepreneurial activities. The economic diversification of the peasant—money-lender—landlord category strengthens the economic as well as the local political power of this group, on whom the regime depends for political support also at the national level.

While the economic and political power of the dominant village groups was considerable at the local level throughout the period of study, their relationship to forces of power at the state level has varied in the concrete historical periods.

The movement for independence from the British in the first half of this century coincided with the emergent political consciousness among the Muslims of Bengal. The rise to political power in the Bengal assembly of the rural-based vernacular élite in the 1930s and 1940s considerably strengthened the economic situation of this class. At the political level the dominant village groups were influential in mobilizing the poorer peasants for the cause of Pakistan.

While during British rule the role of the Bengal economy was subordinated to metropolitan interests, during the Pakistan period it became subordinated to the interests of the dominant social classes in West Pakistan. At the time of

154

independence of Pakistan the political strength of the vernacular élite of Bengal was not reflected at the all-Pakistan state level which was dominated by the power bloc of West Pakistan, nor at the provincial level where important political posts were given to other factions of the Bengali political élite sharing the economic interests of the dominant classes in West Pakistan.

During the course of the Pakistan period, the upper peasantry came to play an important role in national politics through the indirect electoral system introduced through the Basic Democracies system of Ayub Khan. The Basic Democrats were elected from among the upper peasantry, and they served not only on the local councils but also as an electoral college for presidential and assembly elections. The system thus not only strengthened the position of the dominant village groups in the local area, it also gave them decisive voice in elections at the national level.

The increased economic and political power bestowed on the Basic Democrats was a deliberate move on the part of Ayub Khan, who sought to build up a loyal power base in East Bengal. However, rival groups among the upper peasantry—based mainly on local political power struggles—joined the rising Bengali nationalist movement under the Awami League Party, the leadership of which was recruited from among the urban middle class and the upper peasantry.

With the independence of Bangladesh, the upper peasantry of Bengal for the first time became a constituent part of the power bloc of the 'intermediate regime' of the Awami League. Although the direct political influence of the upper peasantry has diminished during the military leadership which followed the Awami League, the influence of this group remains considerable, not only through its influence in the rural areas, but also because of the government's dependence on its political support at the national level.

During the course of the political mobilization of the Bengali people ideology played a dominant role, but while the content of the ideology varied, its function remained the same, viz. to interpellate the individuals as subjects in non-class terms, thus neutralizing their potential antagonisms. During the movement of independence from the British the East Bengalis were inter-pellated as religous subjects, and during the nationalist movement against Pakistan, they were interpellated as Bengali subjects. In both situations the peasants were rooted in the relations of production basic to society, but because of the nature of the leadership of the two movements (feudal lords, urban middle class as well as the vernacular élite in the former, and petty bourgeoisie and upper peasants in the latter), the ideological discourse was transformed into 'people'/power-bloc confrontations, i.e. between Muslim peasants and imperialism and Hindus during the movement for Pakistan, and between the Bengali people and the Pakistan power bloc during the movement for Bangladesh. In mobilizing the masses the leadership used radical rhetoric, but once in power, its vested interest in the existing system became apparent. The absence of fundamental changes during the power of the vernacular élite in the Bengal assembly during the 1930s and 1940s was paralleled by the Awami League's refusal to honour its election pledges to introduce land reforms and land distribution in independent Bangladesh.

B. Development strategies

With the departure of the British from the Indian subcontinent, power was handed over to ruling classes who were not interested in changing the social structure, and—as was the case in other newly independent countries—'national independence and the formation of the national state led to the creation of social strata between imperial capitalism and the labour force . . . rooted in the state bureaucracy it has access to the power of the state, including revenues and expenditures'.[1] As argued in Chapter IV, the Pakistan state followed a development strategy which Petras has referred to as the 'national development model' where the surplus is concentrated in the hands of state and/or private national entrepreneurs, and which does not involve redistribution. Because of the absence of a national bourgeoisie in Pakistan at the time of independence, the state also had to create such a class, and at the same time act as the 'midwife' of the capitalist mode of production, in the terminology used by Ziemann and Lanzendörfer.[2]

As shown in Chapter IV, political independence in Pakistan did not mean that the state severed its economic ties to the capitalist countries. Rather through economic and military assistance these were strengthened and accompanied by a policy of 'external integration', i.e. 'grafting on to the police and military apparatus the ideology and orientation of the metropole'.[3] This policy further strengthened the power of the military as well as the bureaucracy, and through their direct involvement in the economic process these two factions of the state bourgeoisie established a place for itself in the emergent relations of production, and it was argued that they came to constitute an effective class.[4]

Through the economic development policy pursued by the Pakistan state a modern industrial sector was created, and the policy further gave rise to an indigenous bourgeoisie, but at the same time it provided the 'crutch' for the non-capitalist modes of production. The result was that capitalist conditions as well as 'social and political anachronisms were produced and reproduced'.[5] At the political level the resultant anachronism was an accommodation between the interests of the landowning classes and the rising bourgeoisie, one of the structural characteristics inherent in Alavi's notion of both the post-colonial state and the colonial mode of production.[6] At the economic level, the anachronism prevented the development of capital relations of production in agriculture.

Through the Pakistan period the entire economy of Bengal was subordinated to the economic and political interests of the dominant classes in Pakistan. The primary role of the Bengal agricultural sector in the overall economy of Pakistan was to provide foreign currency through the export of jute.

As was the case at the time of independence in Pakistan, the social classes which came to power in Bangladesh after liberation were not interested in changing the social structure. In the initial phase the economic development policy pursued by the Awami League government had many of the characteristics of what Petras has called the 'national-popular' strategy, where the national regime extends the areas of national control through nationalization, reinvests the surplus of the national economy or promotes a redistribution of income within the national class structure.[7] However, as argued in Chapter V, the radical aspects of the Awami League government's economic policy were few and only introduced in order to honour the pledges and to meet the expectations raised during the course of political mobilization. Given the 'intermediate' nature of the Awami League regime, i.e. the rich peasant and lower-middle class background of the ruling classes, its commitment to socialism soon turned out to be no commitment at all. As Petras has pointed out, 'the striking characteristic of this type of regime is the frequency with which they have appeared in the periphery, (as well as) their short duration as "national-popular" regimes'. Usually they are either overthrown or evolve into one of the two variants.[8] The economic policy of the Awami League government soon evolved into the 'national development' model, and because of the absence of an indigenous bourgeoisie, capitalism was 'sponsored' by the state, thus paving the way for private investors to grow in size and power.[9]

The Awami League government considerably curbed bureaucratic power through political appointments to the civil services and through the appointment of party officials to manage the state enterprises. With the overthrow of the Awami League government bureaucratic power has re-emerged, and this social strata has access to the economic powers of the state through control over revenue and expenditures. Because of the inability to achieve self-sufficiency in food and a self-reliant economy, the country becomes increasingly dependent on foreign aid, which in turn enhances bureaucratic power.

Through the policy of sponsored capitalism pursued by the state, a modern sector characterized by capitalist relations of production may emerge. However, given the political necessity not to alienate the landowning class and the compatibility of interest between this class, the emergent bourgeoisie and the state bourgeoisie, the state's police is also likely to continue to act as 'crutch' for non-capitalist relations of production.

C. The 'mode of production' in agriculture

In Chapter VIII it was argued that capitalist relations of production had not taken root in Bangladesh agriculture. Exploitation based on usury continued to dominate, thus perpetuating the economic and political influence of the peasant-landlord-money-lender-category in the rural areas. Alamgir has described this mode of production as semi-feudal, but although the characteristics inherent in this concept—not least the multiple roles of the dominant groups as landowner, money-lender, merchant capitalist and village broker and intermediary—aptly describes the situation in rural Bangladesh, it was argued that the structural characteristics underlying the concept of the colonial mode of production provides a better tool for analysing the situation. The major structural characteristic of the colonial mode of production is that as a result of the colonial impact the pre-capitalist relations of production were transformed, and the small peasant farming community was drawn into the orbit of capitalist commodity production and exploitation through its subordination to (usurer's and) merchant capital. The colonial mode of production thus does not constitute by itself a distinct mode, but is integrally a part of the capitalist mode of production, and its structural characteristics can only be defined with reference to its integration into capitalism'.[10]

In Chapter VIII it was further shown how, during the colonial period, the small peasant farming community was drawn into the orbit of capitalist commodity production and exploitation. This exploitation made it possible to export agricultural surpluses to the metropolitan centre. The system functioned through depressing the level of consumption of the peasants who were forced to sell at low prices. Because of the perpetual indebtedness of the poor peasants, usurious interests were high, and for the big peasants with investable surplus, money-lending was more attractive than investment in agricultural production. The result was that the structure acted as a built-in depressor within the village economy.

Without any change in the rural social structure perpetual indebtedness of the majority of the rural population continues, and because of the high profits to be made through usurious loans, investment in agricultural production remains unattractive to the surplus farmers.

Through the government's rural development programmes inputs are provided at subsidized prices, and the surplus farmers do avail themselves of these opportunities to cultivate new high-yielding varieties, thus producing an agricultural surplus which is exported to the urban areas. However, while the surplus farmers do avail themselves of the low-cost inputs provided by the government, the profit earned from increased agricultural production is not reinvested in agricultural production, but in money-lending or non-agricultural activities, through a process which has been referred to as economic diversification. Because of the continued indebtedness of the poor peasants, these are still forced to sell at low prices, and, as Patnaik has pointed out, capitalist production in agriculture cannot emerge as long as it is surrounded by petty production, 'unless the level of capitalist rent (surplus profit over and above "normal profit") at least equals that of pre-capitalist rent (surplus of output value over necessary cost for petty producers). As long as a majority of the producers are poor peasants who are enforced to rely for a livelihood on those who monopolise landed property, precapitalist rent remains high . . .'.[11]

The absence of a development towards capitalist relations of production in agriculture and the continued dominance of usurious exploitation in Bangladesh has also been demonstrated for southern India through two analyses of rural social structure.

In a village study from the northern part of Tamil Nadu, Djurfeldt and Lindberg showed that 'Capital occurs almost exclusively in its pre-capitalist forms, i.e. in usury and commerce; and moreover, it is almost totally subordinated to landed property, in the sense that landownership evidently is a prerequisite for accumulation of money-capital, and, thereby, for entry into usury and commerce on a larger scale'.[12] As regards the use of investable surplus, the situation parallels the one observed in Bangladesh. As they point out, 'if a rich peasant is interested in augmenting his income', agricultural investment is not the only alternative, as 'he can as well go into usury, buy more land, go into commercial exploitation, or some other form of unproductive parasitic exploitation'. And they conclude that 'there are many indications that, on the national level, the rich farmers have preferred this alternative even in recent years, when Government agencies have put such a premium on "modernization" by subsidizing the inputs'.[13]

The other study referred to above was conducted by Harriss, also in Tamil Nadu, and not far from the village studied by Djurfeldt and Lindberg; but that village was located in an area with good irrigation facilities, and where the peasants had adopted new high-yielding varieties on a large scale. Nevertheless it was found that the 'investment preferences' of rich farmers included not only investment in tractors,[14] but also in property and housing, in trade and retailing and in ceremonies.[15] Although in that area, money-lending profits have not notably constrained capitalism developments in agriculture since the introduction of HYV, usury remains an important factor in the agrarian economy. As Harriss pointed out, this is due to the continuing dependence of many farmers upon paddy or groundnut dealers for production credit and of the marginal and subsistence farmers for consumption credit.[16] In his conclusion Harriss suggested that 'while the introduction of the new technology has been instrumental in bringing about some expansion of capital in agricultural production . . . it has also consolidated more backward forms of capitalist domination in so far as it has intensified the dependence upon the market of large numbers of marginal and subsistence farmers who rely on consumption loans and loans for circulation capital. But rather than this process being instrumental in squeezing out the small producers, there is a good deal of evidence to suggest that the small-scale producers continue to reproduce themselves'. Referring to Patnaik's argument quoted above, he continues: 'The fact that profits from usury and the uses of capital in trade continue to compete with those from production in agriculture, is in itself a demonstration of the likelihood of this'.[17]

The results from the two local studies from Tamil Nadu have been quoted at length, because in their analyses of their data both authors relate their conclusions to the problematic central to the present study, viz. a discussion of the mode of production at the abstract level, as well as the implication for the determination for the social formation.

In summing up their analysis, Djurfeldt and Lindberg conclude, that 'if we keep to the *form* of the relations, the formation in Thaiyur can be described as a mixture of formally different "modes" of production, (where) many formally different pre-colonial and other relations of production may co-exist, subordinated to the dominant structure'.[18] This conclusion significantly differs from the notion of the colonial mode of production postulated above as prevailing in Bangladesh agriculture. Although the authors may not agree with the inference drawn from their conclusion, it is argued that the difference is not so fundamental as it would first appear. In the above quotation the authors stress the *form* of the relations and, in fact, further on, their argument comes close to postulating a mode of production with the characteristics inherent in the concept of the colonial mode: 'Clearly, the formation is *one* system, produced by the colonial transformation . . . The main agrarian classes thus grew out of one and the same process, and this can be used as an argument against treating them as involved in different modes of production. We prefer to treat the agrarian class-structure as one system . . .'[19]

As shown above, the conclusions reached by Harriss are quite similar to those of Djurfeldt and Lindberg. However, he points out that the introduction of high-yielding varieties did bring about some expansion of capital in agricultural production, implying some development of the forces of production. This leads him to question one of the arguments put forward by the former: 'The difference stems from the over-determinate conception of the relationship between the relations and the forces of production which is taken by Djurfeldt and Lindberg, and which seems almost to deny the possibility of the emergence of contradictions between the development of the forces of production and the relations of production . . .'[20] In order to explain the 'underdevelopment' of the agrarian economy he puts forward an alternative model which emphasizes the importance of 'the State' in determining the formation of the agrarian structure, as well as the feedback relationship between that structure and the formation of the State. His argument that the 'agrarian structure cannot be understood except in terms of the relations of the agrarian classes with other classes within the State'[21] in fact closely follows the lines of argument provided throughout this study.

It may be mentioned that Harriss points out that such an approach 'may be unacceptable to some Marxists . . . because it allows for a degree of "determination" of the *infrastructure* (combination of forces and relations of production) by the *superstructure*'.[22] As pointed out in Chapter II, it was exactly the focus on the superstructure which led many critics to reject Alavi's concept of post-colonial societies. However, while the concept of an 'overdeveloped' superstructure was not found to be particularly useful, the analyses provided in Chapters IV and V show quite clearly that the existence of a powerful state apparatus was of importance not only for the political development but also for the relationship between the various social classes in Pakistan as well as in Bangladesh. Along similar lines Alamgir has argued that 'it is very important to have a clear understanding of the role of the bureaucracy (which in the post-colonial era) was entrusted with the additional responsibility of supervising development activities initiated by the national government. Over time, the bureaucracy was able to further consolidate its position by obtaining complete control over all mechanisms for resource allocation and resource utilization . . . It may be mentioned here that in a country, when there is an ideological vacuum it becomes easy for the bureaucracy to maintain its dominant role . . . It is indeed unfortunate that until now, Bangladesh has had to depend on this class to implement measures which are supposed to better the lot of the masses. It is no wonder that the final outcome in most cases is perverse'.[23]

D. *The relationship between agrarian classes and other classes in Bangladesh*

The relations of the agrarian classes with other classes within the state also play a central role in Djurfeldt's and Lindberg's analysis. As they point out: 'The parasitic exploitation of the big landowners restricts the growth of the productive forces, not only in agriculture, but also in industry by strangling the demand for industrial goods. Since the expansive potentials of industrial capitalism thus are contained by its relations to agriculture, we can with some sense also conclude that capitalism is dominated by agriculture and the agrarian production relations'. And they conclude that 'by virtue of this mutual domination of interdependence, the bourgeoisie is caught in a passionate but strangulating embrace with landed property. They dominate each other in such a way that they gain about equal weight in the ruling class alliance produced by the structure of the social formation'.[24]

A similar interdependence and strangulation result from the agrarian production relations as well as the government's development strategy in Bangladesh. As pointed out in Chapter V, the major aim of the government's rural develement policy is to increase agricultural production, and especially to increase the marketable surplus. The process which has been observed for other areas, has also taken place in Bangladesh: 'Given the needs of the urban areas for cheap and abundant wage goods and for a continuation of the subsidy to industry from agriculture, the best thing that could happen, did happen: the 'green revolution . . . the introduction of high yielding foodgrains . . . has enabled the marketable surplus to be increased, and the resource transfer (from agriculture) to continue . . .'[25]

As pointed out above, due to the indebtedness of the poor peasants, these continue to be forced to sell at low prices. Moreover, the increase in landlessness and increased rural unemployment continues to depress agricultural wages.[26] Without any employment opportunities outside agriculture, the increase of marketable surplus under existing relations of production produces a vicious circle. As Jacoby has argued, 'It is obvious that the increase in rural unemployment, which is not balanced by additional employment possibilities in urban areas, will have serious repercussions on the domestic market and price developments. The multiplied supply of marketable food crops will be met by a declining effective demand for food due to the rising unemployment. This will cause declining food prices . . .'[27]

Although the introduction of high-yielding varieties has led to some increase in output in Bangladesh, the lack of effective demand for agricultural products, and the resultant decline in food prices, will in the long run cause stagnation in agricultural production. As pointed out above, the higher profits to be made from money-lending and investment in non-agricultural activities have led the big farmers not to invest in agricultural production. In Bangladesh, the government's food subsidy policy has further militated against agricultural investment.

Besides the rice procured from the rural areas, rice (and wheat) is also made available to the urban consumers from abroad, mainly from food aid. Most of this food is distributed through the government's ration system, and according to the way the system works, it is primarily the middle classes who are the main beneficiaries. As a FAO Agricultural Mission observed, 'the higher the income, the less one generally pays for food'.[28] And according to official estimates, only around ten per cent of the food supplied through the ration system reaches the poor.

The government's food subsidy system thus militates against achieving the government's proclaimed aim of securing 'economic and social justice'. Besides, the ration system serves as a disincentive to agricultural production. By selling imported food grains at highly subsidized prices, 'the government reduces the market for domestically produced food, while keeping food prices artificially low'.[29] As pointed out in a recent SIDA report, 'it is one of the great paradoxes of Bangaldesh's . . . development strategy that while the agricultural policy is officially extremely production-oriented, with a heavy emphasis on attempts to make the farmers adopt the "green revolution" package of modern inputs, the food policy is totally counter-productive in that it actually depresses prices and thereby reduces the farmer's investable surplus and discourages production of food for the market'.[30]

Thus the feedback relationship between the agrarian structure and the policy of the state consolidates backward forms of capitalist domination. While the rich farmers' investment preferences remain usury and non-agricultural activities, they have at the same time benefited from the government's rural development programmes by obtaining inputs at subsidized prices. Through the diversification of their economic activities they have also become small rural entrepreneurs, thus bringing village and rural towns closer together in one system. This has further consolidated 'the strong coalition of urban and rural rich that holds political power (and which) has been able to use its control over the state apparatus to provide general favours to the urban population while at the same time giving selected favours to the large and middle peasants'.[31] As shown in Chapter V, the influence of the rural rich in the Assembly elected in 1979 is considerable, and as MPs these are able to prevent any policies aiming at curbing their economic position.

The compatibility of interests between the rural rich and the rising bourgeoisie is thus quite obvious: the rural rich continue to thrive on usurious exploitation, thus maintaining their economic and political power in the local areas. The bourgeoisie is able to pay industrial workers low wages because of the supply of cheap food. However, the apparent compatibility of interests is not without its contradictions. As argued above, the low prices paid to the producers do reduce the farmer's investable surplus, and the increasing pauperization of broader and broader sections of the population further reduces effective demand, also of industrial goods, which in the long run militates against growth also in the industrial sector. Thus, as was argued for the Indian case, the bourgeoisie's embrace with landed property has a strangulating effect on the entire economy.

The lack of effective demand is further accentuated by the government's industrial development policy. Because of its desire to obtain 'rapid industrialization', the government gives private investors a variety of concessions which all contribute to make the use of capital goods of foreign origin as attractive as possible. Most of these capital goods are highly capital-intensive,[32] and few new jobs are created. Thus what little industrialization takes place does not significantly increase the purchasing power of industrial labour, and thus effective demand remains low.

The 'capital bias' prevailing in the industrial sector, is also—though to a lesser extent—found in the agricultural sector. Because of its emphasis on agricultural growth, the government has invested heavily in irrigation, and figures show that allocations for this programme have primarily gone to large-scale capital-intensive schemes—which turn out to be the less efficient—an investment policy which the FAO Agricultural Mission termed 'nearly perfectly perverse'.[33]

E. The peripheral state and foreign dependency

The heavy reliance on capital-intensive techniques in order to achieve rapid growth, as well as the government's food ration system, financed primarily from abroad, has made Bangladesh increasingly dependent on foreign aid. As shown in Chapter V, foreign aid finances about 80 per cent of the government's development expenditures. However, a close scrutiny of the budget reveals that the percentage is in fact much higher. Thus the World Bank has shown that because public savings have actually been negative during the last few years, external assistance has not only financed total public investment, but also some public consumption. Thus, foreign aid has exceeded the amount of public investment, and has accounted for almost ten per cent of the GDP.[34]

The dependence on foreign aid has serious consequences. Firstly, the availability of aid services as a cushion for the government. As a U.S. aid official has pointed out, 'Not only does food aid develop budgetary dependence, but it clearly reduces the political pressures on the government to invest in the countryside'.[35] The dependence on aid thus militates against the government's alleged aim of achieving self-sufficiency in food and a self-reliant economy.

Secondly, the increasing dependence on economic aid reduces the country's political independence.[36] As shown in Chapter V, there have been several instances where the policy of the country has been influenced by pressure from donor countries.

The analysis provided in the preceding pages as well as throughout the study shows that the state in Bangladesh exhibits traits in its structures which are characteristic of peripheral social formations. As a result of capitalist expansion during the colonial period, the structures of the traditional society were transformed, primarily through the integration of the traditional small-peasant farming community in the international capitalist system. The social structure was adapted to perform a complementary and subsidiary role within the metropolitan system. At the local political level, the interests of the dominant village groups coincided with those of the social classes in power at the state level, not only during the colonial time, but also in independent Bangladesh. Neither economic crises nor several wars produced a revolution in Bangladesh, as the political leadership throughout the period of study was interested in sustaining, rather than changing the structures of power.

In order to sustain the structures of power and prevent changes in the social structure, the various regimes in Bangladesh (as well as in Pakistan) have relied heavily on foreign aid which has further strengthened the structural dependency of the economy. In their attempts to 'develop' the economy, the various governments in Bangladesh have adopted a growth strategy which has included steps to build up a modern industry, where capitalist relations of production may evolve. Due to the predominance of the agricultural sector in Bangladesh economy, the mode of production is dominated by production relations in agriculture. As argued in Chapter VIII, the mode of production prevailing in Bangladesh agriculture is best described as post-colonial, where backward forms of capitalist domination are consolidated.

As the colonial mode of production can only be defined with reference to its integration into capitalism, so the peripheral nature of the social formation can only be defined and analysed with reference to its integration into the world system. As shown above, the structural dependency of the Bangladesh economy is an integral determinant of the social formation.

The role of Bengal for the economy of Britain during colonial rule was obvious. The import of foodgrains and raw materials from Bengal, and elsewhere, significantly contributed to the industrial revolution in Britain. In countries endowed with raw materials necessary for the Western industrial nations, the continued interest in the Third World countries is also quite obvious. The same holds true for countries where western private companies can make profits through private investment. Neither of these situations, however, is applicable to Bangladesh, so the continued foreign interest and 'donors' willingness to dispose of surplus grains and to support the prevailing power structure in Bangladesh'[37] must be sought elsewhere.

It is beyond the scope of the present study to go into a detailed discussion and analysis of the relationship between the Third World and the developed, industrialized countries. It is suggested that part of the explanation for the western countries' interest in Bangladesh is based on the same rationale as the one underlying the United States' policy towards the Pakistan regime in the 1950s and 1960s. As shown in Chapter IV, the United States was interested in seeking cold-war allies and in supporting strong governments which could prevent revolutionary upheavals. In a more subtle form, the same policies continue today, and it is suggested that this is the rationale behind the 'Basic Needs Strategy', now adopted as official policy by major donor countries.[38]

The hypothesis advanced above is supported by the following statement made by McNamara in his 1972 Annual Address as president of the World Bank: 'We know, in effect, that there is no rational alternative to moving toward policies of greater social equity. When the highly privileged are few and the desperately poor are many—and when the gap between them is worsening rather than improving—it is only a question of time before a decisive choice must be made between the political costs of reform and the political risks of rebellion. That is why the policies specifically designed to reduce the deprivation among the poorest 40 per cent in developing countries are prescriptions not only of principle but of prudence. Social justice is not merely a moral imperative. It is a *political imperative* as well'.[39]

F. *Political mobilization*

As pointed out above, the characterization of Bangladesh as a peripheral social formation implies a structural dependency relationship. As discussed in Chapter II, this relationship is often analysed within the framework of the centre-periphery model, a model which may also be used to analyse contradictions between the national centre (or satellite, to use Frank's terminology) and the hinterland. Failure to solve centre-periphery contradictions give rise to political movements directed against the centre, either through reactive or pro-active mobilization.[40] As shown above and in Chapters III – V, through the period of the study, the people of Bengal have been mobilized against the centre on several occasions, but on all occasions they have been mobilized against a centre dominated by non-Bengalis, and the interpellations used have always been of a non-class nature.

In order to maintain its hegemony, the government of Bangladesh uses the ideology of national unity, and this non-class interpellation aims at neutralizing potential antagonisms. However, as has been documented repeatedly throughout this study, the economic policy pursued by the various goverments in Bangladesh have resulted in the increasing pauperization of broader and broader sections of the population. Neither this pauperization nor the parallel process of social polarization has, so far, significantly developed class consciousness among the poor. Although some studies do report on increased militancy along class lines in the rural areas,[41] the political culture continues to be characterized by structural fragmentation, fomenting atomization of individual economic interests. Even poor people try to maximize their economic goals by 'attaching themselves to persons who are powerful and prestigious'.[42] It is an open question how long this aspect of the political culture will prevail over efforts at political mobilization along class lines.

NOTES TO CHAPTER I

1   For further elaboration, see Hettne and Friberg, especially Introduction.
2   For a review and a critique of the concept, see Rudebeck 1974.
3   ibid., p. 244.
4   Hindess and Hirst 1975, pp. 9–10.
5   Alavi 1978, p. 14.
6   ibid.
7   See, e.g. Nicholas 1968.
8   Alavi 1974.
9   Like the concept of the mode of production, the concept of social formation belongs to the Marxist theoretical framework. While the former is an abstract concept, the latter is concrete. Here the term is used according to the definition provided by Poulantzas: 'The only thing which really exists is a historically determined social formation, i.e. a social whole, in the widest sense, at a given moment in its historical existence . . . the social formation itself constitutes a complex unity in which a certain mode of production dominates the others which compose it. It is a social formation historically determined by a given mode of production . . . In this way a historically determined social formation is specified by a particular articulation . . . of its different economic, political, ideological and theoretical levels or instances' (Poulantzas 1973, p. 15).

According to Poulantzas, the 'political structures (what are called the "political superstructure") of a mode of production and of a social formation consist of the *institutionalized power of the state*' (ibid., p. 42, italics in original), where 'the state has the particular function of constituting the factor of cohesion between the levels of a social formation' (ibid., p. 44), in such a manner that the function corresponds 'to the political interests of the dominant class' (ibid., p. 54).

It is this concept of state and state power which has been used in the theoretical approach adopted in this study. As Poulantzas writes, it is clear that the cohesive function of the state 'takes on different forms according to which mode of production and social formation is under consideration' (ibid., p. 46). Although the object of Poulantzas' original work on *Political Power and Social Classes* was 'in particular the political superstructure of the state in CMP' (capitalist mode of production) (ibid., p. 16), his analysis regarding state power provides tools applicable also to peripheral capitalist social formations. Thus, the concept of overdetermination of the state's political function—allowed for within Poulantzas' framework regarding the capitalist mode of production in European social formations—is very applicable to the countries in the Third World, not least because of the overdetermining relation of the bureaucracy to the political structure (cf. ibid., p. 54, pp. 84–5, and pp. 276–9). (This 'centrality' of the state is further elaborated in the discussion of Alavi's theory of the post-colonial state in Chapter II, and also relates to the argument in Chapter X.)

As pointed out in the following pages and further elaborated in Chapter II, the theoretical framework of the present study is not limited to class analysis (which is the focus of Poulantzas' approach), but issues such as national integration, among others, are articulated into that discourse.

NOTES TO CHAPTER II

1   Hindess and Hirst p. 6, see also Poulantzas 1973, p. 24.
2   Alavi 1973b.
3   ibid., p. 147.
4   ibid., p. 161.
5   ibid., p. 148.

6 ibid., p. 150.
7 ibid., p. 152.
8 ibid., p. 163.
9 ibid., p. 163.
10 ibid., p. 148.
11 Saul 1974, pp. 150 – 1.
12 ibid., p. 351.
13 Leys 1976.
14 ibid., p. 42.
15 ibid., p. 43.
16 ibid., p. 43.
17 Alavi 1973b, p. 145.
18 Westergaard 1978.
19 W. Ziemann and M. Lanzendörfer 1977.
20 ibid., p. 159.
21 Amin 1974.
22 Ziemann and Lanzendörfer, p. 150.
23 Chapter VIII.
24 Cf. the discussion of articulation of modes of production, Chapter VIII.
25 Ziemann and Lanzendörfer, p. 148, see also Poulantzas, pp. 256 – 7 and p. 281 – 2.
26 Ziemann and Lanzendörfer, p. 149, (italics added).
27 ibid., p. 149.
28 ibid., p. 162.
29 Sonntag, p. 136 and p. 170.
30 Ziemann and Lanzendörfer, p. 162.
31 ibid., p. 164.
32 ibid., p. 164.
33 ibid., p. 164.
34 ibid., p. 150.
35 Poulantzas 1973, p. 84 and p. 332.
36 ibid., p. 336, italics in original.
37 von Freyhold, p. 76.
38 Poulantzas 1973, p. 334.
39 With reference to a capitalist social formation, hegemony covers the political practices of the dominant classes in these formations. The hegemonic class is the one which concentrates in itself, at the political level, the double function of representing the general interest of the people/nation and of maintaining a specific dominance among the dominant classes and factions (Poulantzas 1973, p. 137 and p. 141).
40 ibid., p. 338 (italics in original).
41 Alavi 1973b, p. 159.
42 ibid., p. 153.
43 ibid., p. 148.
44 ibid., p. 161.
45 Saul 1974, p. 353.
46 Ziemann and Lanzendörfer, p. 159.
47 ibid., p. 162.
48 Langdon, p. 230.
49 Alavi 1973b, p. 158.
50 Deutsch 1966.
51 ibid., p. 104, italics in original.
52 This also applies to some European countries, e.g. Ireland and Belgium.
53 See e.g. Myron Weiner 1965.
54 Cf. the subtitle of Rounaq Jahan's book *Pakistan: Failure in national integration*.
55 Wertheim 1974.
56 ibid., p. 108 and p. 114.
57 ibid., p. 246, pp. 257 – 9, and p. 295.
58 Galtung 1971.

59   Kothari, p. 11.
60   ibid., pp. 12 – 13.
61   Frank, especially pp. 8 – 12.
62   Ziemann and Lanzendörfer, p. 155.
63   Kothari, p. 12.
64   Hettne and Friberg, p. 12.
65   B. Jessup, p. 55.
66   Rokkan *et al.*, pp. 97 – 8.
67   Hettne and Friberg, pp. 1 – 12.
68   Laclau 1977.
69   ibid., p. 158.
70   This term is adopted from Althusser and refers to the 'recruitment' of subjects (as political, religious, familial, etc., subjects) among individuals (Laclau 1977, pp. 100 – 101).
71   ibid., p. 161.
72   ibid., p. 159.
73   For a critique, see Mouzelis, p. 57.
74   Laclau, p. 164.
75   ibid., same page (italics added, K.W.).
76   ibid., p. 166.
77   ibid., p. 164.
78   ibid., p. 172.
79   ibid., p. 173.
80   ibid., pp. 172 – 3.
81   ibid., p. 175.
82   Laclau's essay on fascism is in fact a polemic against Poulantzas' book *Fascism and Dictatorship* (Poulantzas 1974), in which he accuses Poultanzas of making such reductionism and determinism.
83   Saul 1976, p. 15.
84   Murray, p. 30.
85   Saul 1976, p. 18.
86   ibid., p. 20.
87   ibid., p. 22.
88   Kalecki 1976.
89   Raj 1973.
90   Kalecki, pp. 32 – 3.
91   Mouzelis, p. 55.
92   ibid., p. 56.
93   Maniruzzaman 1975b, p. 91.
94   Mouzelis, p. 54.
95   Alavi 1978.

NOTES TO CHAPTER III

1   Broomfield, p. 53.
2   ibid., p. 56.
3   Jahan 1973, p. 199.
4   Broomfield, p. 47.
5   Westergaard 1978.
6   Mukherjee 1973, p. 403.
7   Sufia Ahmed, pp. 118 – 9.
8   ibid., pp. 166 – 7.
9   For life sketches of Nazimuddin, Suhrawardy and Fazlul Huq, see Kazi Ahmed Kamal.

10 As Rounaq Jahan has pointed out, the difference between the vernacular and the non-vernacular élite is not merely in the languages they speak; it also lies in their socio-economic backgrounds, socialization process, and their philosophies and policy priorities. The vernacular élite generally come from poor or lower-middle-class families in rural areas or small towns, while the non-vernacular élite come from economically well-off urban families . . . who could afford to send their children to English language schools and universities (Jahan 1973, pp. 38 – 9).

11 Sufia Ahmed, p. 281.

12 The sources on this period are very much coloured by the political affiliations of the writers. Thus a pro-Muslim League scholar (Sufia Ahmed, p. 251) writes that most Muslims favoured partition, while a Bengali nationalist scholar (Kamruddin Ahmed 1975, p. 2) writes that the rising Muslim bourgeoisie was against. However, it is a fact that it was the Nawab (prince) of Dacca (Nazimuddin's family) who became the mouthpiece of the Muslim League in Bengal, whereas the founders of the Mussalman Association were lawyers and intellectuals.

13 These were for the first time to be completely popularly elected following the Government of India Act of 1935.

14 Kamruddin Ahmad 1975, pp. 32 – 4.

15 Sayeed 1967, p. 34.

16 59 and 55 seats, compared to 60 for Congress (Kamruddin Ahmad, p. 35).

17 Broomfield, p. 52.

18 Kamal, p. 10.

19 Later, in 1945, the resolution was interpreted by the Muslim League as a call for one sovereign state. When during the 1960s the Bengalis raised their claim for autonomy, reference was made to the early interpretation of the Lahore (Pakistan) resolution demanding two states.

20 Kamruddin Ahmad, p. 48.

21 Abdullah 1976, p. 87.

22 Kamruddin Ahmad, p. 58.

23 ibid., p. 42.

24 Sayeed 1967, p. 55.

25 Kamruddin Ahmad, p. 56.

26 Sayeed 1967, p. 95.

27 For a discussion of the impact of Islam on the political culture, see Sayeed 1967, Chapter 7, especially pp. 176 – 8.

28 See Chapter II.

29 Sayeed 1967, p. 59.

30 Here the analysis differs from the one provided by John Martinussen who has argued that from its inception, the Pakistan social formation was dominated by the capitalist mode of production, primarily because of the subordination of the rural sector by the urban sector which dominated 'indirectly' through the existence of commodity production and a monetary economy in the rural sector (Martinussen 1974, pp. 201 – 2. See, however, also p. 203 and p. 273 where he modified his arguments). As argued in the following chapter, the present analysis concludes that not even the urban sector was dominated by the capitalist mode of production at the time. Furthermore, the arguments provided by Martinussen regarding the rural sector are not sufficient indices of the capitalist mode of production.

31 Broomfield, p. 52.

32 Cf. Alavi 1975, p. 1247.

33 Poulantzas 1973, pp. 13 – 5

NOTES TO CHAPTER IV

1 Feroz Ahmed, p. 420.

2 Alavi 1973a, pp. 57 – 8.

3 Sayeed 1967, p. 83.

4   ibid., pp. 87 – 8.
5   Feroz Ahmed, p. 420.
6   Sayeed 1967, p. 62.
7   Nations 1971, p. 5.
8   For the early period, see Alavi 1967, p. 27.
9   Sayeed 1968, p. 251.
10   Sayeed 1967, p. 63.
11   ibid., p. 62.
12   Alavi 1973b, p. 103, p. 163.
13   Sayeed 1967, p. 76.
14   Sayeed 1968, p. 299.
15   Feroz Ahmed, p. 420.
16   ibid., p. 421.
17   G. W. Choudhury 1969, p. 4.
18   Kamruddin Ahmad, pp. 103 – 4, see also Sayeed 1967, p. 66.
19   Sayeed 1967, p. 83.
20   Quoted in Sayeed 1967, p. 64.
21   Feroz Ahmed, p. 425.
22   It has been pointed out that 'the politicians, especially the members of the Provincial Assembly, were conspicuous by their absence in the Committee. It was by and large a demand of the younger generation, and the students of the Dacca University led the movement' (Kamruddin Ahmad, p. 99).
23   See Choudhury, pp. 69 – 72.
24   ibid., p. 72.
25   Kamruddin Ahmad, p. 103.
26   ibid., p. 110.
27   Sayeed 1967, p. 190 – 1.
28   Kamruddin Ahmad, pp. 113 – 4.
29   Cf. Wertheim's theoretical discussion, 1974, p. 114.
30   Sayeed 1967, p. 73.
31   Choudhury, p. 74.
32   Quoted in Sayeed 1967, p. 77.
33   Sayeed 1967, p. 78.
34   ibid., pp. 73 – 4.
35   For details, see Choudhury, pp. 84 – 93.
36   ibid., p. 97.
37   Kamruddin Ahmad, pp. 119 – 21.
38   See Choudhury, p. 94 and Sayeed 1967, p. 84.
39   Choudhury, pp. 97 – 8.
40   Cf. Laclau's analysis, Chapter II, Section D(2).
41   Choudhury, p. 136 (italics added, K.W.).
42   Alavi 1973b, p. 152.
43   Kamruddin Ahmad, p. 135.
44   Jahan 1972, p. 43.
45   The study was undertaken by Alex Inkeles from among Dacca University students and Polytechnic students, quoted in ibid., p. 44.
46   Sayeed 1967, p. 88.
47   Talukder Maniruzzaman 1966, p. 88.
48   Sayeed 1967, p. 62.
49   Choudhury, p. 68.
50   Stephen R. Lewis, Jr. 1970, p. 3.
51   Papanek, p. 25. and p. 82.
52   R. Nations, p. 16.
53   See, e.g. ibid., p. 5.
54   Lewis 1970, p. 65.
55   ibid., p. 142.
56   See also Papanek, especially p. 23 and pp. 185 – 225.

57 Lewis 1970, pp. 141 – 6.
58 ibid., p. 80.
59 Papanek, p. 22.
60 When questioned, nearly two-thirds of West Pakistan civil servants said that they believed regional considerations influenced the decisions of public servants (Muneer Ahmed 1964, p. 112).
61 Lewis 1969, pp. 1 – 3.
62 Lewis 1970, p. 47.
63 Papanek, pp. 67 – 8.
64 ibid., p. 70.
65 Maniruzzaman 1966, p. 89.
66 ibid., p. 90.
67 Alavi 1973b, p. 163; see also pp. 157 – 8.
68 Abdullah 1976, p. 85.
69 The discussion on the mode of production will be treated in more detail in Chapter VIII.
70 Alamgir 1978, p. 53. (The term is taken from Mao Tse-tung.)
71 ibid., p. 55.
72 See Chapter III, and Alamgir op cit.
73 ibid., pp. 70 – 1.
74 Alavi 1973b, p. 153.
75 Jahan 1972, p. 53, Tariq Ali, p. 87, and Alavi 1973b, pp. 152 – 3.
76 Ayub Khan, *Speeches*, quoted in Jahan 1972, p. 55.
77 For the text of the entire memorandum, see Karl von Vorys, Appendix A, pp. 299 – 306.
78 ibid., p. 304.
79 ibid., p. 299, italics in original.
80 For the various measures adopted, see e.g. ibid., pp. 189 – 90.
81 Jahan 1972, pp. 112 – 3 and von Vorys, p. 196.
82 von Vorys, p. 302.
83 The national average was 60%; in East Pakistan 52%, and in the town of Karachi (West Pakistan) 35%.
84 Ziring, p. 18.
85 For an analysis of the various recommendations, see von Vorys, pp. 208 – 29, and for the text of the Constitution, see same author, Appendix B.
86 Sayeed 1967, p. 105.
87 von Vorys, p. 149.
88 ibid., p. 238.
89 The Muslim League had been about wiped out in East Pakistan in the 1954 provincial election.
90 Ziring, p. 30.
91 von Vorys, p. 227.
92 For a discussion of this point, see von Vorys, pp. 253 – 264 and Jahan 1972, p. 127 – 9.
93 For details, see e.g. von Vorys, pp. 260 – 4.
94 For details, see Section 4 in this chapter.
95 Sobhan 1968, p. 253.
96 von Vorys, p. 283.
97 Jahan 1972, p. 152.
98 See, e.g. Sayeed 1967, pp. 97 – 8.
99 Part VI (4) of the Constitution, as reprinted in von Vorys, Appendix B, p. 329.
100 The figures for the 1960s are calculated from Jahan 1972, pp. 73 – 4, and the figures for the 1950s are taken from Lewis 1970, pp. 156 – 8.
101 See, e.g. Ziring, p. 86.
102 Lewis 1970, p. 8.
103 Papanek 1967, p. 20.
104 Jahan 1972, p. 213.
105 Lewis 1970, p. 148.
106 Papanek, p. 10; Ali, p. 153.
107 Mohiuddin Alamgir 1974, pp. 772 – 4.

108 Azizur Rahman Khan 1970.
109 Lewis 1970, p. 8.
110 Sayeed 1967, p. 226.
111 ibid., p. 96.
112 ibid., p. 114.
113 Lewis 1970, p. 146.
114 Jahan 1972, p. 75.
115 Lewis 1970, p. 146.
116 Alavi 1973, p. 169 – 70; Jahan 1972, pp. 87 – 8.
117 For details, see M. Rashiduzzaman 1968, pp. 9 – 19.
118 Ayub Khan, *Speeches*, quoted in Jahan 1972, p. 111.
119 Raziduzzaman 1968, p. 91.
120 Najmul Abedin 1973, p. 170.
121 The Rural Works Programme was designed to build up rural infrastructure. It was financed by U.S. P.L. 480 counterpart funds, and the workers were paid in kind (wheat).
122 Sobhan 1968, pp. 105 – 10.
123 ibid., p. 243.
124 Jahan 1972, p. 122.
125 Raziduzzaman, p. 43.
126 The above data are based on surveys, see ibid., pp. 37 – 9.
127 ibid., p. 43.
128 See also Ramkrishna Mukherjee 1973, p. 407.
129 See Chapter IX.
130 Sobhan 1968, pp. 253 – 4.
131 ibid., p. 50.
132 ibid., p. 251.
133 Abedin, pp. 383 – 4.
134 Gunnar Myrdal, Vol. I, p. 152.
135 Gardezi, p. 136.
136 Lord Curzon's 'Memorandum on Commissions for Indians', quoted in Alavi 1967.
137 Alavi 1967, p. 40; see also Muneer Ahmed.
138 See, e.g. Sayeed 1967, p. 152.
139 Tariq Ali 1970, p. 89.
140 This dual role of civil servants both as bureaucrats and industrialists is not peculiar to Pakistan. For an interesting account of the symbiotic relationship between civil servants and private industry in Thailand, see F. Riggs, *Thailand, the Modernization of a Bureaucratic Polity*, Hololulu 1957.
141 Alavi 1973b, p. 153.
142 ibid., p. 157.
143 Sayeed 1967, pp. 154 – 5.
144 ibid., p. 157 and Jahan 1972, pp. 95 – 6.
145 Sayeed 1967, p. 195.
146 Gardezi, p. 136.
147 Alavi 1967, p. 30.
148 Quoted in Feroz Ahmed, p. 429.
149 Ayub Khan, p. 59.
150 Sayeed 1967, p. 109.
151 Petras, p. 296.
152 ibid., pp. 297 – 8.
153 Feroz Ahmed, p. 426.
154 Lewis 1970, p. 55.
155 Alavi 1967, p. 17.
156 Papanek, p. 220.
157 Sayeed 1967, p. 269.
158 For a discussion of this point, see ibid., pp. 240 – 1.
159 See also Ziring, pp. 98 – 9.

160 The problematic concerning the mode of production will be discussed in detail in Chapters VIII and X.
161 Alavi 1975, pp. 1257–9.
162 Jahan 1972, p. 159.
163 Hettne and Friberg 1975, pp. 1.11–1.12.
164 Jahan 1972, p. 155.
165 ibid., pp. 146–7.
166 Alavi 1973b, p. 167.
167 Quoted in T. Maniruzzaman 1975b, p. 36.
168 Sheikh Mujibur Rahman, 'East Pakistan Awami League Draft Manifesto', as summarized in Rashiduzzaman 1970, p. 583.
169 Rashiduzzaman 1968, p. 582. For a discussion of the two-economy theory, see Jahan 1972, pp. 88–9.
170 Bengali had been accepted as a national language already in 1956.
171 Maniruzzaman 1975b, p. 35.
172 ibid., p. 36.
173 In 1967 the party split into a pro-Moscow and a pro-Peking faction. The pro-Moscow faction supported the Awami League.
174 See Jahan 1972, p. 170.
175 A total of 33 persons were charged with conspiring to bring about East Pakistan secession in the so-called Agartala conspiracy case, named after the Indian town of Agartala where the conspirators were alleged to have met with Indian officials.
176 ibid., p. 111.
177 ibid., p. 107.
178 Quoted in ibid., p. 113.
179 Maniruzzaman 1975b, p. 37.
180 ibid., p. 38.
181 Quoted in ibid., p. 39.
182 ibid., p. 39.
183 For a break-down of the nominees, see ibid., p. 40.
184 ibid., p. 41.
185 ibid., p. 37 and Jahan 1972, p. 87 and p. 139.
186 Jahan 1972, p. 176.
187 Alavi 1973b, p. 170.
188 Sobhan 1977, p. 38.
189 Jahan 1976, pp. 360–1.
190 Sobhan 1977, pp. 38–9.
191 Maniruzzaman 1975b, p. 30.
192 ibid., p. 53.
193 ibid., p. 41.
194 Jahan 1972, p. 191.
195 Maniruzzaman 1975b, p. 42.
196 ibid., p. 43.
197 Sobhan 1977, p. 43.
198 At a press conference on 25 March 1971 Bhutto declared that the autonomy demand was very close to independence (personal notes, K.W.).
199 See, e.g. Maniruzzaman 1975b, p. 44 and Sobhan 1977, p. 41.
200 A. G. Choudhury 1977.
201 Alamgir 1978, p. 76.
202 Laclau 1977, p. 174.

NOTES TO CHAPTER V

1 For details, see e.g. Maniruzzaman 1975b, pp. 43 – 53.
2 He later became President of Bangladesh in 1977.
3 Maniruzzaman 1975b, p. 49.
4 For a discussion of the division within the army, see p. 1324, Lifschultz.
5 In August 1971 India had signed a friendship treaty with Russia.
6 Sobhan 1977, p. 44.
7 In an interview with author, a former prominent Muslim Leaguer—later a member of the BNP government—justified his participation in the Peace Committee as an attempt to save people's lives. As he said, the Awami League had made no preparation for fighting the war.
8 Jahan 1980, p. 95.
9 Cf. Laclau's discussion of populism, Chapter II and Chapter IV.
10 Jahan 1973, p. 200.
11 ibid., p. 203.
12 ibid., same page.
13 See in particular various issues of the Bengali weekly, *Holiday*, October 1972.
14 Sobhan 1977, p. 46.
15 Maniruzzaman 1975a, p. 906.
16 For a discussion, see Nurul Islam, pp. 26 – 7, and pp. 220 – 2.
17 For a study of the Awami League's policy within this framework, see also Sobhan and Ahmad 1980.
18 For a discussion, see Chapter II; cf. also Jahan 1980, p. 105.
19 Nurul Islam, p. 3 and p. 19. See also Chapter IV.
20 ibid., p. 217.
21 Sobhan 1977, p. 46.
22 Nurul Islam, p. 100.
23 ibid., p. 13.
24 K. N. Raj, p. 1193.
25 Cf. Chapter III.
26 Jahan 1973, p. 200 and 1974, pp. 129 – 30.
27 Nurul Islam, p. 6. For a discussion of the bureaucracy, see also pp. 52 – 81.
28 For a discussion of the army at the time of independence, see Lifschultz, pp. 1327 – 8.
29 The exile government had made him president, but he preferred the more important political post as prime minister. He stepped down as president the day after his return, announcing a provisional constitutional order which stipulated a unitary parliamentary government.
30 Jahan 1973, p. 205 and Maniruzzaman 1975c, p. 905 and p. 907.
31 ibid., pp. 893 – 4.
32 Jahan 1974, p. 128.
33 Maniruzzaman 1975c, p. 894.
34 For a similar diversification of income among surplus farmers, cf. the data from the local study, Chapter VII.
35 For a discussion of the background of the MPs as well as their role in the rural areas, see Jahan 1976, p. 357 ff.
36 Jahan 1973, p. 207.
37 This radical faction is alleged to have been formed as early as 1962 as a 'nucleus' within the Awami League. From the very beginning they considered the A.L. as being 'Two parties in one', and when the appropriate moment came, one would emerge from the other (Lifschultz, pp. 1319 – 21).
38 Maniruzzaman 1975c, p. 896.
39 Cf. the local election study, Chapter IX.
40 Jahan 1974, pp. 132 – 3, and Maniruzzaman 1975c, p. 905.
41 Jahan 1974, p. 133.
42 Maniruzzaman 1975a, p. 122.
43 Maniruzzaman 1975c, pp. 903 – 4.
44 Planning Commission 1973. The first five-year plan 1973 – 8, p. 10.

45   ibid., p. 2.

46   Anisur Rahman 1973.

47   Maniruzzaman 1975c, p. 895, footnote 12.

48   These figures are taken from Maniruzzaman 1975a, pp. 118–9.

49   Q. K. Ahmad 1974, p. 679.

50   *Statistical Pocket Book of Bangladesh 1978*, p. 178.

51   Nurul Islam, p. 229.

52   ibid., same page, and p. 14.

53   *Holiday*, 9 June, 1974.

54   Maniruzzaman 1975a, p. 119.

55   See Alamgir 1978, p. 21. and various issues in *Economic and Political Weekly* (Bombay), August to November, 1974.

56   Personal information gathered in Dacca in January, 1975.

57   K. N. Raj, p. 1195.

58   Nurul Islam, p. 18, and pp. 244–7.

59   Maniruzzaman 1975a, pp. 119–20.

60   Nurul Islam, pp. 147–9 and p. 246.

61   Maniruzzaman 1975a, p. 120.

62   ibid., same page.

63   Sobhan 1977, p. 49.

64   Nurul Islam, p. 245.

65   Maniruzzaman 1975a, p. 124.

66   Nurul Islam, p. 247.

67   Cf. Chapter II and Chapter IV.

68   This section of the political situation in 1974 and 1975 is based on Maniruzzaman 1975a and 1976.

69   Independence was considered the first revolution.

70   According to one source, the idea of the one-party system was sold to Sheikh Moni by 'the embassy of the most powerful socialist state' (Maniruzzaman 1976, p. 120). Given the support to the idea on the part of the pro-Moscow parties this statement does not seem unlikely.

71   Cf. Chapter II.

72   Nurul Islam, p. 249.

73   Jahan 1980, p. 95.

74   The number of districts were to be enlarged from 19 to 61.

75   Jahan 1980, p. 117.

76   ibid., p. 135.

77   Maniruzzaman 1976, p. 121.

78   Saul 1976, p. 13.

79   Cf. Chapter II.

80   Chapter II.

81   This account is based on Maniruzzaman 1976, pp. 122–3 and Lifschultz, p. 1305. Both confirm information the author was able to gather in Bangladesh, where she was at the time of the coup.

82   See above two sources.

83   Lifschultz, p. 1305.

84   Besides Mushtaque, 10 Awami League ministers were retained in the new government. The pro-Indian and the 'radical' factions were excluded.

85   Jahan 1980, p. 137.

86   ibid., p. 138.

87   ibid., p. 139.

88   Maniruzzaman 1976, p. 124.

89   This account is based on Lifschultz, pp. 1305–7 and Maniruzzaman 1976, pp. 124–5. The lack of enthusiasm for the 3 November coup—as well as the overwhelming enthusiasm for the 7 November coup—was apparent to anyone who was in Bangladesh at the time (the author happened to be in Dacca).

90 In fact the Indian enthusiasm was so strong, that many believed India had engineered the coup. However, as is the case regarding the 15 August coup, there is no firm evidence of foreign involvement.

91 See notes 88 and 89 above. The most detailed information is given by Lifschultz. I have no way of checking the accuracy of the information, but it should be pointed out that his entire essay is primarily a defence of Colonel Taher and the JSD.

92 *Bangladesh Times*, 8 November, 1975.

93 Within a week of the coup a Martial Law Regulation was made, providing for death penalty for offences including attempts to cause disaffection among officers and men of the Defence Services or interference with the discipline or the performance of duties by them. This regulation was deemed to have come into force on 2 November, 1975 (*Bangladesh Times*, 11 November, 1975).

94 ibid., 26 November, 1975. See also Maniruzzaman 1976, p. 126.

95 Maniruzzaman 1977, p. 195.

96 ibid., p. 196.

97 *Bangladesh Observer*, 31 March, 1976.

98 Maniruzzaman 1977, p. 200.

99 ibid., pp. 192–3.

100 During the author's stay in a rural area at that time, this was the one issue which occupied the villagers who—in that area—were otherwise not politically conscious.

101 See e.g. Zia's speech at a widely attended rally in Dacca on 7 May, 1976 (*Bangladesh Observer*, 9 May, 1976).

102 Cf. Chapter II.

103 By this I do not want to play down the Indian attempts at making Bangladesh subservient to Indian interests.

104 In fact during 1976 the 'official' history of Bangladesh was being rewritten for the second time. During the rule of Sheikh Mujib, the official line had—incorrectly—been that Mujib had declared Bangladesh independent, after which he was taken as prisoner by the Pakistan army. After his downfall, this version was revised, and at the same time the role played by the East Pakistan Regiment in Chittagong in late March 1971 was given prominence, at the expense of the role of the Awami League and Sheikh Mujib as leader of the nationalist movement. (See various issues of English language newspapers in Dacca, especially during late March 1976.)

105 Jahan 1980, p. 114.

106 For a thorough discussion of the issue of secularism in the Bangladesh context, see O'Connell 1976. For this observation, see p. 72.

107 ibid., p. 66.

108 C. W. Smith, quoted in ibid., p. 80.

109 See e.g. Jahan 1980, p. 138, and Maniruzzaman 1977, p. 194.

110 *Bangladesh Times*, 23 April, 1977.

111 For the entire text of the proclamations (amendment) order, see ibid.

112 Maniruzzaman 1977, p. 200.

113 For the entire text of the 19-point programme, see *Bangladesh Times*, 1 May, 1977.

114 Nurul Islam, pp. 254–5.

115 *Bangladesh Times*, 5 and 8 December, 1975.

116 ibid., 13 and 17 January, 1976.

117 Maniruzzaman 1977, p. 199.

118 *Bangladesh Times*, 21 January, 1976.

119 Maniruzzaman 1977, p. 199.

120 The percentage for food grains is calculated from World Bank's Annual Report 1978, and the other figures are taken from Maniruzzaman 1977, p. 199.

121 This support was observed during a visit in Jan./Feb. Especially in the rural areas the declining cost of living was repeatedly mentioned in praising the government.

122 The influence of the surplus farmers in the elected Assembly was so strong that 'even a small tax on affluent agriculturalists had to be hurriedly withdrawn minutes before the Budget was placed before the Assembly'. (*Holiday*, 10 June, 1979).

123 World Bank, op. cit., p. 87.
124 A. R. Khan 1978, p. 40.
125 *Holiday*, 10 June, 1979.
126 A. R. Khan, op. cit., and World Bank, op. cit., p. 85.
127 Maniruzzaman 1977, p. 198.
128 *Bangladesh Times*, 23 April, 1977.
129 These will be discussed in Chapter IX.
130 Rashiduzzaman 1978, p. 129.
131 ibid., pp. 126 – 7.
132 ibid., p. 127.
133 For a similar view, see Mukhopadhyay, p. 904.
134 Rashiduzzaman 1979, p. 192.
135 The omission of the word 'democratic' from the new party 'did not pass unnoticed', as a Bengali reporter noted (*The New Nation*, 8 August, 1978).
136 *Bangladesh Times*, 2 September, 1978.
137 For a discussion of factionalism, see Rashiduzzaman 1979, pp. 192 – 4.
138 Haque, p. 219.
139 ibid., 7 April, 1979.
140 Personal information, collected in Bangladesh in April 1979.
141 Jahan 1980, p. 197.
142 Haque 1981, p. 199.
143 Quoted in Haque 1980, p. 221.
144 Quoted in ibid., p. 225.
145 Jahan 1980, p. 214.
146 Haque 1980, p. 225.
147 Haque 1981, p. 201.
148 ibid., p. 198.
149 Haque 1980, p. 222.
150 See Alam 1980/81. This study confirms observations made by the author in various parts of Bangladesh during 1981.
151 Jahan 1980, p. 216.
152 See Chapter V, Section C (2) b (iii).
153 Franda, p. 1987.
154 Quoted in Haque 1981, p. 191.
155 For the various theories, see Franda, pp. 1389 – 90.
156 ibid., p. 1389.
157 Z. R. Khan, p. 169.
158 ibid., p. 165.
159 ibid., p. 166.
160 For the entire text of Ershad's November 28 statement, see *Holiday*, 6 December, 1981, p. 5.
161 For details, see various articles in ibid., 28 March, 1982. See also *Far Eastern Economic Review*, 19 March and 2 April, 1982.
162 The events surrounding the 1981 and 1982 coups were written in April 1982.
163 Franda, p. 1394.
164 Cf. Chapter V, Section B (4).
165 Cf. Ziemann's and Lanzendörfer's analysis, Chapter II, Section A (2).
166 See Chapter VIII, Section B.
167 See note 165.
168 Cf. Chapter II.
169 Cf. Laclau's discussion, referred to in Chapter II, Section D (2).
170 Jahan 1980, p. 217.
171 Haque 1981, p. 189.
172 Sobhan 1981, p. 333.
173 See the theories by Ziemann and Lanzendörfer as well as by Sonnatag discussed in Chapter II, Section A (2).
174 Sobhan op. cit., p. 346.

NOTES TO CHAPTER VI

1   *Statistical pocket-book of Bangladesh 1978*, Tables 2.6 and 10.1.
2   World Bank 1978, Appendix table 2.2.
3   SIDA 1979, p. 27.
4   Lipton 1977, p. 347.
5   Cf. ibid., and SIDA 1979, pp. 23 – 33.
6   Alamgir 1975, p. 288.
7   Rahim and Hoque, p. 4.
8   Mukhopadhyaya 1978, quoted in SIDA op cit., p. 29.
9   Alamgir 1974, pp. 740 – 9.
10 For a discussion of the food policy, see SIDA 1979, pp. 29 – 33 and pp. 41 – 6.
11 For the figures quoted, see World Bank 1978, Appendix tables 7.4 – 7.6.
12 Azizur R. Khan 1977, p. 147.
13 Alamgir 1978, pp. 2 – 3.
14 Wood 1978, p. 9 and Table 6, p. 24.
15 Alamgir 1978, pp. 94 – 5.
16 USAID 1977, p. 41.
17 Alamgir 1978, p. 101.
18 Abdullah *et al.* 1976, p. 211 and Table A – 1, p. 257.
19 Alamgir 1978, p. 113.
20 Azizur R. Khan 1977, p. 159.
21 ibid., p. 159 and Alamgir 1978, pp. 102 – 10.
22 See, e.g. Alamgir op cit., chapter 6.
23 Faaland and Parkinson, pp. 88 – 9.
24 See, e.g. Abdullah *et al.* 1974, and Planning Commission's Evaluation 1974.
25 Bangladesh Academy for Rural Development (Comilla) 1975.
26 Wood 1976, p. 145.
27 For a detailed description, see Nafis Ahmad, Chapter I.
28 Census Commission 1974, Bull. 2, Table 1.
29 For a comparison of the data from some of the recent studies, see SIDA 1977, p. 80.
30 See, e.g. Faidley and Esmay, p. 130.
31 See Chapter VII.
32 See Bertocci 1976, p. 159 ff. and Chapter VII below.
33 Wood 1978, p. 2.
34 For a study of a village in the jute belt, see Arn 1978.
35 Cf. the title of Wood's 1976 study: 'Class Differentiation and Power in Bondokgram: The Minifundist Case'.
36 The approach followed in presenting the detailed data from one local area (Chapter VII) and in analysing these data in the broader context of Bangladesh rural social structure and at the abstract level of the 'mode of production' (Chapter VIII), has been used in several analyses. The rationale of the approach has been well argued by Harriss who writes: 'The logic of the method is that the internal properties of any part should be studied in terms of its relations within the whole reproductive totality to which it belongs. It is possible by studying processes at village level to contribute to understanding of the greater whole: the village is in a sense a *conjuncture* of much wider processes and relationships' (Harriss, p. 26).
37 Sayeed 1967, p. 223.
38 Jahan 1972, pp. 152 – 4.

NOTES TO CHAPTER VII

1   A slightly different and more detailed version of the local area study is published by the Bogra Academy (Westergaard 1980). Most of the material in this chapter was collected by the author who spent seven months in Boringram in 1975 – 6 and revisited the area in 1977, 1979 and 1981.

2   For a discussion of villages as a social unit, see Bertocci 1970.
3   Cf. Chapter VI.
4   This is also a fictitious name.
5   The Biharis are non-Bengali Muslims who came from India at the time of partition.
6   Mukherjee 1971, p. 122. The Mukherjee study was undertaken in another area of the Barind tract north of Sherpur thana.
7   1 maund = 82 lbs, and 1 acre = 0.4 hectare.
8   For average yields see Ahmad, p. 67, and for uncertainty in calculation, see Elkinton, p. 68.
9   Ahmad, p. 69.
10 See, e.g. Mukherjee, p. 156, and Alamgir 1974, p. 809.
11 This calculation is based primarily on Mukherjee (p. 156) who gives an average per capita requirement of rice as 6.17 maunds per year (for males 7.5 mds, for females 7.0 mds, and for children below 12 years 4.0 mds). This gives an average daily consumption per person of 0.66 seers (22 ounces). This is considerably lower than the figures given by the villagers who calculate with 1 seer per adult per day. On the other hand, it is higher than the cereal consumption estimates carried out by the National Nutrition Survey for 1962 – 64 (see Chen, Apr. 1975, p. 112) where per capita cereal consumption is given as 18 ounces per day. In order to get 6 maunds of rice it is necessary to produce about 8.5 mds of paddy (1 maund = 40 seers, and from 1 maund of paddy 28 seers of rice is produced). Thus to get 6 maunds (240 seers) of rice we need

$$\frac{1 \text{ maund x } 240 \text{ seers}}{28 \text{ seers}} = 8.6 \text{ mds of paddy}$$

12 This figure is based on the actual production of the individual households of *aman*, *aus* and *boro* (production from own land—share-cropped and leased out, + share-cropped and leased in).
13 This kind of mortgage is much less harsh than elsewhere in Bangladesh, where the person who borrows money has to give not only his land in mortgage but also to pay interest on the loan, and often repay the loan advanced. If the money is not repaid after a fixed number of years, the landowner loses the ownership right to his land which becomes the property of the money-lender. In one study of the Comilla area it was found that mortgage was the principal means of land transactions (Wood 1976, p. 141).
14 Land Occupancy Survey 1977, Table VI.
15 Cf. USAID 1977 and Alamgir 1978. For national figures, see Land Occupancy Survey Report, Table IX.
16 Taka 30 = £1 (1982).
17 The salaries paid to hired labourers thus constitute a minumum reproduction cost, if we accept that rice constitutes one-half of the rural population's basic needs (see text). At the time of investigation day-labourers were paid Tk. 3.00 plus meals for most of the period. At that time the price of rice was around Tk. 3,000 per seer.
18 For a description of female work in processing and the sexual division of labour, see Westergaard 1982.
19 In a traditional rural economy like that of Bangladesh it is not always clearcut how best to define a rural household, as for instance, in some cases a father and his sons may cultivate the land together but have separate economies. In Boringram this problem was a minor one, as there were only four borderline cases, and in all, the decision whether or not to classify a unit as a household was made on the basis of the eating unit. This is quite common in anthropological analysis and also corresponds to the villagers' own perception. A household is thus defined as a unit which most often has a distinct separate economy and which always comprises one eating unit. Thus defined, a household may comprise an extended family or a nuclear family.
20 As mentioned in note 11, it is necessary to produce 8.5 maunds of paddy per person a year to meet the rice requirement, and 17 maunds to meet daily needs. With an average yield of 15 maunds per acre of *aman* and 9 maunds of *aus* (which is cultivated on about one-third of the cultivated land), the minimum land requirement per person is at least 0.9 acres to meet basic needs and 0.45 acres to meet rice requirement (0.9 acres of *aman* at 15 maunds = 13.5 maunds, + 0.3 acres of *aus* at 9 maunds = 2.7 maunds. This gives a total of 16.2 maunds).
21 For a detailed break-down of land distribution, see Table 7.8.

22   No Marginal Peasant HH maintain their families from their landownership alone; they either take outside work or rent in land, or both. n.s. = not significant.

23   These data are based on actual production from each household (own land + rented land − rented out).

24   This is based on peasants' own information. For the small and medium peasants the numbers listed are put in parenthesis. On a strict criterion they should be listed under surplus peasants, but as the boundaries are not absolute (cf. e.g. the question of household size), they are excluded in this division according to land size..

25   Alamgir 1978, p. 36.

26   These are all the landowning households − 6 marginal and 1 small peasant, all of whom have rented out all their land, + 4 landless households who sharecrop in land.

27   Bernstein 1977.

28   Cf. Lenin 1899.

29   Bernstein, op. cit., p. 8.

30   ibid., p. 10.

31   Bertocci 1979, p. 11.

32   Béteille, quoted in ibid., p. 11.

33   The percentage of owner-cum-tenants is higher than the average for Bangladesh. The 1977 Land Occupancy Survey lists 32% as owner-cum-tenants (Land Occupancy Survey 1977, Table IV). No breakdown for districts is available from the 1977 survey, but the 1960 agricultural census recorded a higher percentage of owner-cum-tenants for the northern division (Rajshahi) than the average for the country, viz. 46% as against 38% for the country (Bertocci 1976, p. 176).

34   Cf. the discussion on the Below Poverty Level Equilibrium Trap in the preceding chapter.

35   Cf. Chapter VI.

36   IRDP Bench Mark Survey No. 2, pp. 59 − 60.

37   For an elaborated view of this argument, see A. Bhaduri. See also Patnaik 1976, p. A-97, who argues that the barriers to development are due to high levels of precapitalist rent on land.

38   Mukherjee studied 5 interior villages and 1 village close to a major town. Where the data are broken down in Mukherjee's study, the data from the 5 interior villages will be used for comparison, as they are more similar to Boringram. The comparison will always by a second best, and I am aware that one cannot *a priori* postulate that the two areas have developed similarly. However, the assumption seems reasonable given the dependence on agriculture, the limited out-migration, and the general population increase, among other things.

39   Mukherjee, p. 5 and p. 83.

40   See Chapter VI, Section A.

41   See Chapter IV, Section A (5) b.

42   Mukherjee, p. 86.

43   ibid., p. 164.

44   ibid., p. 187 − 8.

45   ibid., p. 216.

46   For a discussion, see Wood 1978, pp. 12 − 13.

47   Bertocci 1972, p. 47.

48   ibid., 1970, p. 103.

49   In the southern part of Bangladesh it comprises several villages (Bertocci 1974, p. 93), whereas it seems to be coterminous with the village in the northern part—at least as far as I could gather from my village study.

50   It is an open question whether the two factions should be referred to as two separate *samaj*. Religious ceremonies take place within the individual *samaj* which is one argument for still referring to the groupings as *samaj* (as the villagers do). On the other hand, it could be argued that factionalism has superseded the unity implied in the *samaj* notion.

51   Nicholas, p. 263.

52   Bertocci 1979, p. 51.

53   ibid., pp. 52 − 3.

54   Little data is available on marketed surplus of rice in Bangladesh as a whole, but a survey conducted in 1973 − 4 suggests that about 30% of the total rice is being marketed (Abdullah 1976, p. 212).

55 Data are available for only 30 persons, including the surplus households. These all knew the name of the president; among the rest only 2 gave a correct answer. (It should be added that the survey was carried out in 1975 – 6 at a time when the President (Sayem) did not figure as prominently as Mujib before him or Zia afterwards.)

56 During a brief revisit to the village in 1979 it was learnt that the co-operative was functioning at the time, but it was not very active, and the local IRDP officers complained of the lack of co-operation on the part of the people in Boringram.

NOTES TO CHAPTER VIII

1 A different version of this chapter has been published in the *Journal of Social Studies* (Westergaard 1978).
2 Saul and Woods 1971, p. 106.
3 ibid., p. 105.
4 Shanin 1973, p. 64.
5 For a more detailed discussion, see e.g. ibid., pp. 67 – 71.
6 Thorner *et al.* 1966, esp. chapter 2.
7 Rajat and Ratna Ray 1973, pp. 122 – 3.
8 ibid., p. 127.
9 ibid., p. 104.
10 ibid., p. 109.
11 ibid., p. 121.
12 ibid., p. 111.
13 ibid., p. 113.
14 ibid., p. 122.
15 Rajat K. Ray 1973, p. 271.
16 ibid., p. 266.
17 R. and R. Ray, p. 127. For a quite similar account of the development in the Deccan, see Banaji, 1977.
18 Mukherjee 1971, pp. 187 – 8.
19 Abdullan *et al.*, 1976, p. 211.
20 Wood 1978, p. 9.
21 ibid., p. 1.
22 ibid., p. 15.
23 ibid., p. 14.
24 B. K. Jahangir 1976, p. 318.
25 ibid., p. 206.
26 ibid., p. 319.
27 Arens and van Veurden 1977.
28 Cf. Wood 1978, p. 14.
29 Abdullah *et al.*, and USAID 1977.
30 Cf. the analysis in the following chapter.
31 Jahangir 1976, pp. 195 – 6, and Wood 1976, pp. 146 – 7.
32 Broomfield, p. 47.
33 Cf. Alavi 1974, cited in Chapter I.
34 For a review of the debate, see e.g. Foster-Carter 1978, pp. 47 – 77.
35 Zeimann and Lanzendörfer 1977, p. 157.
36 Much of this summary of the articulation theory is based on the work of Meillassoux, see in particular 1972 and 1975.
37 Zeimann and Lanzendörfer, p. 159.
38 Alavi 1975, p. 1253.
39 ibid., p. 1247.
40 Banaji 1972, p. 2500.

41   Banaji advances a more extreme view in a later article in which he argues that the relations of production which tie the enterprise of small commodity producers to capital are such that 'the "price" which the producer receives is no longer a pure category of exchange, but a category, that is, a relation, of production, a concealed wage' (Banaji 1977, p. 34).
42   Alavi 1978 (quoted with permission of the author).
43   Alavi 1975, p. 1259.
44   Foster-Carter 1978, p. 72.
45   McEachern 1976, p. 451.
46   It may be pointed out that in a later article Alavi juxtaposes the capitalist mode of production with peripheral capitalism and does not use the concept of a post-colonial mode of production (Alavi 1981, see especially Table p. 477).
47   Alamgir 1978, p. 67. See also, p. 68.
48   Bhaduri, 1973.
50   McEachern, p. 451.
51   It is this reasoning which underlies the arguments concerning pauperization discussed in the previous section.
52   Patnaik 1976, p. A-96. For Patnaik's contribution to the debate, see also Patnaik 1971a and b, and 1972a and b.
53   Banaji 1972, p. 2498.
54   Wood 1978, p. 9.
55   Alavi 1978, pp. 22 – 3.
56   Mukherjee 1971, pp. 71 – 3.
57   Banaji 1977, p. 1398.
58   Peter Bertocci 1970, p. 103.
59   Patnaik 1971a, p. A-148.
60   Wood 1978, see especially pp. 8 – 9.
61   R. and R. Ray 1973, p. 127.
62   Patnaik 1976, p. A-98.
63   Abdullah *et al.*, pp. 252 – 3.
64   For a similar conclusion, however, see the analysis from South India provided by Harriss and referred to in Chapter X.
65   Wood 1978, p. 11.
66   See e.g., Abdullah *et al.*, and various annual reports of the Bangladesh Academy for Rural Development, Comilla.
67   Wood 1976, p. 146.

NOTES TO CHAPTER IX

1   Much of the analysis in this chapter was presented at the VIth European Conference on Modern South Asian Studies in Paris in 1978.
2   Cf. Chapter V.
3   Cf. Chapter V.
4   O'Connell, pp. 72 – 3.
5   In the sitting chairman's family a split arose at the time of the 1977 election. The older brother—who had been member of the Union Councils during the Ayub regime—wanted to run as chairman, but as the youngest brother insisted on supporting his father-in-law the oldest brother withdrew his candidacy and supported the third candidate.
6   It should be noted that also in the traditional families economic diversification is now taking place in the younger generation. As mentioned in Chapter VII, the fourth son in the traditional family in Boringram is heavily engaged in trade in the local area. The oldest grandson in this same family is emerging as the biggest entrepreneur in the village (during a revisit to Boringram in 1979 it was learnt that he had just bought a rice mill).
7   See Rashiduzzaman's 1978 study, referred to in Chapter V.

8   Cf. Sobhan's analysis, referred to in Chapter IV.
9   Arn, 1978.
10   See Chapter V.
11   *Holiday*, 21 August and 4 September, 1977.
12   The ninth chairman was in jail at the time of the 1979 general election.

NOTES TO CHAPTER X

1   Cf. Petras analysis referred to in Chapter IV.
2   Cf. the arguments advanced in Chapter IV.
3   Petras, p. 297.
4   See Chapter IV; cf. also Poulantzas, argument referred to in Chapter II.
5   See Ziemann's and Lanzendörfer's arguments, Chapter II.
6   See Chapter II and Chapter VIII.
7   Petras, p. 298.
8   ibid., p. 300.
9   Cf. Chapter V.
10   Cf. Alavi's argument in Chapter VIII.
11   Cf. Patnaik's argument discussed in Chapter VIII.
12   Djurfeldt and Lindberg, p. 164.
13   ibid., p. 173.
14   This was not so much a productive investment, but used for custom hire services.
15   Harriss, p. 286.
16   ibid., pp. 291 – 2.
17   ibid., p. 194.
18   Djurfeldt and Lindberg, p. 204 and p. 208 (italics in original).
19   ibid., p. 205 and p. 203 (italics in original).
20   Harriss, p. 444.
21   ibid., p. 446.
22   ibid., same page (italics in original).
23   Alamgir 1978, p. 85.
24   Djurfeldt and Lindberg, p. 208.
25   Griffin, quoted in SIDA 1979, p. 115.
26   Official statistics show that real wages of agricultural workers in Bangladesh were between 30 and 40 per cent lower in 1972 – 5 than in 1949 (Clay 1976, pp. 423 – 4).
27   Jacoby, quoted in SIDA 1979, pp. 113 – 4.
28   FAO Agricultural Mission, p. 21, quoted in ibid., p. 31.
29   SIDA 1969, p. 32.
30   ibid., pp. 32 – 3.
31   ibid., p. 33.
32   ibid., pp. 70 – 2.
33   FAO Agricultural Mission, p. 12, quoted in ibid., p. 73. For investment figures and efficiency, see also SIDA, p. 74.
34   SIDA 1979, p. 35.
35   McHenry and Bird, p. 79, quoted in ibid., p. 45.
36   For a further elaboration on this point, see Sobhan 1981.
37   SIDA, p. 46.
38   For a discussion of the 'Basic Needs' approach and its limitations, see e.g., Steward and Streeten 1976, and OECD *Development and Co-operation Review* 1978, Chapter V.
39   IBRD, Summary Proceedings, 1972 Annual Meeting of the Boards of Governors, p. 26 (italics added, K.W.).
40   Cf. the discussion of mobilization in Chapter II.
41   See e.g. Jahangir 1976.
42   Cf. Bertocci's discussion of political culture, referred to in Chapter VII, Section F.

BIBLIOGRAPHY

Abdullah, Abu, 1976. 'Land Reform and Agrarian Change in Bangladesh', *Bangladesh Development Studies*, Vol. IV, No. 1.

Abdullah, Abu, M. Hossain and R. Nations, 1974. 'Issues in agrarian development and the IRDP', Appendix I to SIDA/ILO Report on Integrated Rural Development Programme, IRDP, Bangladesh (mimeo), Dacca.

Abdullah, Abu, M. Hossain and R. Nations, 1976. 'Agrarian Structure and the IRDP —Preliminary Considerations', *Bangladesh Development Studies*, Vol. IV, No. 2.

Abedin, Najmul, 1973. *Local Administration and Politics in Modernising Societies; Bangladesh and Pakistan*. Dacca.

Ahmad, Kamruddin, 1975. *A Socio-Political History of Bengal and the Birth of Bangladesh*. Fourth Ed., Dacca.

Ahmad, Nafis, 1976. *A New Economic Geography of Bangladesh*. New Delhi.

Ahmad, Q.K., 1974. 'Aspects of Management of Nationalized Industries in Bangladesh', *Bangladesh Development Studies*, Vol. II, No. 3.

Ahmed, Feroz, 1973. 'The Structural Matrix of the Struggle in Bangladesh', in: *Imperialism and Revolution in South Asia*. K. Gough and H.P. Sharma, eds. New York.

Ahmed, Muneer, 1964. *The Civil Servant in Pakistan*. Oxford.

Ahmed, Sufia, 1974. *Muslim Community in Bengal 1884 – 1912*. Dacca (Oxford Univ. Press).

Alam, Manjur-ul, 1980 – 1. 'Leadership Pattern Under Swanirvar Gram Sarker in Bangladesh: An Experimentation of Some Characteristic of Gram Prodhans in Selected Areas of Comilla District', *Journal of the Bangladesh Academy For Rural Development*, Comilla, Vol. X, Nos. 1 – 2.

Alamgir, M., 1974. 'Some Analysis of Distribution of Income, Consumption, Saving and Poverty in Bangladesh', *Bangladesh Development Studies*, Vol. II, No. 4.

———— 1975. 'Some Aspects of Bangladesh Agriculture: Review of Performance and Evaluation of Policies', ibid., Vol. III, No. 3.

———— 1978. *Bangladesh. A case of below poverty level equilibrium trap*. Dacca (Bangladesh Institute of Development Studies).

Alavi, Hamza, 1967. 'The Army and the Bureaucracy in Pakistan Politics', (mimeo). (An abridged version has been published in *Armée et Nations dans les Trois Continents*, A. Abdel-Malek, ed.

———— 1973a. 'Peasant Classes and Primordial Loyalties', *Journal of Peasant Studies*, Vol. 1, No. 1.

———— 1973b. 'The State in Postcolonial Societies: Pakistan and Bangladesh', in: *Imperialism and Revolution in South Asia*, K. Gough and H.P. Sharma, eds. New York.

———— 1974. 'Rural Bases of Political Power in South Asia', *Journal of Contemporary Asia*, Vol. IV, No. 4.

———— 1975. 'India and the Colonial Mode of Production', *Economic and Political Weekly*, August 1975.

———— 1978. 'Capitalism and Colonial Transformation', provisional paper presented in the Seminar on 'Underdevelopment and Subsistence Reproduction in Southeast Asia', Bielefeld, April 1978.

———— 1981. 'Structure of Colonial Formations', *Economic and Political Weekly*, Vol. XVI, Nos. 10 – 12.

Ali, Tariq, 1970. Pakistan. *Military Rule or People's Power?* London.

Amin, Samir, 1974. *Accumulation on a world scale: A critique of the theory of underdevelopment.* New York.

Arens, J. and J. van Beurden, 1977. *Jhagrapur. Poor Peasants and Women in a Village in Bangladesh.* Amsterdam.

Arn, Ann-lisbet, 1978. 'A case study of an integrated village in Mymensingh District, Bangladesh', (mimeo). Gotherburg University, Department of Peace and Conflict Research.

Banaji, Jairus, 1972. 'For a Theory of Colonial Modes of Production'. *Economic and Political Weekly*, August 1975.

———— 1977. 'Modes of Production in a Materialist Conception of History', *Capitalist and Class*, Autumn 1977.

Bangladesh Academy For Rural Development, 1975. *Integrated Rural Development Program in Comilla District—An Evaluation.* Comilla.

———— 1972 – 1978. *Annual Report* (various issues). Comilla.

Bangladesh Government, Bureau of Statistics, 1977. 'Summary Report of the 1977 Land Occupancy Survey of Rural Bangladesh', (mimeo).

———— 1978. *Statistical Pocket Book of Bangladesh 1978.*

———— Census Commission, 1974. *Bangladesh Population Census 1974.*

———— Integrated Rural Development Programme, 1976. 'Problems of Rural Development: Some Household Level Indicators', Benchmark Survey Report Series, No. 2 (Ahmadullah Mia).

———— Planning Commission, 1973. *The First Five-Year Plan 1973 – 78.*

———— 1974. *Integrated Rural Development Programme, an Evaluation.*

Bangladesh Observer (English Language Daily). Dacca, 31 March 1976 and 9 May 1976.

Bangladesh Times (English Language Daily). Dacca, various issues 1975, 1976, 1977, 1979.

Bernstein, Henry, 1977. 'Notes on Capital and Peasantry', *Review of African Political Economy*, No. 10.

Bertocci, Peter, 1970. 'Elusive Villages, Social Structure and Community Organization in Rural East Pakistan'. Ph.D. thesis, Michigan State University (mimeo).

———— 1972. 'Community Structure and Social Rank in Two Villages in Bangladesh', *Contributions to Indian Sociology*, New Series, No. VI.

———— 1974. 'Rural Communities in Bangladesh: Hajipur and Tinpara', in: *South Asia: Seven Community Profiles*, C. Maloney, ed. New York.

———— 1976. 'Social Organization and Agricultural Development in Bangladesh', in: *Rural Development in Bangladesh and Pakistan*, R.D. Stevens, H. Alavi and P. Bertocci, eds. Honolulu.

———— 1979. 'Structural Fragmentation and Peasant Class in Bangladesh', *Journal of Social Studies* (Dacca), No. 5.

Béteille, André, 1975. *Studies in Agrarian Social Structure.* London.

Bhaduri, A., 1973. 'A Study in Agricultural Backwardness under Semi-Feudalism', *Economic Journal*, Vol. 83 (329).

Broomfield, John H., 1976. 'Peasant Mobilization in Twentieth-Century Bengal', in: *Forging Nations: A Comparative View of Rural Ferment and Revolt*, J. Spielberg and Whiteford, eds. Michigan State Univ. Press.

Chen, Lincoln, C., 1975. 'An Analysis of Per Capita Foodgrain Availability, Consumption and Requirement in Bangladesh: A Systematic Approach to Food Planning', *Bangladesh Development Studies*, Vol. III, No. 2.

Choudhury, A.G., 1977. 'Introduction' to *Sheikh Mujib. A Commemorative Anthology*, A.G. Choudhury, ed. London.

Choudhury, G.W., 1969. *Constitutional Development in Pakistan.* Vancouver, Second ed.

Clay, E.J., 1976. 'Institutional Change and Agricultural Wages in Bangladesh', *Bangladesh Development Studies*, Vol. IV, No. 4.

Deutsch, Karl W., 1966. *Nationalism and Social Communication.* M.I.T. Press.

Djurfeldt, G. and S. Lindberg, 1975. *Behind Poverty. The Social Formation in a Tamil Village.* Copenhagen (Scandinavian Institute of Asian Studies).

Elkinton, Charles, M., 1976. 'East Pakistan's Agricultural Planning and Development, 1955 – 1969: Its Legacy for Bangladesh', in: *Rural Development in Bangladesh and Pakistan*, R.D. Stevens, *et al.*, eds. Honolulu.

Faaland, Just and Parkinson, J.R., 1976. *Bangladesh: The test case of Development.* Dacca (University Press Ltd., also: Hurst & Co. Ltd., London).

Faidley, L. and Esmay, M.L., 1976. 'Introduction and Use of Improved Rice Varieties: Who Benefits?', in: *Rural Development in Bangladesh and Pakistan*, R.D. Stevens, *et al.*, eds.

FAO, UNDP, Government of Bangladesh, 1977. 'Agricultural Mission, Selected Policy Issues and Working Papers'. Dacca.

Far Eastern Economic Review (weekly, Hongkong), March 19, and April 2, 1982.

Foster-Carter, 1978. 'The Modes of Production Controversy', *New Left Review*, 107.

Franda, Marcus, 1981. 'Bangladesh after Zia: A Retrospect and Prospect', *Economic and Political Weekly*, Vol. XVI, No. 34.

Frank, Andre Gunder, 1967. *Capitalism and Underdevelopment in Latin America.* New York.

Galtung, J., 1971. 'A structural theory of imperialism', *Journal of Peace Research*, No. 2.

Gardezi, Hassan N., 1973. 'Neocolonial Alliances and the Crisis of Pakistan', in: *Imperialism and Revolution in South Asia*, K. Gough and H.P. Sharma, eds. New York.

Griffin, Keith, 1974. *The Political Economy of Agrarian Change.* London.

Haque, Azizul, 1980. 'Bangladesh 1979: Cry for a Sovereign Parliament', *Asian Survey*, Vol. XX, No. 2.

———— 1981. 'Bangladesh in 1980: Strains and Stresses—Opposition in the Doldrums', ibid., Vol. XXI, No. 2.

Harriss, John, 1977. 'Capitalism and Peasant Farming: A Study of Agricultural Change and Agrarian Structure in northern Tamil Nadu'. Ph.D. thesis, University of East Anglia, (mimeo).

Hettne, Björn and Friberg, M., 1975. 'A tenatative approach to mobilization research', Part I (mimeo), Göteborg.

Hindess, B. and Hirst, P.Q., 1975. *Pre-capitalist Modes of Production*, London.

Holiday (English Language Weekly), Dacca. Various issues 1972 – 1982.

International Bank for Reconstruction and Development, International Finance Corporation, and International Development Association, 1972. *1972 Annual Meetings of the Boards of Governors.* Summary Proceedings. Washington, D.C.

Islam, Nurul, 1977. *Development Planning in Bangladesh. A Study in Political Economy.* London.

Jahan, Rounaq, 1972. Pakistan. *Failure in National Integration.* New York.

———— 1973. 'Bangladesh in 1972: Nation Building in a New State', *Asian Survey*, Vol. XIII, No. 2.

———— 1974. 'Bangladesh in 1973: Management of Factional Politics', ibid., Vol. XIV, No. 2.

———— 1976. 'Members of Parliament in Dacca', *Legislative Studies Quarterly*, I, 3.

———— 1980, *Bangladesh Politics: Problems and Issues* (A collection of articles written between 1970 and 1980), Dacca University Press.

Jahangir, B.K., 1979. *Differentiation, Polarization and Confrontation in Rural Bangladesh*. Dacca.

Jessup, B., 1972. *Social Order, Reform and Revolution*. London.

Kalecki, Michal, 1976. 'Observations on Social and Economic Aspects of 'Intermediate Regimes', in: *Essays on Developing Economies*. Harvester Press.

Kamal, Kazi Ahmed, 1970. *Fazlul Huq, Suhrawardy and Moulana Bhashani*. Dacca.

Khan, A.R., 1978. 'The Two-Year Plan: Some Aspects of Financing and Domestic Resource Mobilization', *Business Review* (Dacca University Business Study Circle), July – October, 1978.

Khan, Ayub, 1967. *Friends Not Masters: A Political Autobiography*. London.

Khan, Azizur Rahman, 1970. 'A New Look at Disparity', *Forum* (Dacca), Vol. 1, No. 7.

Khan, Z.R., 1982. 'Bangladesh in 1981: Change, Stability and Leadership', *Asian Survey*, Vol. XXII, No. 2.

Kothari, Rajni, 1976. 'State and Nationbuilding in the Third World', in *State and Nation Building. A Third World Perspective*, R. Kothari, ed. New Delhi.

Laclau, E., 1977. 'Fascism and Ideology' and 'Towards a Theory on Populism', in: *Politics and Ideology in Marxist Theory*. London.

Langdon, Steven, 1979. 'Multinational Corporations and the State in Africa', in: *Transnational Capitalism and National Development*, J.J. Villamil, ed. Harvester Press.

Lenin, 1899. *The Development of Capitalism in Russia*.

Lewis, Stephen R., 1969. *Economic Policy and Industrial Growth in Pakistan*. London.

———— 1970. *Pakistan. Industrialization and Trade Policies*. Oxford University Press.

Leys, Colin, 1976. 'The "Overdeveloped" Post Colonial State: A re-evaluation', *Review of African Political Economy*, No. 5.

Lifschultz, L., 1974a. 'A State of Siege', *Economic and Political Weekly*, 30 August.

———— 1974b. 'Reaping a Harvest of Misery', ibid., 25 October.

———— 1974c. 'A Death Trap Called Rangpur', ibid., 15 November.

———— 1977. 'Abu Taher's Last Testament. Bangladesh: The Unfinished Revolution', ibid., Special No., August.

Lipton, M., 1977. *Why Poor People Stay Poor. A Study of Urban Bias in World Development*. London.

Maniruzzaman, T., 1966. 'Group Interests in Pakistan Politics, 1947 – 1958', *Pacific Affairs*, Vol. XXXIX, Nos. 1 – 2.

———— 1975a. 'Bangladesh in 1974: Economic Crisis and Political Polarization', *Asian Survey*, Vol. XV, No. 2.

———— 1975b. *Radical Politics and the Emergence of Bangladesh*. Dacca.

———— 1975c. 'Bangladesh: An Unfinished Revolution?', *Journal of Asian Studies*, Vol. XXXIV. No. 4.

———— 1976. 'Bangladesh in 1975: The Fall of the Sheikh Mujib Regime and its Aftermath', *Asian Survey*, Vol. XVI, No. 2.

———— 1977. 'Bangladesh in 1976: Struggle for Survival as an Independent State', ibid., Vol. XVII, No. 2.

Martinussen, John, 1974. 'Bidrag til en analyse af den pakistanske stat' (Contributions to an analysis of the Pakistan State, in Danish), mimeo, Aarhus University.

McEachern, D., 1976. 'The Mode of Production in India', *Journal of Contemporary Asia*, Vol. 6, No. 4.

McHenry, D.F., and K. Bird, 1977. 'Food Bungle in Bangladesh', *Foreign Policy*, No. 27.

Meillassoux, C., 1972. 'From Reproduction to Production', *Economy and Society*, Vol. 1, No. 1.

————— 1975. *Femmes, greniers et capitaux*. Paris.

Mouzelis, Nicos, 1978. 'Ideology and Class Politics. A Critique of Ernesto Laclau', *New Left Review*, No. 112.

Mukherjee, Ramkrishna, 1971. *Six Villages of Bengal*. Bombay.

————— 1973. 'The Social Background of Bangladesh', in: *Imperialism and Revolution in South Asia*, K. Gough and H.P. Sharma, eds. New York.

Mukhopadhyaya, A., 1978a. 'Preparing for Parliamentary Polls', *Economic and Political Weekly*, 26 August.

————— 1978b. 'Bangladesh. The Economic Millstone of Foreign Aid', ibid., 28 October.

Murray, R., 1967. 'Second Thoughts on Ghana', *New Left Review*, No. 42.

Myrdal, Gunnar, 1968. *Asian Drama*.

Nations, R., 1971. 'The Economic Structure of Pakistan: Class and Colony', *New Left Review*, No. 68.

New Nation (English Language Weekly), Dacca, September 2, 1978.

Nicholas, Ralph W., 1968. 'Structure of Politics in the Villages of Southern Asia', in: *Structure and Change in Indian Society*, M. Singer and B.S. Cohn, eds. Chicago.

O'Connell, 1976. 'Dilemmas of Secularism in Bangladesh', *Journal of Asian and African Studies*, XI, 1 – 2.

OECD, 1978. *Development and Co-operation Review*. Paris.

Papanek, Gustav F., 1967. *Pakistan's Development. Social Goals and Private Incentives*, Harvard University Press.

Patnaik, Utsa, 1971a. 'Capitalist Development in Agriculture: A Note', *Economic and Political Weekly*, 25 September.

————— 1971b. 'Capitalist Development in Agriculture: A Further Comment', *ibid.*, 25 December.

————— 1972a + b. 'Capitalism in agriculture', *Social Scientist*, No. 2 and 3.

————— 1976. 'Class Differentiation within the Peasantry', *Economic and Political Weekly*, 25 September.

Petras, James F., 1975. 'New Perspectives on Imperialism and Social Classes in the Periphery', *Journal of Contemporary Asia*, Vol. 5, No. 3.

Poulantzas, Nicos, 1973. *Political Power and Social Classes*. London.

————— 1974. *Fascism and Dictatorship*. London.

Rahman, Anisur, 1973. 'Foreign Aid vs. Self-Help', *Business Review*, (Dacca), January.

Rahim, A.M.A. and A.K.M. Hoque, 1978. 'The Terms of Trade of Bangladesh: 1972 – 76. An Analysis and Policy Implications', *Bangladesh Bank Bulletin*, Vol. 58, April.

Raj, K.N., 1973. 'The Politics and Economics of "Intermediate Regimes" ', *Economic and Political Weekly*, Vol. VIII, No. 27.

Rashiduzzaman, M., 1968. *Politics and administration in the local councils. A study of union and district councils in East Pakistan*. Dacca.

————— 1970. 'The Awami League in the Political Development of Pakistan', *Asian Survey*, Vol. X, No. 7.

————— 1978. 'Bangladesh in 1977: Dilemmas of the Military Rulers', ibid., Vol. XVIII, No. 2.

———— 1979. 'Bangladesh in 1978: Search for a Political Party', ibid., Vol. XIX, No. 2.

Ray, Rajat K., 1973. 'The Crisis of Bengal Agriculture: 1870–1927. The Dymanics of Immobility', *Indian Economic and Social History Review*, Vol. X, No. 3.

Ray, Rajat and Ratna, 1973. 'The Dynamics of Continuity in Rural Bengal under the British Imperium: A Study of quasi-stable Equilibrium in underdeveloped Societies in a changing World', ibid., Vol. X, No. 2.

Riggs, Fred W., 1966. *Thailand. The Modernization of a Bureaucratic Polity*. Honolulu.

Rokkan, Stein, *et al.*, 1970. 'Nation-Building, Cleavage Formation and the Structuring of Mass Politics', in: *Citizens, Elections, Parties*. Oslo.

Rudebeck, Lars, 1974. *Guinea-Bissau. A Study of Political Mobilization*. Uppsala.

Saul, John S., 1974. 'The State in Post-colonial Societies: Tanzania', *Socialist Register*.

———— 1976. 'The Unsteady State: Uganda, Obote and General Amin', *Review of African Political Economy*, No. 5.

Saul, John S., and Roger Woods, 1971. 'African Peasantries', *Peasants and Peasant Societies*, T. Shanin, ed., Penguin.

Sayeed, Khalid B., 1967. *The Political System of Pakistan*. Boston.

———— 1968. *Pakistan. The Formative Phase 1857–1948*. Oxford University Press, Second Edition.

Shanin, T., 1973. 'The Nature and Logic of the Peasant Economy: A Generalization', *Journal of Peasant Studies*, Vol. 1, No. 1.

Smith, W.C., 1962. *Pakistan as an Islamic State*. Lahore.

Sobhan, Rehman, 1968. *Basic Democracies, Works Programme and Rural Development in East Pakistan*. Dacca.

———— 1977. 'Sheikh Mujibur Rahman and the contradictions of bourgeois society in Bangladesh', in *Sheikh Mujib. A Commemorative Anthology*, A.G. Choudhury, ed. London.

———— 1981. 'Bangladesh and the World Economic System: The Crisis of External Dependence', *Development and Change*, Vol. 12, No. 3.

Sobhan, Rehman and Muzaffer Ahmad, 1980. *Public Enterprise in an Intermediate Regime. A Study of the Political Economy of Bangladesh*. The Bangaladesh Institute of Development Studies, Dacca.

Sonntag, Heinz Rudolf, 1973. 'Der Staat des unterentwickelten Kapitalismus', *Kursbuch*, Berlin, May.

Stewart, F. and Streeten, P., 1976. 'New Strategies for Development: Poverty, Income Distribution, and Growth', *Oxford Economic Papers*, Vol. 28, No. 3.

Swedish International Development Authority (SIDA), 1977. *Bangladesh. Landanalys.* (Country Analysis). (Daniel Asplund).

———— 1979. *Contradictions and Distortions in a Rural Economy. The Case of Bangladesh*. (Report from Policy Development and Evaluation Division, by Stefan de Vylder and Daniel Asplund), Stockholm.

Thorner, D. *et al.*, 1966. *The Theory of Peasant Economy* (A.V. Chayanov). Homewood, Illinois.

United States Agency for International Development (USAID), 1977. *Report on the Hierarchy of Interests in Land in Bangladesh*.

von Freyhold, Michela, 1977. 'The Post-colonial State and Its Tanzanian Version', *Review of African Political Economy*, No. 8.

von Vorys, Karl, 1965. *Political Development in Pakistan*. Princeton.

Weiner, Myron, 1965. 'Political Integration and Political Development', *Annals of the American Academy of Political and Social Sciences*.

Wertheim, W.F., 1974. *Evolution and Revolution. The rising Waves of Emancipation.* London.

Westergaard, Kirsten, 1978. 'Mode of Production in Bangladesh', *Journal of Social Studies* (Dacca), No. 2.

———— 1979. 'Local Politics and Its Relation to State Power in Bangladesh', Proceedings from the VIth European Conference on Modern South Asian Studies, *Asie du Sud. Traditions et changements.* Centre National de la Recherche Scientifique, Paris.

———— 1980. *Boringram. An Economic and Social Analysis of a Village in Bangladesh.* Bogra Rural Academy.

———— 1983. Pauperization and Rural Women in Bangladesh. A Case Study. Bangladesh Academy for Rural Development, Comilla.

Wood, G.D., 1976. 'Class Differentiation and Power in Bandakgram: The Minifundist Case', in: *Exploitation and the Rural Poor.* M. Ameerul Huq, ed. Comilla, Bangladesh.

———— 1978. 'The Nature of Rural Class Differentiation in Bangladesh' (mimeo). Reissued by Agricultural Development Agencies in Bangladesh.

World Bank, 1978. *Bangladesh. Current Trends and Development Issues.* Washington, D.C.

Ziemann, W. and M. Lanzendörfer, 1977. 'The State in Peripheral Societies', *The Socialist Register.*

Ziring, Lawrence, 1971. *The Ayub Khan Era. Politics in Pakistan, 1958–1969.* Syracuse University Press.